W9-CRU-770

An Introduction to Probability and Inductive Logic

This is an introductory textbook on probability and induction written by one of the world's foremost philosophers of science. The book has been designed to offer maximal accessibility to the widest range of students (not only those majoring in philosophy) and assumes no formal training in elementary symbolic logic. It offers a comprehensive course covering all basic definitions of induction and probability, and it considers such topics as decision theory, Bayesianism, frequency ideas, and the philosophical problem of induction.

The key features of this book are:

- A lively and vigorous prose style
- Lucid and systematic organization and presentation of ideas
- Many practical applications
- A rich supply of exercises drawing on examples from such fields as psychology, ecology, economics, bioethics, engineering, and political science
- Numerous brief historical accounts of how fundamental ideas of probability and induction developed
- A full bibliography of further reading

Although designed primarily for courses in philosophy, the book could certainly be read and enjoyed by those in the social sciences (particularly psychology, economics, political science, and sociology) or medical sciences (such as epidemiology) seeking a reader-friendly account of the basic ideas of probability and induction.

Ian Hacking is University Professor in Philosophy at the University of Toronto and a Professor at the Collège de France in Paris. He is the author of many books; his previous books with Cambridge University Press include *The Logic of Statistical Inference, The Emergence of Probability,* and *The Taming of Chance.*

AN INTRODUCTION TO

Probability and Inductive Logic

IAN HACKING
University of Toronto
Collège de France

CAMBRIDGE
UNIVERSITY PRESS

CAMBRIDGE UNIVERSITY PRESS
Cambridge, New York, Melbourne, Madrid, Cape Town, Singapore,
São Paulo, Delhi, Dubai, Tokyo

Cambridge University Press
32 Avenue of the Americas, New York, NY 10013-2473, USA

www.cambridge.org
Information on this title: www.cambridge.org/9780521775014

© Ian Hacking 2001

This publication is in copyright. Subject to statutory exception
and to the provisions of relevant collective licensing agreements,
no reproduction of any part may take place without the written
permission of Cambridge University Press.

First published 2001
9th printing 2009

A catalog record for this publication is available from the British Library.

Library of Congress Cataloging in Publication Data

Hacking, Ian.
An introduction to probability and inductive logic / Ian Hacking.
    p.   cm.
Includes bibliographical references and index.
ISBN 0-521-77287-7 – ISBN 0-521-77501-9 (pbk.)
1. Probabilities.   2. Induction (Logic).   I. Title.
BC141.H33   2001
160–dc21   00-045503

ISBN 978-0-521-77287-7 Hardback
ISBN 978-0-521-77501-4 Paperback

Cambridge University Press has no responsibility for the persistence or
accuracy of URLs for external or third-party Internet Web sites referred to in
this publication and does not guarantee that any content on such Web sites is,
or will remain, accurate or appropriate.

For Sam

Contents

A Note on the Cover Illustration

The Allegory of Fortune, by Dosso Dossi (1486–1542)

The young woman on the right is the classical Goddess *Fortuna,* whom today we might call *Lady Luck.*

The young man on the left is *Chance.*

Fortuna is holding an enormous bunch of fruits, symbolizing the good luck that she can bring. But notice that she has only one sandal. That means that she can also bring bad luck. And she is sitting on a soap bubble! This is to indicate that what you get from luck does not last.

Chance is holding lottery tickets. Dosso Dossi was a court painter in the northern Italian city of Ferrara, which is near Venice. Venice had recently introduced a state lottery to raise money (see page 86). It was not so different from modern state-run lotteries, except that Venice gave you better odds than any state-run lottery today. Art critics say that Dosso Dossi believed that life is a lottery for everyone.

Do you agree that life is a lottery for everyone?

The painting is in the J. Paul Getty Museum, Los Angeles, and the above note is adapted from notes for a Dossi exhibit, 1999.

Foreword

Inductive logic is unlike deductive or symbolic logic. In deductive reasoning, when you have true premises and a valid argument, the conclusion must be true too. Valid deductive arguments do not take risks.

Inductive logic takes risks. You can have true premises, a good argument, but a false conclusion. Inductive logic uses probability to analyse that kind of risky argument.

Good News

Inductive reasoning is a guide in life. People make risky decisions all the time. It plays a much larger part in everyday affairs than deductive reasoning.

Bad News

People are very bad when reasoning about risks. We make a lot of mistakes when we use probabilities.

This book starts with a list of seven Odd Questions. They look pretty simple. But most people get some of the answers wrong. The last group of nine-year-olds I tested did better than a group of professors. Try the Odd Questions. Each one is discussed later in the book.

Practical Aims

This book can help you understand, use, and act on probabilities, risks, and statistics. We live our lives taking chances, acting when we don't know enough. Every day we experience a lot of uncertainties. This book is about the kinds of actions you can take when you are uncertain what to do. It is about the inferences you can draw when your evidence leaves you unsure what is true.

We Are Drowning in Probabilities and Statistics

Nowadays you can't escape hearing about probabilities, statistics, and risk. Everything—jobs, sex, war, health, sport, grades, the environment, politics, astronomy, genetics—is wrapped up in probabilities.

This is new. If your grandparents lived in North America they seldom came across anything much more complicated than "9 out of 10 Hollywood stars use Lux beauty soap" (a famous line on a weekly radio show). Now we get polls, surveys, and digests of opinion all the time. No public decision can be made without statistical analysis, risk analysis, environmental impact reports.

It is pretty hard to understand what all the numbers mean. This book aims at helping you understand them. How to use them. How they are abused. When inductive reasoning is fallacious or uses sloppy rhetoric. How people get fooled by numbers. How numbers are often used to conceal ignorance. How not to be conned.

Philosophy

There is a famous problem in philosophy called the problem of induction. That comes at the end of the book.

There are ethical questions about risk. Some philosophers say we should always act so as to maximize the common good. Others say that duty and right and wrong come before cost-benefit thinking. These questions arise in Chapter 9.

There are even some probability arguments for, and against, religious belief. One comes up in Chapter 10.

There are philosophical arguments about probability itself. Right now there are big disagreements over the basic ideas of inductive inference. Different schools of thought approach practical issues in different ways. Most beginning statistics courses pretend that there is no disagreement. This is a philosophy book, so it puts the competing ideas up front. It tries to be fair to all parties.

Calculation

To get a grip on chances, risks, or probabilities, you need numbers. But even if you hate calculating you can use this book. Don't be put off by the formulas. This book is about *ideas* that we represent by numbers. A philosophy book is concerned with the ideas behind calculations. It is not concerned with computing precise solutions to complicated problems.

You do not need a pocket calculator for most of the exercises, because the numbers usually "cancel" for an easy solution. Students who learn not to use calculators solve most of the problems more quickly than students who use them.

Gambling

Many simple examples of probability mention games of chance. You may not like this. People have different attitudes toward gambling for money. Some think it is fun. Some are addicted to it. Some find it boring. Many people think it is immoral. Governments all over the world love legalized forms of gambling such as lotteries, because they are an easy way to produce extra revenue. Gamblers, as a group, always lose, and lose a lot. This book is not an advertisement for gambling. Quite the opposite! Aside from friendly occasions—a bet on the ball game, or a late night poker party among friends—gambling is a waste of time, money, and human dignity.

Nevertheless, in our risky lives we "gamble" all the time. We make decisions under uncertainty. We draw inferences from inconclusive data, not for fun, but because we do not know enough. Models based on games help us to understand these decisions and inferences. They can clarify the ways in which we think about chance.

That is why we so often turn to dice and other randomizers used in betting. They crop up in the Odd Questions. Yet they soon lead to practical issues like testimony in court (Odd Question 5) and medical diagnosis (Odd Question 6).

Odd Questions

Try your luck at these questions, without any calculating. Each question will be discussed in the text. Do not be surprised if you make mistakes!

1. About as many boys as girls are born in hospitals. Many babies are born every week at City General. In Cornwall, a country town, there is a small hospital where only a few babies are born every week.

   A **normal** week is one where between 45% and 55% of the babies are female. An **unusual** week is one where more than 55% are girls, or more than 55% are boys.

   Which of the following is true:

   _____ (a) Unusual weeks occur equally often at City General and at Cornwall.
   _____ (b) Unusual weeks are more common at City General than at Cornwall.
   _____ (c) Unusual weeks are more common at Cornwall than at City General.

   Discussed on page 192.

2. Pia is thirty-one years old, single, outspoken, and smart. She was a philosophy major. When a student, she was an ardent supporter of Native American rights, and she picketed a department store that had no facilities for nursing mothers. Rank the following statements in order of probability from 1 (most probable) to 6 (least probable). (Ties are allowed.)

   _____ (a) Pia is an active feminist.
   _____ (b) Pia is a bank teller.
   _____ (c) Pia works in a small bookstore.
   _____ (d) Pia is a bank teller and an active feminist.
   _____ (e) Pia is a bank teller and an active feminist who takes yoga classes.
   _____ (f) Pia works in a small bookstore and is an active feminist who takes yoga classes.

   Discussed on page 65.

3. In Lotto 6/49, a standard government-run lottery, you choose 6 out of 49 numbers (1 through 49). You win the biggest prize—maybe millions of dol-

lars—if these 6 are drawn. (The prize money is divided between all those who choose the lucky numbers. If no one wins, then most of the prize money is put back into next week's lottery.)

Suppose your aunt offers you, *free*, a choice between two tickets in the lottery, with numbers as shown:

A. You win if 1, 2, 3, 4, 5, and 6 are drawn.
B. You win if 39, 36, 32, 21, 14, and 3 are drawn.

Do you prefer A, B, or are you indifferent between the two?

Discussed on page 30.

4. To throw a total of 7 with a pair of dice, you have to get a 1 and a 6, or a 2 and a 5, or a 3 and a 4.

   To throw a total of 6 with a pair of dice, you have to get a 1 and a 5, or a 2 and a 4, or a 3 and another 3.

   With two fair dice, you would expect:

   _____ (a) To throw 7 more frequently than 6.
   _____ (b) To throw 6 more frequently than 7.
   _____ (c) To throw 6 and 7 equally often.

Discussed on page 43.

5. You have been called to jury duty in a town where there are two taxi companies, Green Cabs Ltd. and Blue Taxi Inc. Blue Taxi uses cars painted blue; Green Cabs uses green cars.

   Green Cabs dominates the market, with 85% of the taxis on the road.

   On a misty winter night a taxi sideswiped another car and drove off. A witness says it was a blue cab.

   The witness is tested under conditions like those on the night of the accident, and 80% of the time she correctly reports the color of the cab that is seen. That is, regardless of whether she is shown a blue or a green cab in misty evening light, she gets the color right 80% of the time.

   You conclude, on the basis of this information:

   _____ (a) The probability that the sideswiper was blue is 0.8.
   _____ (b) It is more likely that the sideswiper was blue, but the probability is less than 0.8.
   _____ (c) It is just as probable that the sideswiper was green as that it was blue.
   _____ (d) It is more likely than not that the sideswiper was green.

Discussed on page 72.

6. You are a physician. You think it is quite likely that one of your patients has strep throat, but you aren't sure. You take some swabs from the throat and send them to a lab for testing. The test is (like nearly all lab tests) not perfect.

If the patient has strep throat, then 70% of the time the lab says YES. But 30% of the time it says NO.

If the patient does **not** have strep throat, then 90% of the time the lab says NO. But 10% of the time it says YES.

You send five successive swabs to the lab, from the same patient. You get back these results, in order:

YES, NO, YES, NO, YES

You conclude:

_____ (a) These results are worthless.

_____ (b) It is likely that the patient does **not** have strep throat.

_____ (c) It is **slightly** more likely than not, that the patient **does** have strep throat.

_____ (d) It is **very much more** likely than not, that the patient **does** have strep throat.

Discussed on page 76.

7. "Imitate" a coin. That is, write down a sequence of 100 H (for heads) and T (for tails) without tossing a coin—but a sequence that you think will fool everyone into thinking it is the report of tossing a fair coin.

Discussed on page 30.

1 Logic

Logic is about good and bad reasoning. In order to talk clearly about reasoning, logicians have given precise meanings to some ordinary words. This chapter is a review of their language.

ARGUMENTS

Logicians attach a special sense to the word *argument*. In ordinary language, it usually takes two to argue. One dictionary defines an argument as:

1 A quarrel.
2 A discussion in which reasons are put forward in support of and against a proposition, proposal, or case.
3 A point or series of reasons presented to support a proposition which is the conclusion of the argument.

Definition (3) is what logicians mean by an argument.

Reasoning is stated or written out in arguments. So logicians study arguments (in sense 3).

An argument thus divides up into:

A point or series of reasons which are called *premises*,
and a *conclusion*.

Premises and conclusion are *propositions*, statements that can be either true or false. Propositions are "true-or-false."

GOING WRONG

The premises are supposed to be reasons for the conclusion. Logic tries to understand the idea of a good reason.

We find arguments convincing when we know that the premises are true, and when we see that they give a good reason for the conclusion.

So two things can go wrong with an argument:

- the premises may be false.
- the premises may not provide a good reason for the conclusion.

Here is an argument:

(*J) If James wants a job, then he will get a haircut tomorrow.
      James will get a haircut tomorrow.
So:
      James wants a job.

The first two propositions are the premises. The third proposition is the conclusion.

Someone might offer this argument, thinking the premises give a conclusive reason for the conclusion. They do not. The premises could be true and the conclusion false, for any number of reasons. For example:

James has a date with a girl who likes tidy men, and his hair is a mess.
He has to go home to his family, who would be disgusted by how he looks.
It is the third Monday of the month, and he always gets a haircut then.
No way does he want a job! Of course, if he did want a job, he'd get a haircut
    tomorrow.

Argument (*J), if offered as a conclusive argument, commits an error—a common error. That is why we labeled it with a "star" in front, as a warning that it is a bad argument.

Argument (*J) commits a *fallacy*. A fallacy is an error in reasoning that is so common that logicians have noted it. Sometimes they give it a name. Argument (*J) commits the fallacy called "affirming the consequent." The first premise in the argument is of the form:

If A, then C.

A is called the *antecedent* of this "if-then" proposition, and C is called the *consequent*.

The second premise of (*J) is of the form "C." So in stating this premise, we "affirm the consequent."

The conclusion is of the form "A." It is a fallacy to infer the antecedent A from the consequent C. That is the fallacy of affirming the consequent.

TWO WAYS TO CRITICIZE

Here is a conclusive argument that only looks a little like (*J):

(J) If James wants a job, then he will get a haircut tomorrow.
    James wants a job.
So:
    James will get a haircut tomorrow.

Here the premises do provide a conclusive reason for the conclusion. If the premises are true, then the conclusion must be true too.

But you might question the premises.

You might question the first premise if you knew that James wants a job as a rock musician. The last thing he wants is a haircut.

You might also question the second premise. Does James really want a job?

There are two basic ways to criticize an argument:

■ Challenge the premises—show that at least one is false.
■ Challenge the reasoning—show that the premises are not a good reason for the conclusion.

The two basic types of criticism apply to any kind of argument whatsoever. But logic is concerned only with reasoning. It cannot in general tell whether premises are true or false. It can only tell whether the reasoning is good or bad.

VALIDITY

Here is another conclusive argument:

(K) Every automobile sold by Queen Street Motors is rust-proofed.
    Barbara's car was sold by Queen Street Motors.
Therefore:
    Barbara's car is rust-proofed.

If the two premises of (K) are true, then the conclusion must be true too. The same goes for (J) above. But not for (*J)!

This idea defines a valid argument. It is logically impossible for the conclusion to be false given that the premises are true.

Validity is best explained in terms of logical form. The logical form of arguments (J) and (K) is:

1. If A, then C.   4. Every F is G.
2. A.   5. b is F.
So: Therefore:
3. C.   6. b is G.

Whenever an argument of one of these forms has true premises, then the conclusion is also true. That is a definition of a valid argument form.

Valid is a technical term of deductive logic. The opposite of *valid* is *invalid*. In ordinary life, we talk about a valid driver's license. We say someone is making a valid point if there is a basis for it, or even if it is true. But we will stick to the special, logicians' meaning of the word. Arguments are valid or invalid.

Argument (*J) above was invalid. Here is another invalid argument:

(*K) Every automobile sold by Queen Street Motors is rust-proofed.
    Barbara's car is rust-proofed.
Therefore:
    Barbara's car was sold by Queen Street Motors.

This is invalid because the conclusion could be false, even when the premises are true. Many companies sell rust-proofed cars, so Barbara need not have bought hers at Queen Street Motors.

TRUE VERSUS VALID

Be careful about *true* and *valid*. In logic:

Propositions are true or false.
Arguments are valid or invalid.

You should also distinguish the argument (K) about Barbara's car from an "if-then" or conditional proposition like this:

If Barbara's car was sold by Queen Street Motors, and if every automobile sold by Queen Street Motors is rust-proofed, then Barbara's car is rust-proofed.

This is a true proposition of the form,

If p and if q, then r.

Or, in finer detail,

If b is F, and if every F is G, then b is G.

Argument (K), on the other hand, is of the form:

4.	p.	Or, in finer detail,	4.	Every F is G.
5.	q.		5.	b is F.
So:			Therefore:	
6.	r.		6.	b is G.

To every argument there is a corresponding conditional proposition "if-then." An argument is valid if and only if the corresponding conditional proposition is a truth of logic.

METAPHORS

There are many ways to suggest the idea of validity:

> The conclusion follows from the premises.
> Whenever the premises are true, the conclusion *must* be true too.
> The conclusion is a logical consequence of the premises.
> The conclusion is implicitly contained in the premises.
> Valid argument forms are truth-preserving.

"Truth-preserving" means that whenever you start out with true premises, you will end up with a true conclusion.

When you reason from true premises using a valid argument, you never risk drawing a false conclusion. When your premises are true, there is no risk that the conclusion will be false.

Textbooks on deductive logic make precise sense of these metaphors. For the purposes of this book, one metaphor says best what matters for validity:

> Valid arguments are risk-free arguments.

SOUND

A *valid* argument never takes you from true premises to a false conclusion.

But, of course, the argument might have a false premise.

We say an argument is *sound* when:

- all the premises are true, **and**
- the argument is valid.

Thus an argument may be unsound because:

- A premise is false.
- The argument is invalid.

Validity has to do with the logical connection between premises and conclusion, and *not* with the truth of the premises or the conclusion.

Soundness for deductive logic has to do with *both* validity *and* the truth of the premises.

LIKE BUILDING A HOUSE

Making a deductive argument is like building a house.

- It may be built on sand, and so fall down, because the foundations are not solid. That is like having a false premise.

■ Or it may be badly built. That is like having an invalid argument.
■ And, of course, a house built on sand with bad design may still stay up. That is like an invalid argument with false premises and a true conclusion.

There are two ways to criticize a contractor who built a house. "The foundations are no good!" Or, "The house is badly built!" Likewise, if someone shows you a deduction you can make two kinds of criticism. "One of your premises is false." Or, "The argument is invalid." Or both, of course.

VALIDITY IS NOT TRUTH!

A valid argument can have a *false premise* but a *true conclusion*. Example:

(R) Every famous philosopher who lived to be over ninety was a mathematical logician.
Bertrand Russell was a famous philosopher who lived to be over ninety.
So:
Bertrand Russell was a mathematical logician.

This argument is valid. The conclusion is true.
But the first premise is false. Thomas Hobbes, the famous political philosopher, lived to be over ninety, but he was not a mathematical logician.
Likewise an argument with *false premises* and a *false conclusion* could be valid. Validity is about the connection between premises and conclusion, not about truth or falsehood.

INVALIDITY IS NOT FALSEHOOD!

An invalid argument can have *true premises* and a *true conclusion*. Example:

(*R) Some philosophers now dead were witty and wrote many books.
Bertrand Russell was a philosopher, now dead.
So:
Bertrand Russell was witty and wrote many books.

Both premises are true. The conclusion is true. But the argument is invalid.

TWO WAYS TO CRITICIZE A DEDUCTION

Both (R) and (*R) are unsound, but for quite different reasons.
You can tell that (*R) is unsound because it is invalid. You can tell it is invalid without knowing *anything* about Bertrand Russell (except that "Bertrand Russell" was someone's name).
Likewise, you can tell that (R) is valid without knowing anything about Bertrand Russell.
But to know whether the premises are true, you have to know something

about the world, about history, about philosophers, about Bertrand Russell and others.

Maybe you did not know that Bertrand Russell was witty or that Thomas Hobbes was a famous political philosopher who lived to be over ninety. Now you do.

You need not know anything special about the world to know whether an argument is valid or invalid. But you need to know some facts to know whether a premise is true or false.

There are two ways to criticize a deduction:

- A premise is false.
- The argument is invalid.

So there is a *division of labor*.

Who is an expert on the truth of premises?

Detectives, nurses, surgeons, pollsters, historians, astrologers, zoologists, investigative reporters, you and me.

Who is an expert on validity?

A logician.

Logicians study the relations between premises and conclusions, but, as logicians, are not especially qualified to tell whether the premises are true or false.

EXERCISES

1 *Propositions.* The premises and conclusion of an argument are propositions. Propositions are expressed by statements that can be either true or false. For brevity, we say that propositions are true-or-false.

   The headline of a newspaper story is:

   SEIZED SERPENTS MAKE STRANGE OFFICE-FELLOWS
   SHIPPING ERROR LANDS OFFICIAL WITH PYTHONS

   There was a bizarre mix-up. A man who runs a tropical fish store in Windsor, Ontario, was delivered a box of ball pythons from a dealer in California. The newspaper tells us that:

   The ball python is a central African ground dweller that can grow to more than a meter on a diet of small mammals.

   (a) Is that true-or-false?
   (b) Do you know whether it is true?
   (c) Is it what logicians call a proposition? [You should give the same answer to (c) as to (a).]

   The newspaper goes on to tell us that:

   The ball python is named for its tendency to curl up into a ball.

(d) Is that true-or-false?

(e) Do you know whether it is true?

The story continues:

> The shipment of tropical fish intended for Windsor went to a snake dealer in Ohio.

(f) Is that a proposition?

In logic, propositions express matters of fact that can be either true or false. Judgments of personal taste, such as "avocados are delicious," are not strictly matters of fact. Avocados taste good to some people and taste slimy and disgusting to others. The proposition that avocados are delicious is not strictly speaking true-or-false. But if I say "avocados taste delicious to me," I am stating something about me, which happens to be true.

Joe, the man who owns the fish store, is quoted as saying:

> Ball pythons are very attractive animals.

(g) Is that true-or-false? Is it a proposition?

Suppose that he had said,

> I think ball pythons are very attractive animals.

(h) Is that true-or-false? Is it a proposition?

The newspaper begins the story by saying "It is not so nice to share your office with a box of snakes for two months." Then it adds, as a full paragraph:

> Especially when it was all a result of being soft-hearted.

(i) Is that a proposition?

Joe has to feed the snakes a lot of live mice. According to the reporter, Joe said,

> I'm not really too thrilled to hear baby mice squeaking and screaming behind me while I'm on the telephone.

(j) Is that a proposition?

Then Joe said,

> Thank God they don't eat every day!

(k) Is that a proposition?

He next asked,

> Do you know any zoos or schools who might want these snakes?

(l) Is that a proposition?

Joe phoned Federal Express, the shipper who had mixed up the deliveries, saying:

> You owe me for my expenses, my trouble, and your mistake.

(m) Is that a proposition?

The story ended happily:

> On Wednesday Federal Express bargained a $1000 payment to Joe.

(n) Is that a proposition?

2 *False all over.* State two arguments—they can be silly ones—in which the premises and conclusion are all false, and such that one argument is (a) valid and the other is (b) invalid.

3 *Unsound.* Is either of your answers to question 2 a sound argument?

4 *Combinations.* Only one of the following eight combinations is impossible. Which one?
   (a) All premises true. Conclusion true. Valid.
   (b) All premises true. Conclusion false. Valid.
   (c) One premise false. Conclusion true. Valid.
   (d) One premise false. Conclusion false. Valid.
   (e) All premises true. Conclusion true. Invalid.
   (f) All premises true. Conclusion false. Invalid.
   (g) One premise false. Conclusion true. Invalid.
   (h) One premise false. Conclusion false. Invalid.

5 *Soundness.* Which of the combinations just listed are sound arguments?

6 *Conditional propositions.* Which of the following is true-or-false? Which is valid-or-invalid? Which is an argument? Which is a conditional proposition?

   (a) Tom, Dick, and Harry died.
       So:
       All men are mortal.

   (b) If Tom, Dick, and Harry died, then all men are mortal.

7 *Chewing tobacco.* Which of these arguments are valid?

   (a) I follow three major league teams. Most of their top hitters chew tobacco at the plate.
       So:
       Chewing tobacco improves batting average.

   (b) The top six hitters in the National League chew tobacco at the plate.
       So:
       Chewing tobacco improves batting average.

   (c) A study, by the American Dental Association, of 158 players on seven major league teams during the 1988 season, showed that the mean batting average for chewers was .238, compared to .248 for non users. Abstainers also had a higher fielding average.
       So:
       Chewing tobacco does not improve batting average.

   (d) In 1921, every major league pitcher who chewed tobacco when up to bat had a higher batting average than any major league pitcher who did not.
       So:
       Chewing tobacco improves the batting average of pitchers.

8 *Inductive baseball.* None of the arguments (7a)–(7d) is valid. Invalid arguments are not conclusive. But some non-conclusive arguments are better than others. They are risky arguments. Each of the arguments (a)–(d) is risky. We have not

done any inductive logic yet, but you probably think some of (7a)–(7d) are better arguments than others. Which is best? Which is worst?

KEY WORDS FOR REVIEW

Argument	Conclusion
Proposition	Valid
True-or-false	Sound
Premise	Conditional

2 What Is Inductive Logic?

Inductive logic is about risky arguments. It analyses inductive arguments using probability. There are other kinds of risky arguments. There is inference to the best explanation, and there are arguments based on testimony.

Valid arguments are risk-free. Inductive logic studies risky arguments. A risky argument can be a very good one, and yet its conclusion can be false, even when the premises are true. Most of our arguments are risky.

Begin with the big picture. The Big Bang theory of the origin of our universe is well supported by present evidence, but it could be wrong. That is a risk.

We now have very strong evidence that smoking causes lung cancer. But the reasoning from all that evidence to the conclusion "smoking causes lung cancer" is still risky. It might just turn out that people predisposed to nicotine addiction are also predisposed to lung cancer, in which case our inference, that smoking causes lung cancer, would be in question after all.

After a lot of research, a company concludes that it can make a profit by marketing a special left-handed mouse for personal computers. It is taking a risk.

You want to be in the same class as your friend Jan. You reason that Jan likes mathematics, and so will take another logic class. You sign up for inductive logic. You have made a risky argument.

ORANGES

Here are some everyday examples of risky arguments.

A small grocer sells her old fruit at half-price. I want a box of oranges, cheap. But I want them to be good, sweet, and not rotten. The grocer takes an orange from the top of a box, cuts it open, and shows it to me. Her argument is:

(A) This orange is good.
So:
   All (or almost all) the oranges in the box are good.

The premise is evidence for the conclusion: but not very good evidence. Most of the oranges in the box may be rotten.

Argument (A) is not a valid argument. Even if the premise is true, the conclusion may be false. This is a risky argument.

If I buy the box at half-price on the strength of this argument, I am taking a big risk. So I reach into the box, pick an orange at random, and pull it out. It is good too. I buy the box. My reasoning is:

(B) This orange that I chose at random is good.
So:
   All (or almost all) the oranges in the box are good.

This argument is also risky. But it is not as risky as (A).

Julia takes six oranges at random. One, but only one, is squishy. She buys the box at half-price. Her argument is:

(C) Of these six oranges that I chose at random, five are good and one is rotten.
So:
   Most (but not all) of the oranges in the box are good.

Argument (C) is based on more data than (B). But it is not a valid argument. Even though five out of six oranges that Julia picked at random are fine, she may just have been lucky. Perhaps most of the remaining oranges are rotten.

SAMPLES AND POPULATIONS

There are many forms of risky argument. Arguments (A)–(C) all have this basic form:

   Statement about a sample drawn from a given population.
   So:
   Statement about the population as a whole.

We may also go the other way around. I might know that almost all the oranges in this box are good. I pick four oranges at random to squeeze a big glass of orange juice. I reason:

   All or almost all the oranges in this box are good.
   These four oranges are taken at random from this box.
   So:
   These four oranges are good.

This too is a risky argument. I might pick a rotten orange, even if most of the oranges in the box are fine. The form of my argument is:

Statement about a population.
So:
Statement about a sample.

We can also go from sample to sample:

These four oranges that I chose at random are good.
So:
The next four oranges that I draw at random will also be good.

The basic form of this argument is:

Statement about a sample.
So:
Statement about a new sample.

PROPORTIONS

We can try to be more exact about our arguments. These are small juice oranges, 60 to the box. A cautious person might express "almost all" by "90%," and then the argument would look like this:

These four oranges, that I chose at random from a box of 60 oranges, are good.
So:
At least 90% (or 54) of the oranges in the box are good.

At least 90% (or 54) of the oranges in this box are good. These four oranges are taken at random from this box.
So:
These four oranges are good.

PROBABILITY

Most of us are happy putting a "probably" into these arguments:

These four oranges, that I chose at random from a box of 60 oranges, are good.
So, probably:
At least 90% (or 54) of the oranges in the box are good.

At least 90% (or 54) of the oranges in this box are good.
These four oranges are taken at random from this box.
So, probably:
These four oranges are good.

These four oranges, that I chose at random from a box of 60 oranges, are good.
So, probably:
The next four oranges that I draw at random will also be good.

Can we put in numerical probability values? That would be one way of telling which arguments are riskier than others. We will use ideas of probability to study risk.

Probability is a fundamental tool for inductive logic.

We will only do enough probability calculations to make ideas clear. *The focus in this book is on the ideas, not on the numbers.*

DEDUCING PROBABILITIES

Inductive logic uses probabilities. *But not all arguments using probabilities are inductive.* Not all arguments where you see the word "probability" are risky. Probability can be made into a rigorous mathematical idea. Mathematics is a deductive science. We make deductions using probability. In chapter 6 we state basic laws, or axioms, of probability. We *deduce* other facts about probability from these axioms.

Here is a simple deduction about probabilities:

This die has six faces, labeled 1, 2, 3, 4, 5, 6.
Each face is equally probable. (Each face is as likely as any other to turn up on a roll of the die.)
So,
The probability of rolling a 4 is 1/6.

This argument is valid. You already know this. Even if you have never studied probability, you make probabilities add up to 1.

You intuitively know that when the events are *mutually exclusive*—the die can land only one face up on any roll—and *exhaustive*—the die must land with one of the six faces up—then the probabilities add up to 1.

Why is the argument valid? Given the basic laws of probability, whenever the premises of an argument of this form are true, then the conclusion must be true too.

Here is another valid argument about probability.

This die has six faces, labeled 1, 2, 3, 4, 5, 6.
Each face is equally probable.
So:
The probability of rolling a 3 or a 4 is 1/3.

Even if you have never studied probability, you know that probabilities add up. If two events are *mutually exclusive*—one or the other can happen, but not both at the same time—then the probability that one or the other happens is the sum of their probabilities.

Given the basic laws of probability, whenever the premises of an argument of this form are true, then the conclusion must be true too. So the argument is valid.

The two arguments just stated are both valid. Notice how they differ from this one:

> This die has six faces, labeled 1, 2, 3, 4, 5, 6.
> In a sequence of 227 rolls, a 4 was rolled just 38 times.
> So:
> The probability of rolling a 4 with this die is about 1/6.

That is a risky argument. The conclusion might be false, even with true premises. The die might be somewhat biased against 4. The probability of rolling a 4 might be 1/8. Yet, by chance, in the last 227 rolls we managed to roll 4 almost exactly 1/6 of the time.

ANOTHER KIND OF RISKY ARGUMENT

Probability is a fundamental tool for inductive logic. But we have just seen that:

■ There are also deductively valid arguments about probability.

Likewise:

■ Many kinds of risky argument need not involve probability.

There may be more to a risky argument than inductive logic. Inductive logic does study risky arguments—but maybe not every kind of risky argument. Here is a new kind of risky argument. It begins with somebody noticing that:

> It is very unusual in our university for most of the students in a large elementary class to get As. But in one class they did.

That is odd. It is something to be explained. One explanation is that the instructor is an easy marker.

> Almost all the students in that class got As.
> So:
> The instructor must be a really easy marker.

Here we are *not* inferring from a sample to a population, or from a population to a sample.

We are offering a *hypothesis* to explain the observed facts. There might be other explanations. Almost all the students in that class got As,

> So:
> That was a very gifted class.

So:
The instructor is a marvelous teacher.
So:
The material in that course is far too easy for well-prepared students.

Each of these arguments ends with a *plausible explanation* of the curious fact that almost everyone in the class got an A grade.

Remember argument (*J) on page 2:

(*J) If James wants a job, then he will get a haircut tomorrow.
      James will get a haircut tomorrow.
So:
      James wants a job.

This is an invalid argument. It is still an argument, a risky argument. Let us have some more details. James gets his hair cut once in a blue moon. He is broke. You hear he is going to the barber tomorrow. Why on earth? Because he wants a job. The conclusion is a *plausible explanation*.

INFERENCE TO THE BEST EXPLANATION

Each of the arguments we've just looked at is an *inference to a plausible explanation*.

If one explanation is much more plausible than any other, it is an *inference to the best explanation*.

Many pieces of reasoning in science are like that. Some philosophers think that whenever we reach a theoretical conclusion, we are arguing to the best explanation. For example, cosmology was changed radically around 1967, when the Big Bang theory of the universe became widely accepted. The Big Bang theory says that our universe came into existence with a gigantic "explosion" at a definite date in the past. Why did people reach this amazing conclusion? Because two radio astronomers discovered that a certain low "background radiation" seems to be uniformly distributed everywhere in space that can be checked with a radio telescope. The best explanation, then and now, is that this background radiation is the result of a "Big Bang."

"ABDUCTION"

One philosopher who thought deeply about probability was Charles Sanders Peirce (1839–1914). Notice that it is spelled PEIrce. His name is not "Pierce." Worse still, his name is correctly pronounced "purse"! He came from an old New England family that spelled their name "Pers" or "Perse."

Peirce liked things to come in groups of three. He thought that there are three types of good argument: deduction, induction, and inference to the best explanation. Since he liked symmetries, he invented a new name for inference to the best explanation. He called it *abduction*. So his picture of logic is this:

	Deduction
Logic	Induction
	Abduction

Induction and abduction are, in his theory, two distinct types of risky argument.

Some philosophers believe that probability is a very useful tool in analyzing arguments to the best explanation. Other philosophers, like Peirce, do not think so. There is a debate about that. We leave that debate to philosophers of science. The issues are very interesting, but this book will not discuss inference to the best explanation.

TESTIMONY

Most of what you believe, you believe because someone told you so.

How reliable are your parents? Your psychology instructor? The evening news? Believing what they say involves risky arguments.

> I know I was born on February 14, because my mother told me so.
> So:
> I was born on February 14.

> My psychology instructor says that Freud was a fraud, and is a worthless guide to human psychology.
> So:
> Freud is a worthless guide to human psychology.

> According to the evening news, the mayor is meeting with out-of-town officials to discuss the effect of the flood.
> So:
> The mayor is meeting with out-of-town officials to discuss the effect of the flood.

These are risky arguments. The evening news may be misinformed. Your psychology instructor may hate Freud, and be a very biased informant.

The argument about your birthday is the least risky. It is still risky. How do you know that your parents are telling the truth?

> You look at your birth certificate. You can't doubt that! Well, maybe your parents lied by a day, so they could benefit from a new law about child benefits that took effect the day after you were born. Or maybe you were born on Friday the thirteenth, and they thought it would be better if you thought you were born on Valentine's Day. Or maybe you were born on a taxi ride to the hospital, and in the excitement no one noticed whether you were born before or after midnight . . .

All the examples are arguments based on the *testimony* of someone else: your family, your instructor, the evening news.

Some kinds of testimony can be analyzed using probability, but there are a lot of problems. Inductive logic touches on testimony, but there is a lot more to testimony than probability.

In this book we will *not* discuss inference to the best explanation, and we will *not* discuss testimony. But if you really want to understand risky arguments, you should think about testimony, and inference to the best explanation. In this book we study only one side of probability.

ROUGH DEFINITION OF INDUCTIVE LOGIC

> Inductive logic analyzes risky arguments using probability ideas.

DECISION THEORY

There is a whole other side to reasoning: *decision*. We don't just reason about what to believe.

We reason about what to do.

The probability theory of practical reasoning is called *decision theory*, and it is very close to inductive logic.

We decide what to do on the basis of two ingredients:

- What we think will probably happen (*beliefs*).
- What we want (*values*).

Decision theory involves both probabilities and values. We measure values by what are called *utilities*.

ROUGH DEFINITION OF DECISION THEORY

> Decision theory analyzes risky decision -making using ideas of probability and utility.

EXERCISES

1 *Fees.* With a budgetary crisis, administrators at Memorial University state that they must either increase fees by 35% or increase class sizes and limit course offerings. Students are asked which option they prefer. There is a sharp difference of opinion.

Which of these risky arguments is from sample to population? From population to sample? From sample to sample?

(a) The student body as a whole is strongly opposed to a major fee increase.
65 students will be asked about the fee increase.
So:
Most of the 65 students will say that they oppose a major fee increase.

(b) A questionnaire was given to 40 students from all subjects and years.
32 said they were opposed to a major fee increase.
So:
Most students are opposed to a major fee increase.

(c) The student body as a whole is strongly opposed to a major fee increase.
So (probably):
The next student we ask will oppose a major fee increase.

(d) A questionnaire was a given to 40 students from all subjects and years.
32 said they were opposed to a major fee increase.
So (probably):
The next student we ask will oppose a major fee increase.

2 *More fees.* Which of these is an inference to a plausible explanation? Which is an inference based on testimony?

(a) The student body as a whole is strongly opposed to a major fee increase.
So:
They prefer to save money rather than get a quality education.

(b) The student body as a whole is strongly opposed to a major fee increase.
So:
Many students are so poor, and loans are so hard to get, that many students would have to drop out of school if fees went up.

(c) Duodecimal Research Corporation polled the students and found that 46% are living below the official government poverty line.
So:
The students at Memorial cannot afford a major fee increase.

3 Look back at the Odd Questions on pages xv–xvii. Each question will be discussed later on. But regardless of which answer is correct, we can see that any answer you give involves an argument.

3.1 *Boys and girls.* Someone argues:

About as many boys as girls are born in hospitals.
Many babies are born every week at City General.
In Cornwall, a country town, there is a small hospital where only a few babies are born every week.
An unusual week at a hospital is one where more than 55% of the babies are girls, or more than 55% are boys.
An unusual week occurred at either Cornwall or City General Hospital last week.
So:
The unusual week occurred at Cornwall Hospital.

Explain why this is a risky argument.

3.2   *Pia.* The premises are as stated in Odd Question 2.
Which is the riskier conclusion, given those premises?
(a) Pia is an active feminist.
(e) Pia is a bank teller and an active feminist who takes yoga classes.

3.3   *Lotteries.* Your aunt offers you as a present one of two free Lotto 6/49 tickets for next week's drawing. They are:

> A. 1, 2, 3, 4, 5, and 6.
> B. 39, 36, 32, 21, 14, and 3.

(a) Construct an argument for choosing (A). If you think it is stupid to prefer (A) over (B), then you can produce a bad or weak argument! But try to make it plausible.
(b) You decide to take (A). Is this a risky decision?

3.4   *Dice.*

> Two dice are fair: each face falls as often as any other, and the number that falls uppermost with one die has no effect on the number that falls uppermost with the other die.

So:

> It is more probable that 7 occurs on a throw of these two dice, than 6.

Is this a risky argument?

3.5   *Taxicabs.* Amos and Daniel are both jurors at a trial. They both hear the same information as evidence, namely the information stated in Odd Question 5. In the end, they have to make a judgment about what happened.

> Amos concludes: So, the sideswiper was blue.
> Daniel concludes: So, the sideswiper was green.

(a) Are these risky arguments?
(b) Could you think of them as risky decisions?

3.6   *Strep throat.* The physician has the information reported in Odd Question 6. She concludes that the results are worthless, and sends out for more tests. Explain why that is a risky decision.

4   *Ludwig van Beethoven.*
(a) What kind of argument is this? How good is it?

Beethoven was in tremendous pain during some of his most creative periods—pain produced by cirrhosis of the liver, chronic kidney stones (passing a stone is excruciatingly painful), and bouts of nonstop diarrhea.
Yet his compositions are profound and often joyous.
So:
He took both pain killers and alcohol, and these drugs produced states of elation when he did his composing.

(b) Give an example of a new piece of information which, when added to the premises, strengthens the argument.

Books on "critical thinking" teach you how to analyze real-life complicated arguments. Among other things, they teach you how to read, listen, and think critically about the things that people actually say and write. This is not a book for critical thinking, but it is worth looking at a few real-life arguments. All are taken from a daily newspaper.

5   *The slender oarfish.*

> A rare deep-sea creature, the slender oarfish, is helping Japanese scientists predict major earthquakes. In Japanese folklore, if an oarfish, which normally lives at depths of more than 200 meters, is landed in nets, then major tremors are not far behind.
>
> Two slender oarfish were caught in fixed nets recently only days before a series of earthquakes shook Japan. This reminds us that one of these fish was caught two days before a major earthquake hit Nijima Island, near Tokyo, in 1963. Moreover, when shock waves hit Uwajima Bay in 1968, the same type of rare fish was caught.
>
> The oarfish has a unique elongated shape, which could make it susceptible to underwater shock waves. It may be stunned and then float to the surface. Or the real reason could be that poisonous gases are released from the Earth's crust during seismic activity. At any rate, whenever an oarfish is netted, a geological upheaval is in progress or about to occur.
>
> And, having just caught some slender oarfish, Japanese seismologists are afraid that another disaster is imminent.

(a) In the first paragraph, there is a statement based on testimony. What is it? On what testimony is it based?

(b) The third paragraph states one conclusion of the entire discussion. What is the conclusion?

(c) The second paragraph states some evidence for this conclusion. Would you say that the argument to the conclusion (b) is more like an argument from population to sample, or from sample to population?

(d) The third paragraph offers two plausible explanations for the facts stated in the second paragraph. What are they?

(e) There are several distinct arguments leading to the final conclusion in the fourth paragraph. Describe how the arguments fit together.

6   *Women engineers.*

> Since 1986, only 11% of engineering school graduates have been women. That showing is particularly poor considering that in other formerly male-dominated fields there are signs of real progress. Some examples from 1986: law, 48%; commerce, 44%; medicine, 45%; and in the biological sciences, nearly 50% of the graduates are women.

(a) What is the conclusion? (b) What kind of argument is it? Valid? Inductive and risky? Inference to a plausible explanation?

7   *Plastic surgery.*

> In her private counseling service for women, Martha Laurence, a professor of social work, tries to get behind the reasons women give for wanting plastic surgery. "Usually it is because they have a lack of confidence in who they are, the way they are," she said. "There is no simple answer, but the real problem is one of equity and of women's control over the self."

Her conclusion is that "the real problem is one of equity and of women's control over the self." What type of argument does she have for this conclusion?

8   *Manitoba marijuana.*

Basement operations are sprouting up in rural Manitoba to supply hydroponically grown marijuana for the Winnipeg market, police say. As Constable Duane Rhone of the rural Selkirk community of Winnipeg said in a recent interview, "It's cheap, it's easy to set up and there is a high return on investment. You can produce more marijuana of a better quality in a small amount of space," he said, adding that the necessary equipment is readily available. "It's become the thing to do. We've been seeing a lot more of this hydroponics marijuana in the last little while. There must be plenty more of these operators that we don't know about."

Conclusion: There are many as-yet undiscovered marijuana growers in rural Manitoba.

What kind of argument is Constable Rhone offering?

KEY WORDS FOR REVIEW

Population   Sample
Inference to the best explanation   Testimony
Inductive logic   Decision Theory

3   The Gambler's Fallacy

Most of the main ideas about probability come up right at the beginning. Two major ones are **independence** and **randomness**. Even more important for clear thinking is the notion of a **probability model**.

ROULETTE

A gambler is betting on what he thinks is a *fair* roulette wheel. The wheel is divided into 38 segments, of which:

- 18 segments are black.
- 18 segments are red.
- 2 segments are green, and marked with zeroes.

If you bet $10 on red, and the wheel stops at red, you win $20. Likewise if you bet $10 on black and it stops at black, you win $20. Otherwise you lose. The house always wins when the wheel stops at zero.

Now imagine that there has been a long run—a dozen spins—in which the wheel stopped at black. The gambler decides to bet on red, because he thinks:

The wheel must come up red soon.
This wheel is fair, so it stops on red as often as it stops on black.
Since it has not stopped on red recently, it must stop there soon. I'll bet on red.

The argument is a risky one. The conclusion is, "The wheel must stop on red in the next few spins." The argument leads to a risky decision. The gambler decides to bet on red. There you have it, an argument and a decision. Do you agree with the gambler?

Since this chapter is called "the gambler's fallacy" there must be something wrong with the gambler's argument. Can you say what?

We will spend some time explaining one way to talk about the argument—and about probability in general. Do not expect formal definitions yet. Try to get some fairly clear ideas.

FAIR

Arguments have premises. The gambler's main premise was that the roulette wheel is **fair**. Fair? What is fair? The word has quite a few meanings.

> A judge may be fair.
> A fair wage.
> A fair settlement.
> A fair grade in this course.
> A fair game.
> A fair coin.
> One greedy child cuts a cake in half; another greedy child chooses which half to take. "That's fair."
> "Affirmative action" to help minorities or women in the workplace: is that fair?

What is the opposite of fair? Something is unfair if it favors one party over another. A judge who is fair is not biased in favor of one party or the other. We use the same word—*biased*—for gambling devices. A gambling setup like a coin or a roulette wheel is unfair if it is biased.

BIASED

If a coin tends to come up heads more often than tails, it is biased.

If spins of a roulette wheel tend more often to be red than black, the wheel is biased.

A biased coin tends to come up heads more often than tails, or vice versa. What do we mean by "tends"? That is a hard question. The coin comes up heads more often than tails. Always? In any sequence of tosses with this setup? No, it must be "on average" or "in the long run." And what does that mean? In the long run we're all dead.

Yet we do seem to have a rough intuitive idea of averages in the long run. We have to start somewhere. We think of these setups as somehow involving "chance." Call them *chance setups*. We can in principle make repeated *trials* on a chance setup: tosses, spins, draws, samples. Trials on a setup have a definite set of possible *outcomes*:

- With a coin: heads, tails.
- With a die: 1, 2, 3, 4, 5, 6.
- With a roulette wheel: each of the 38 segments.

We have the idea of how frequently different outcomes occur on repeated trials. If each outcome occurs as often as every other, we say the setup is unbiased.

> A chance setup is **unbiased** if and only if the relative
> frequency in the long run of each outcome is equal to that
> of any other.

Since this is a philosophy book, we will come back and worry about what we
mean by "long run," "tends," and "relative frequency." We do seem to have some
intuitions about what these ideas mean, and we start with those intuitions. Later
on, philosophical analysis tries to get clearer about what they mean.

INDEPENDENCE

There are many ways to be unfair. A coin tossing device is "unfair" if it regularly
gives heads more often than tails. It is biased. But that is not the only way to be
unfair.

You can very easily learn to toss a coin, flipping it with your thumb and
catching it on your wrist, so that it almost always appears heads if you last
tossed tails, and tails if it last fell heads. (You may not believe this, but practice
for five minutes and then you can amaze your friends. You are on your way to
becoming a magician.) When you get the knack, heads and tails come up equally
often:

H T H T H T H T H T H T H T

Your system is **unbiased**. But would you count that as "fair" tossing? No. Something is fishy about this kind of tossing. A gambler would have a field day. He
does not have to wait until he sees 12 tails in a row (he never will). He sees one
tails—and then bets heads. He is sure to win!

Hence lack of bias in the system does **not** guarantee that a chance setup is
fair. We need more than that. The idea of a fair tossing device seems to involve
there being *no regularity* in the outcomes. Or they should be *random*. Randomness
is a very hard idea. Outcomes from a chance setup are random (we think) if
outcomes are not *influenced* by the outcomes of previous trials.

The setup should not have a *"memory."* A fair setup does not know, at any
trial, what happened on previous trials.

There are even more ways to think about this. For example, if a gambler knew
that two heads in a row are usually followed by tails, then he could place bets so
as to make a profit. But trials on that setup would not be independent. Randomness is sometimes defined as: *no successful gambling system is possible.*

The idea of *complexity* is also used. Random sequences are so complex that
we cannot predict them. The complexity of a sequence can be measured by the
length of the shortest computer program needed to generate the sequence. A
sequence is called random, relative to some computational system, if the shortest
program needed to generate it is as long as the sequence itself.

Here we have a family of related ideas:

random	no influence from previous trials
no regularity	no memory of previous trials
complexity	impossibility of a gambling system

Some students like the metaphor of "no memory." Others focus on randomness. People happy with computers like complexity. Each of these ideas gets at a central notion. We say that the outcome of each trial should be *independent* of the outcome of other trials on the setup. A more precise account of independence is given in chapter 6. For the present this will suffice:

> Trials on a chance setup are **independent** if and only if the probabilities of the outcomes of a trial are not influenced by the outcomes of previous trials.

This is not a definition. It is an explanation of an idea. A chance setup is **fair** if and only if:

■ It is **unbiased**, and
■ outcomes are **independent** of each other.

TWO WAYS TO BE UNFAIR

Hence a chance setup can be "unfair" in two different ways. It can be biased. For example, heads tends to come up more often than tails. But there could also be some regularity in the sequence of outcomes. Trials may not be independent of each other. Since there are two ways to be unfair, there are four possible combinations:

Fair: unbiased, independent.
Unfair: unbiased, not independent.
Unfair: biased, independent.
Unfair: biased, not independent.

Here are examples of each combination.

UNBIASED AND INDEPENDENT

A favorite model for probability is a big container of balls, an urn, from which we draw balls "at random." Imagine an urn with 50 balls in it, numbered 1 to 50, but otherwise as round and smooth and as similar as could be—the same circumference, the same weight. There is lots of room to spare. A trial consists of shaking the urn very well, drawing a ball, noting the number, and putting it back. This is called *sampling with replacement*. We expect each number to be drawn as often as every other. We imagine that the draws are *unbiased* and *independent*.

BIASED BONES, INDEPENDENT OUTCOMES

People gambled a long time ago. In the beginning they did not have dice. They used bones. The heelbones of a running animal like a deer or a horse can land in only four ways. They are natural randomizers. These bones are sometimes called "knucklebones." They are ancestors of our dice. Some gamblers still talk about "rolling the bones."

Of course, every knucklebone is different. One class tossed a knucklebone from Turkey, about 6,000 years old. Three outcomes were labeled with colored spots: red, black, blue. The fourth outcome was left unmarked.

The bone was tossed 300 times. Here is a summary of results:

    unmarked: 110   blue: 88
    red: 50   black: 52

Or in percentages, rounding off:

    unmarked: 37%   blue: 29%
    red: 17%   black: 17%

Although red and black seem to occur almost equally often, unmarked comes up more often than red and black combined. These bones are clearly *biased*.

But we could not detect any regularity in the rolls. It did not look as if the outcome of any roll depended on previous rolls. Rolls of this bone seem to be *independent*.

UNBIASED DRAWS, DEPENDENT OUTCOMES

Imagine an urn with an equal number of red and green balls. At the first draw, we might think that there will be no bias for red or green. But suppose we sample *without replacement*. That is, once a ball is drawn, we draw another without replacing, until the urn is empty; then, if we want, we restore all the balls to the urn and start again. If we draw a green ball the first time, then at the next draw there is one more red ball in the urn than there are green balls. So we would expect a better chance of getting a red ball than a green one, the next time around.

Hence the result of the second draw is *not* independent of the result of the first draw. Yet overall, green and red balls are drawn equally often. The setup is *unbiased* (red and green come up equally often), but trials are influenced by previous outcomes. They are *not independent*.

BIAS AND DEPENDENCE

Now imagine that 90% of the balls are red, and 10% are green. We sample without replacement. Then there is a *bias* in favor of red. And trials are *not independent*.

THE GAMBLER'S FALLACY

We have just seen that a chance setup can be unfair in two different ways. It can be biased. And trials may not be independent. The difference matters. *Fallacious Gambler* said:

> I think this is a fair roulette wheel.
> I have just seen twelve black spins in a row.
> Since the wheel is fair, black and red come up equally often.

Hence:

> Red has to come up pretty soon.
> I'd better start betting red.
> Maybe red won't come up the very next time, but a lot of reds have to come up soon.

This is called "the gambler's fallacy." We commit many fallacies in inductive reasoning.

What is the gambler's fallacy? The fallacy does not involve *bias*. It involves *independence*.

The gambler thinks that a sequence of twelve blacks makes it more likely that the wheel will stop at red next time. *If so, a past sequence affects future outcomes.* So trials on the device would not be independent, and the device would not be fair after all.

Thus the gambler is being *inconsistent*. His premises are:

- The setup is fair, and
- there have been twelve black spins in a row.

He infers:

- Some reds must turn up soon.

That conclusion would follow only if outcomes from the setup were not independent. That would be inconsistent with the gambler's first premise.

IMPOSSIBILITY OF A SUCCESSFUL GAMBLING SYSTEM

There are many ways to think about randomness and independence. One definition says that *outcomes are random if and only if a successful gambling system is impossible*. That does not mean that you can't win. Someone has to win. A gambling system is impossible if no betting system is guaranteed to win.

For example, suppose a coin-tossing setup has a "memory." It is made so that every time there has been heads followed by tails, the coin falls tails. Every time there has been tails followed by heads, the coin falls heads. It can never produce the sequences HTH or THT. So you might see this sequence:

H T T T T H H T T H H T

But not this one:

H T T T T H T T T H H T

If the setup never allows THT or HTH, a very profitable gambling system is possible: when you see HT, bet on T next; when you see TH, bet on H next; otherwise don't bet. So for the first sequence above you bet like this:

HT (bet T) TTTH (bet H) HT (bet T) TH (bet H) HT

You win every bet you make.

Our fallacious gambler dreams that a profitable gambling system is possible. His system is, in part, "When you see 12 blacks in a row, bet red." This system would work only if the spins of the roulette wheel were not independent. And, of course, they may not be! But if the gambler's premise is that the roulette wheel is fair, then he should think the spins are independent of each other. So his fallacy is thinking **both** that the roulette wheel is fair, **and** that a gambling system is possible.

COMPOUND OUTCOMES

There is yet another way to think of a fair setup. A coin is unbiased if on average the two outcomes heads and tails come up equally often. But we can also think of all outcomes of two trials, namely,

HH   HT   TH   TT

If trials are independent, then each of these four compound outcomes will occur on average equally often. Likewise, each sequence of 13 outcomes from the roulette wheel, made up of just B and R, will come up equally often. Thus on average,

B B B B B B B B B B B B R

occurs neither more nor less frequently than

B B B B B B B B B B B B B.

Half the time a sequence of 12 blacks is followed by red. Half the time a sequence of 12 blacks is followed by black.

ODD QUESTION 3

In Lotto 6/49, a standard government-run lottery, you choose 6 out of 49 numbers (1 through 49). You win the biggest prize—maybe millions of dollars—if these 6 are drawn. (The prize money is divided between all those who choose the lucky numbers. If no one wins, then most of the prize money is put back into next week's lottery.)

Suppose your aunt offers you, *free*, a choice between two tickets in the lottery, with numbers as shown:

A. You win if 1, 2, 3, 4, 5, and 6 are drawn.
B. You win if 39, 36, 32, 21, 14, and 3 are drawn.

Do you prefer A, B, or are you indifferent between the two?
     If the lottery is fair, then any sequence of outcomes will be as probable as any other. Some people might prefer ticket A because it is simpler to check the ticket to see if you have won. That's practical.
     Some people might prefer ticket B because they have a kid brother who is fourteen years old and a little sister who is three. That is superstition.
     If you choose your tickets *simply by the probability*, then you should have no preference between A and B.
     But! There might be a real advantage in choosing A over B!
     The very large prizes are split between all the people who chose the lucky numbers that win. It may be that most people like irregular-looking outcomes like B. They cannot believe that a regular sequence like A would occur. So fewer people choose sequence A than choose sequence B. Hence, if sequence A is drawn, the prize may be bigger, for each winner, than if sequence B is drawn.
     But! Maybe enough people know this so that they try to outwit the herd, and become a little herd themselves. When government lotteries were finally introduced into Great Britain late in the twentieth century, a lot of people chose 1, 2, 3, 4, 5, 6 because they thought that no one else would. If it had come up (it did not) the payoff would have been quite small, because the prize would have been split among so many players.

ODD QUESTION 7

"Imitate" a coin. That is, write down a sequence of 100 H (for heads) and T (for tails) without tossing a coin—but a sequence that you think will fool everyone into thinking it is the report of tossing a fair coin.

That sounds easy, and it is. But most people try to build in *too much* irregularity to make the sequence look random. It is the same instinct that inclines most of us to think, for a moment, that B is a better choice for a lottery ticket than A.

A *run* is a sequence of identical outcomes—like the run of 12 blacks at roulette. Most people think that a sequence of 100 tosses will fluctuate a good deal between heads and tails.

Hardly anyone making up a sequence of 10 tosses puts in a run of seven heads in a row. It is true that the chance of getting 7 heads in a row, with a fair coin, is only $1/64$ ($\frac{1}{2} \times \frac{1}{2} \times \frac{1}{2} \times \frac{1}{2} \times \frac{1}{2} \times \frac{1}{2} \times \frac{1}{2}$). But in tossing a coin 100 times, you have at least 93 chances to start tossing 7 heads in a row, because each of the first 93 tosses could begin a run of 7.

It is more probable than not, in 100 tosses, that you will get 7 heads in a row. It is certainly more probable than not, that you will get at least 6 heads in a row. Yet almost no one writes down a pretend sequence, in which there are even 6 heads in a row.

This example may help some people with the gambler's fallacy. We have this feeling that if there have been 12 blacks in a row, then the roulette wheel had better hurry up and stop at a red! Not so. There is, so to speak, all the time in the world for things to even out.

THE ALERT LEARNER

We began with a person we call *Fallacious Gambler*. He meets *Stodgy Logic*. *Stodgy Logic* says to *Fallacious Gambler*:

> Your premise was that the setup is fair. But now you reason as if the setup is not fair! You think the only ingredient in unfairness is bias. You forgot about independence. That's your fallacy.

They meet a third party, *Alert Learner*. She reasons:

> We've been spinning black with this wheel all too frequently. I thought that the wheel was unbiased. But that must be wrong. The wheel must be biased toward black! So I'll start betting on black.

She has made an inductive argument: to the risky conclusion that the wheel is biased. *Alert Learner* bets black. *Fallacious Gambler* bets red. *Stodgy Logic* says there is no point in betting either way. Who is right?

Alert Learner might be right. Maybe the wheel *is* biased. Pure logic cannot tell you. You have to know more about this casino, how it gets its roulette wheels, and so on. In a real-life casino we would guess that the wheel is not loaded for black. There would be no point. People would catch on quickly, and all the alert learners in this world would be getting rich.

I expect that *Alert Learner* is wrong. I think so because I am worldly-wise. My belief that she is wrong has nothing to do with inductive logic. It depends on what I know about casinos, wheels, and gamblers. I may be wrong. Another risky argument.

RISKY AIRPLANES

Vincent and Gina have been visiting their grandparents and have to fly home. Two companies fly their route, Alpha Air and Gamma Goways. Gamma has just crashed one of its planes.

> VINCENT: Let's take Gamma—they crash only one flight in a million, and they've just had their crash!
>
> GINA: Don't be crazy. This accident shows that Gamma is negligent; we had better take Alpha.

Who is right? Gina is thinking like *Alert Learner*. But her grandmother may say: "Gamma will be extra careful and check all its planes for just the fault that caused the crash. So Gamma is the one to fly." Gina's boyfriend says: "No way! Gamma has a long record of safety violations. Moreover, its pilots are poorly trained. Their planes are old, cheap, and poorly maintained. Their cabin staff are underpaid. There is no way they can fix things in a week—or in a year."

Vincent, Gina, grandma, and the boyfriend all argue differently. Each brings in different premises. A premise may be false. Logic cannot tell which premises are true. Logic can only tell when premises are good reasons for a conclusion. All logic can tell us is that *if* Vincent is reasoning like the fallacious gambler, *then* he is wrong. And it seems that he is.

MODELS

In reasoning using probability, we often turn to *simple and artificial models* of complex situations. Real life is almost always complicated, except when we have deliberately made an apparatus and rules—as in a gambling situation. People made the roulette wheel to have some symmetries, so that each segment turns up as often as every other. Real life is not like that. But artificial games may still be useful *probability models* that help us to think about the real world.

A basic strategy of probability thinking: make simple and artificial models. Compare the models to a real-life situation. We can apply precise and often mathematical or logical concepts to the models. That is why they help us to think clearly. But we also have to see how applicable they are to a real-life problem.

For example: it is very hard to find a place to park on my street. The fine for illegal parking is $20. My guest wants to park illegally. How likely is it that she will get a ticket this evening? The parking inspector comes around only one evening a week. So I make a model using a lottery, in which one red card and six green cards are put in a hat, and one is drawn at random. I compare a red card to getting a fine, and a green one to a free parking place.

Another guest says: "What *is* the right model of this situation? I got a ticket parking outside last night." We believe the inspectors almost never come around two days running. Now we make a new model of the situation, in which trials are not independent.

The question for Vincent and Gina is: what is the right model of the situation with Gamma Goways?

TWO WAYS TO GO WRONG WITH A MODEL

Serious thinking about risks, which uses probability models, can go wrong in two very different ways.

- The model may not represent reality well. That is a mistake about the real world.
- We can draw wrong conclusions from the model. That is a logical error.

Alert Learner said, "Bet on black." This is because she thought we were using the wrong model, and were making a mistake about the real world.

Fallacious Gambler said, "Bet on red." He made a logical error. He forgot about independence.

These two kinds of error recall the two ways to criticize an argument.

- Challenge the premises—show that at least one is false.
- Challenge the reasoning—show that the premises are not a good reason for the conclusion.

Criticizing the model is like challenging the premises. Criticizing the analysis of the model is like challenging the reasoning.

EXERCISES

1 *Roulette wheels.* At North American casinos, roulette wheels have two "zeros" where the house collects all. In Europe the rules are similar, but there is only one zero.
(a) If you had to bet, would you rather play roulette in Europe or North America?
(b) Does the difference in odds make any difference to the gambler's fallacy?

2 *Shuffling.* In card games such as bridge, cards are shuffled before each deal. The deal usually has a "memory" of previous games, because shuffling is imperfect. After a deal, cards stay in an order that still reflects the order present before the deal. Even professional dealers are not perfect. A pack must be shuffled at least seven times by a professional to eliminate all traces of its previous order.

Suppose some good friends are playing, and they shuffle the pack only twice before each deal.
(a) In repeated playing, are the hands that are dealt biased?
(b) Are they independent?
(c) Is the setup fair, according to our definition of a fair setup?

3 *Lotto.* Two mathematicians from Stanford University analyzed data from the Canadian Lotto 6/49. Using a model of choices people made, they calculated that the least popular ticket was 20, 30, 39, 40, 41, 48. If you are going to buy a Lotto ticket, would that be a good number to choose?

4 *Numerals.* We can produce a sequence of numerals by rolling a die. The *trials* consist of rolling the die. The possible *outcomes* are 1 through 6. What about the numerals produced by the following setups? Are these setups unbiased? Are trials independent?

   (a) *Birth weights.* Newborn babies at a large hospital are weighed to the nearest gram. Take just the last digit in the birth weight in grams to generate a sequence of numerals from 0 through 9. A trial consists of a birth, weighing, and recording. The possible outcomes are 0 through 9. What if the babies were weighed only to the nearest pound, and the last digit were used?

   (b) *Telephone poles.* A telephone line runs alongside a long straight road in the prairies. The poles are numbered consecutively. Trials, in order, consist of noting the last digit on successive poles.

   (c) *Books.* A book has exactly 600 pages, numbered 1–600. You open the pages at random. Each time, you note the last digit of the left-hand page.

   (d) *Cruise ships.* The captain on a cruise ship reports, at noon each day, the number of nautical miles the ship has sailed in the past twenty-four hours. Each day, passengers bet on the last digit in the distance. Twenty percent of the stakes go to charity. The rest is divided among those who bet on the right digit. (Might you have any reason for betting on one digit rather than another?)

5 *Fallacious Gambler strikes back.* "I've been reading this old book, *A Treatise on Probability*, published in 1921 by the famous economist John Maynard Keynes. He says that a German psychologist, Dr. Marbe, studied 80,000 spins of roulette at Monte Carlo, and found that long runs do not occur nearly as often as theory predicts. A run of 13 blacks is more improbable than anyone believes, so having seen 12 blacks in a row, I am going to bet red!" (a) Is our friend still a fallacious gambler? (b) How would you explain Dr. Marbe's data?

6 *Counting.* In varieties of poker known as blackjack, "twenty-one," etc., when played at a casino, the odds favor the house. But not by much. Hands of blackjack used to be dealt until the pack was exhausted. That was like sampling *without replacement*. Explain why a *gambling system* should be possible when a game is played according to these rules.

7 *The American draft.* During the Vietnam War, there was much criticism of the way in which young American men were drafted into the army. The poorer you were, the more likely you were to get conscripted. Blacks and Hispanics were more likely to be drafted than other Americans. So the old system was replaced by a lottery: 365 balls were placed in a large rotating urn. The balls were labeled, one for each day of the year (an extra ball was added for leap years).

   The draw was done in public, on television. To show the public that every ball went in, no cheating, the balls were put in the urn in order, starting with 365 (it was not a leap year) and going down to 1. Pretty young women then reached into the urn and drew one ball at a time.

   The first men to be drafted were those whose birthdays were drawn early in the draw. The army drafted men who had the first birthday drawn, then the second, and so on, until it had as many soldiers as it wanted.

   The first few balls that were drawn did seem to come from anywhere in the year, but after a while, there was a pronounced tendency for the balls to be from the early months. So if you were born in February, you had a good chance of being drafted. If you were born in December, you had little chance of being drafted.

(a) Was this sampling with, or without, replacement?

(b) Do you think the draws were biased?

(c) If so, the set-up was not "fair" in the sense of this chapter. Was it unfair to the men of draft age?

(d) Suggest at least two explanations of what was happening.

8 *X rays* are potentially harmful. They may damage a cell that then becomes cancerous.

Sara says to her dentist: "Please do not take any X rays. I had a terrible skiing accident three years ago and broke many leg bones, and so had many X rays then. I don't want any more, because that would make cancer even more likely."

Dentist: "Nonsense. Your past X rays make no difference to the danger of future X rays. To think otherwise is to commit the gambler's fallacy!"

Continue the argument.

9 *A dry August.* A man started a farm in arid but fertile land. Weather records show that during each month from March through August there is a fifty-fifty chance of one good rainfall, enough to let him irrigate for the whole season. A completely dry growing season occurs less than once in sixty years.

It is now mid-August. There has been no rain since a big storm at the end of last year. The farmer has run out of water. His crops are dying. He is optimistic, because he thinks:

It will almost certainly rain soon. The statistics prove it!

Has he committed the gambler's fallacy? Are there any errors in the argument which are different from the gambler's fallacy?

10 *The inverse gambler's fallacy.* Albert enjoys gambling with dice.

(a) If Albert rolls four fair dice simultaneously, what is the probability that on a single roll he gets 6, 6, 6, 6?

(b) Trapper: "Albert was rolling four dice last night, and got four sixes." Nelson: "I bet he rolled the dice many times to get four sixes!" Is Nelson's conclusion reasonable?

(c) Lucie visits Albert. As she enters, he rolls four dice and he shouts "Hooray!" for he has just rolled four sixes. Lucie: "I bet you've been rolling the dice for a long time tonight to get that result!" Now Lucie may have many reasons for saying this—perhaps Albert is a lunatic dice-roller. But simply on the evidence that he has just rolled four sixes, is her conclusion reasonable?

11 *Lucky aunt.* (a) "Did you know your aunt won a medium prize in the lottery last year?"—"Oh, I suppose she played every week." Is that a good inference? (b) The lottery numbers have just been announced on TV. Phone rings, it is your aunt. "I just won the lottery!"—"Oh, I suppose you've been playing every week." Is that a good inference?

12 *The argument from design.* There is a famous argument for the existence of a Creator. If you found a watch in the middle of a desert, where "no man has been before," you would still infer that this well-designed timekeeping instrument had been made by a craftsman or factory. Here we are in the midst of an extraordinarily organized and well-designed universe, where there is an extraordinary adjust-

ment of causes, and of means to ends. Therefore, our universe too must have a Creator.

A common objection: The emergence of a well-organized universe just by chance would be astonishing. But if we imagine that matter in motion has been around, if not forever, at least for a very long time, then of course sooner or later we would arrive at a well-organized universe, just by chance. Hence the argument from design is defective.

Is this a sound objection?

KEY WORDS FOR REVIEW

Relative frequency	Gambling system
Chance setup	Complexity
Biased/unbiased	Independence
Random	Probability model

4   Elementary Probability Ideas

This chapter explains the usual notation for talking about probability, and then reminds you how to add and multiply with probabilities.

WHAT HAS A PROBABILITY?

Suppose you want to take out car insurance. The insurance company will want to know your age, sex, driving experience, make of car, and so forth. They do so because they have a question in mind:

What is the probability that you will have an automobile accident next year?

That asks about a *proposition* (statement, assertion, conjecture, etc.):

"You will have an automobile accident next year."

The company wants to know: *What is the probability that this proposition is true?* The insurers could ask the same question in a different way:

What is the probability of your having an automobile accident next year?

This asks about an *event* (something of a certain sort happening). Will there be

"an automobile accident next year, in which you are driving one of the cars involved"?

The company wants to know: *What is the probability of this event occurring?* Obviously these are two different ways of asking the same question.

PROPOSITIONS AND EVENTS

Logicians are interested in arguments from premises to conclusions. Premises and conclusions are propositions. So inductive logic textbooks usually talk about the probability of propositions.

Most statisticians and most textbooks of probability talk about the probability of events.

So there are two languages of probability, propositions and events.

Propositions are true or false.
Events occur or do not occur.

Most of what we say in terms of propositions can be translated into event-language, and most of what we say in terms of events can be translated into proposition-language.

To begin with, we will sometimes talk one way, sometimes the other.

The distinction between propositions and events is not an important one now. It matters only in the second half of this book.

WHY LEARN TWO LANGUAGES WHEN ONE WILL DO?

Because some students will already talk the event language, and others will talk the proposition language.

Because some students will go on to learn more statistics, and talk the event language. Other students will follow logic, and talk the proposition language.

The important thing is to be able to understand anyone who has something useful to say.

There is a general moral here. Be very careful and very clear about what you say. But do not be dogmatic about your own language. Be prepared to express any careful thought in the language your audience will understand. And be prepared to learn from someone who talks a language with which you are not familiar.

NOTATION: LOGIC

Propositions or events are represented by capital letters: A, B, C . . .

Logical compounds will be represented as follows, no matter whether we have propositions or events in mind:

Disjunction (or): AvB for (A, or B, or both). We read this "A or B."

Conjunction (and): A&B for (A and B).

Negation (not): ~A for (not A).

Example in the proposition language:
Let Z be the proposition that the roulette wheel stops at a zero. Let B be the proposition that the wheel stops at black.

ZvB is the proposition that the wheel stops at a zero or black.

Example:

Let Z: the wheel stops at a zero.
Let B: the wheel stops at black.

Then: ZvB = one or the other of those events occurs = the wheel stops at black or a zero.
Let R: the wheel stops at red.
In roulette, the wheel stops at a zero or black (ZvB) if and only if it does not stop at red (~R). So,

~R is equivalent to (ZvB).
R is equivalent to ~(ZvB).

NOTATION: SETS

Statisticians usually do not talk about propositions. They talk about **events** in terms of **set theory**. Here is a rough translation of proposition language into event language.

The **disjunction** of two propositions, AvB, corresponds to the **union** of two sets of events, A∪B.

The **conjunction** of two propositions, A&B, corresponds to the **intersection** of two sets of events, A∩B.

The **negation** of a proposition, ~A, corresponds to the **complement** of a set of events, often written A'.

NOTATION: PROBABILITY

In courses on probability and statistics, textbooks usually write P( ) for probability. But our notation for probability will be:

Pr ( ).

In the roulette example (Z for zero, R for red, B for black), all these are probabilities:

Pr(Z)   Pr(ZvB)   Pr(~(ZvB))   Pr(R)

Earlier on this page we said that ~R is equivalent to (ZvB). So:

Pr(~R) = Pr(ZvB).

That is, the probability of not stopping at a red segment is the same as the probability of stopping at a zero or a black segment.

TWO CONVENTIONS

All of us—whether we were ever taught any probability theory or not—have got into the habit of expressing probabilities by percentages or fractions. That is:

Probabilities lie between 0 and 1.

In symbols, for any A,

$0 \leq Pr(A) \leq 1$

At the extremes we have 0 and 1.

In the language of propositions, what is certainly true has probability 1.

In the language of events, what is bound to happen has probability 1.

In probability textbooks, the sure event or a proposition that is certainly true is often represented by the last letter in the Greek alphabet, omega, written as a capital letter: Ω. So our convention is written:

$Pr(\Omega) = 1$

The probability of a proposition that is certainly true, or of an event that is sure to happen, is 1.

MUTUALLY EXCLUSIVE

Two propositions are called *mutually exclusive* if they can't both be true at once. An ordinary roulette wheel cannot both stop at a zero (the house wins) and, on the same spin, stop at red. Hence these two propositions cannot both be true. They are mutually exclusive:

The wheel will stop at a zero on the next spin.
The wheel will stop at red on the next spin.

Likewise, two events which cannot both occur at once are called *mutually exclusive*. They are also called *disjoint*.

ADDING PROBABILITIES

There are some things about probability that "everybody" in college seems to know. For the moment we will just use this common knowledge. "Everybody" knows how to add probabilities.

More carefully: *the probabilities of mutually exclusive propositions or events add up.*

If A and B are **mutually exclusive,** Pr(AvB) = Pr(A) + Pr(B).

Thus if the probability of zero, in roulette, is 1/19, and the probability of red is 9/19, the probability that one or the other happens is:

Pr(ZvR) = Pr(Z) + Pr(R) = 1/19 + 9/19 = 10/19.

Example: Take a *fair* die.
Let: E = the die falls with an even number up.

E = (the die falls 2, 4, or 6).   Pr(E) = ½

Why? Because Pr(2) = 1/6. Pr(4) = 1/6. Pr(6) = 1/6.

The events 2, 4, and 6 are mutually exclusive.
Add (1/6) + (1/6) + (1/6). You get ½.

People who roll dice call the one-spot on a die the *ace*.
Let M = the die falls either ace up, or with a prime number up.

M = (the die falls 1, 2, 3, or 5).   Pr(M) = 4/6 = 2/3

But you cannot add Pr(E) to Pr(M) to get

** Pr(EvM) = 7/6. (*WRONG*)

(We already know probabilities lie between 0 and 1, so 7/6 is impossible.)
Why can't we add them up? Because E and M *overlap*: 2 is in both E and M. E and M are not mutually exclusive.
In fact, (EvM) = (the die falls 1, 2, 3, 4, 5, or 6), so that,

Pr(EvM) = 1.

You cannot add if the events or propositions "overlap."

Adding probabilities is for mutually exclusive events or propositions.

INDEPENDENCE

Intuitively:

Two events are independent when the occurrence of one does not influence the probability of the occurrence of the other.

> Two propositions are independent when the truth of one does not make the truth of the other any more or less probable.

Many people—like *Fallacious Gambler*—don't understand independence very well. All the same, "everybody" seems to know that probabilities can be multiplied. More carefully: *the probabilities of independent events or propositions can be multiplied*.

MULTIPLYING

> If A and B are **independent**, $Pr(A\&B) = Pr(A) \times Pr(B)$.

We are rolling two fair dice. The outcome of tossing one die is independent of the outcome of tossing the other, so the probability of getting

> a five on the first toss $(Five_1)$
> and a six on the second toss (Six_2) is:
>
> $Pr(Five_1 \& Six_2) = Pr(Five_1) \times Pr(Six_2) = 1/6 \times 1/6 = 1/36.$

Independence matters! Here is a mistake:

> The probability of getting an even number (E) with a fair die is $1/2$.
> We found that the probability of M, of getting either an ace or a prime number, is $2/3$.
> What is the probability that on a single toss a die comes up both E and M? We cannot reason:
>
> ** $Pr(E\&M) = Pr(E) \times Pr(M) = 1/2 \times 2/3 = 1/3.$ (*WRONG*)

The two events are not independent. In fact, only one outcome is both even and prime, namely 2. Hence:

> $Pr(E\&M) = Pr(2) = 1/6.$

Sometimes the fallacy is not obvious. Suppose you decide that the probability of the Toronto Blue Jays playing in the next World Series is 0.3 [Pr(J)], and that the probability of the Los Angeles Dodgers playing in the next world series is 0.4 [Pr(D)]. You cannot conclude that

> ** $Pr(D\&J) = Pr(D) \times Pr(J) = 0.4 \times 0.3 = 0.12.$ (*WRONG*)

This is because the two events may not be independent. Maybe they are. But maybe, because of various player trades and so on, the Dodgers will do well only if they trade some players with the Jays, in which case the Jays won't do so well.

> Multiplying probabilities is for independent events or propositions.

SIXES AND SEVENS: ODD QUESTION 4

Odd Question 4 went like this:

> To throw a total of 7 with a pair of dice, you have to get a 1 and a 6, or a 2 and a 5, or a 3 and a 4.
> To throw a total of 6 with a pair of dice, you have to get a 1 and a 5, or a 2 and a 4, or a 3 and another 3.
> With two fair dice, you would expect:
> _____(a) To throw 7 more frequently than 6.
> _____(b) To throw 6 more frequently than 7.
> _____(c) To throw 6 and 7 equally often.

Many people think that 6 and 7 are equally probable. In fact, 7 is more probable than 6.

Look closely at what can happen in one roll of two dice, X and Y. We assume tosses are independent. There are 36 possible outcomes. In this table, (3,5), for example, means that X fell 3, while Y fell 5.

(1,1)	(2,1)	(3,1)	(4,1)	(5,1)	(6,1)
(1,2)	(2,2)	(3,2)	(4,2)	(5,2)	(6,2)
(1,3)	(2,3)	(3,3)	(4,3)	(5,3)	(6,3)
(1,4)	(2,4)	(3,4)	(4,4)	(5,4)	(6,4)
(1,5)	(2,5)	(3,5)	(4,5)	(5,5)	(6,5)
(1,6)	(2,6)	(3,6)	(4,6)	(5,6)	(6,6)

Circle the outcomes that add up to 6. How many?

Put a square around the outcomes that add up to 7. How many?

We can get a **sum of seven** in six ways: (1,6) or (2,5) or (3,4) or (4,3) or (5,2) or (6,1).

Each of these outcomes has probability 1/36. (*Independent tosses*) So,

Pr(7 with 2 dice) = 6/36 = 1/6. (*Mutually exclusive outcomes*)

But we can get a **sum of six** in only five ways: (1,5) or (2,4) or (3,3) or (4,2) or (5,1). So,

Pr(6 with 2 dice) = 5/36.

COMPOUNDING

Throwing a 6 with one die is a single event. Throwing a sum of seven with two dice is a *compound* event. It involves two distinct outcomes, which are combined in the event "the sum of the dice equals 7."

A lot of simple probability reasoning involves compound events. Imagine a fair coin, and two urns, Urn 1 and Urn 2, made up as follows:

Urn 1: 3 red balls, 1 green one.
Urn 2: 1 red ball, 3 green ones.

In a fair drawing from Urn 1, the probability of getting a Red ball is $Pr(R_1)$ = 3/4.

With Urn 2, it is $Pr(R_2) = 1/4$.

Now suppose we pick an urn by tossing a fair coin. If we get heads, we draw from Urn 1; if tails, from Urn 2. Assume independence, that is, that the toss of the coin has no effect on the urns.

What is the probability that we toss a coin **and then** draw a red ball from Urn 1? We first have to toss heads, and then draw a red ball from Urn 1 (R_1).

$$Pr(H\&R_1) = 1/2 \times 3/4 = 3/8.$$

The probability of tossing a coin and then drawing a red ball from Urn 2 (R_2) is:

$$Pr(T\&R_2) = 1/2 \times 1/4 = 1/8.$$

What is the probability of getting a red ball, using this setup? That is a compound event. We can get a red ball by getting heads with the coin, and then drawing red from Urn 1, ($H\&R_1$), **or** by getting tails, and then drawing red from Urn 2 ($T\&R_2$).

These are mutually exclusive events, and so can be added.

$$Pr(Red) = Pr(H\&R_1) + Pr(T\&R_2) = 3/8 + 1/8 = 1/2.$$

So the probability of drawing red, in this set-up, is 1/2.

A TRICK QUESTION

Suppose we select one of those two urns by tossing a coin, and then make *two* draws from *that* urn with replacement. What is the probability of drawing two reds in a row in this setup?

We know the probability of getting one red is 1/2.

Is the probability of two reds $(1/2)(1/2) = 1/4$? NO!

The reason is that we can get two reds in a row in two different ways, which we'll call X and Y:

X: By tossing heads (an event of probability ½), and then getting red from Urn 1 (R_1, an event of probability 3/4) followed by replacing the ball and again drawing red from Urn 1 (another event of probability 3/4).

Y: By tossing tails (probability 1/2), and then getting red from Urn 2 (R_2), followed by replacing the ball and again drawing red from Urn 2 (another R_2).

The probabilities are:

- $Pr(X) = (1/2)(3/4)(3/4) = 9/32.$
- $Pr(Y) = (1/2)(1/4)(1/4) = 1/32.$

Hence,

Pr(first ball drawn is red & second ball drawn is red)
= Pr(X) + Pr(Y) = 10/32 = 5/16.

UNDERSTANDING THE TRICK QUESTION

Did you think that the probability of two reds would be 1/4? Here is one way to understand why not. Think of doing two different experiments over and over again.

Experiment 1. Choose an urn by tossing a coin, and then draw a ball.

Results 1. You draw a red ball about half the time.

Experiment 2. Choose an urn by tossing a coin, and then draw two balls with replacement. (After you have drawn a ball, you put it back in the urn.)

Results 2. You get two red balls about 5/16 of the time, two green balls about 5/16 of the time, and a mix of one red and one green about 6/16 = 3/8 of the time.

Explanation. Once you have picked an urn with a "bias" for a given color, it is more probable that both balls will be of that color, than that you will get one majority and one minority color.

LAPLACE

This example was a great favorite with P. S. de Laplace (1749–1827), a truly major figure in the development of probability theory. He wrote the very first introductory college textbook about probability, *A Philosophical Essay on Probabilities*. He wrote this text for a class he taught at the polytechnic school in Paris in 1795, between the French Revolution and the rule of Napoleon.

Laplace was one of the finest mathematicians of his day. His *Analytic Theory of Probabilities* is still a rich source of ideas. His *Celestial Mechanics*—the mathematics of gravitation and astronomy—was equally important. He was very popular with the army, because he used mathematics to improve the French artillery. He used to go to Napoleon's vegetarian lunches, where he gave informal talks about probability theory.

EXERCISES

1   *Galileo.* Don't feel bad if you gave the wrong answer to Odd Question 4, about rolling dice. A long time ago someone asked a similar question, about throwing three dice. Galileo (1564–1642), one of the greatest astronomers and physicists ever, took the time to explain the right and wrong answers.

    Explain why you might (wrongly) expect three fair dice to yield a sum of 9 as often as they yield a sum of 10. Why is it wrong to think that 9 is as probable as 10?

2   *One card.* A card is drawn from a standard deck of fifty-two cards which have been well shuffled seven times. What is the probability that the card is:

(a) Either a face card (jack, queen, king) or a ten?
(b) Either a spade or a face card?

3   *Two cards.* When two cards are drawn in succession from a standard pack of cards, what are the probabilities of drawing:
(a) Two hearts in a row, with replacement, and (b) without replacement.
(c) Two cards, neither of which is a heart, with replacement, and (d) without replacement.

4   *Archery.* An archer's target has four concentric circles around a bull's-eye. For a certain archer, the probabilities of scoring are as follows:

Pr(hit the bull's-eye) = 0.1
Pr(hit first circle, but not bull's-eye) = 0.3.
Pr(hit second circle, but no better) = 0.2.
Pr(hit third circle, but no better) = 0.2.
Pr(hit fourth circle, but no better) = 0.1.

Her shots are independent.
(a) What is the probability that in two shots she scores a bull's-eye on the first shot, and the third circle on the second shot?
(b) What is the probability that in two shots she hits the bull's-eye once, and the third circle once?
(c) What is the probability that on any one shot she misses the target entirely?

5   *Polio from diapers* (a news story).

> *Southampton, England*: A man contracted polio from the soiled diaper of his niece, who had been vaccinated against the disease just days before, doctors said yesterday. "The probability of a person contracting polio from soiled diapers is literally one in three million," said consultant Martin Wale. What did Dr. Wale mean?

6   *Languages.* We distinguish between a "proposition-language" and an "event-language" for probability. Which language was used in:
(a) Question 2. (b) Question 3. (c) Question 4. (d) Dr. Wale's statement in question 5?

KEY WORDS FOR REVIEW

Events	Addition
Propositions	Independence
Mutually exclusive	Multiplication

5 Conditional Probability

The most important new idea about probability is the probability that something happens, on condition that something else happens. This is called conditional probability.

CATEGORICAL AND CONDITIONAL

We express probabilities in numbers. Here is a story I read in the newspaper. The old tennis pro Ivan was discussing the probability that the rising young star Stefan would beat the established player Boris in the semifinals. Ivan was set to play Pete in the other semifinals match. He said,

The probability that Stefan will beat Boris is 40%.

Or he could have said,

The chance of Stefan's winning is 0.4.

These are *categorical* statements, no ifs and buts about them. Ivan might also have this opinion:

Of course I'm going to win my semifinal match, but if I were to lose, then Stefan would not be so scared of meeting me in the finals, and he would play better; there would then be a 50–50 chance that Stefan would beat Boris.

This is the probability of Stefan's winning in his semifinal match, *conditional* on Ivan losing the other semifinal. We call it the *conditional probability*. Here are other examples:

Categorical: The probability that there will be a bumper grain crop on the prairies next summer.

Conditional: The probability that there will be a bumper grain crop next summer, given that there has been very heavy snowfall the previous winter.

Categorical: The probability of dealing an ace as the second card from a standard pack of well-shuffled cards (regardless of what card is dealt first).

There are 4 aces and 52 cards, any one of which may come up as the second card. So the probability of getting an ace as the second card should be $4/52 = 1/13$.

Conditional: The probability of dealing an ace as the second card *on condition that* the first card dealt was a king.

If a king was dealt first, there are 51 cards remaining. There are 4 aces still in the pack, so the *conditional probability* is 4/51.

Conditional: The probability of dealing an ace as the second card on condition that the first card dealt was also an ace.

When an ace is dealt first, there are 51 cards remaining, but only 3 aces, so the conditional probability is 3/51.

NOTATION

Categorical probability is represented:

Pr( )

Conditional probability is represented:

Pr(/).

Examples of categorical probability:

Pr(S wins the final) = 0.4.
Pr(second card dealt is an ace) = 1/13.

Examples of conditional probability:

Pr(S wins his semifinal/I loses his semifinal) = 0.5.
Pr(second card dealt is an ace/first card dealt is a king) = 4/51.

BINGO

Bingo players know about conditional probability.

In a game of bingo, you have a 5×5 card with 25 squares. Each square is marked with a different number from 1 to 99. The master of ceremonies draws numbered balls from a bag. Each time a number on your board is drawn, you fill in the corresponding square. You win (BINGO!) when you fill in a complete column, row, or diagonal.

Bingo players are fairly relaxed when they start the game. The probability that they will soon complete a line is small. But as they begin to fill in a line they get very excited, because the conditional probability of their winning is not so small.

PARKING TICKETS

If you park overnight near my home, and don't live on the block, you may be ticketed for not having a permit for overnight parking. The fine will be $20. But the street is only patrolled on average about once a week.

What is the probability of being fined?

Apparently the street is never patrolled on two consecutive nights. What is the probability of being ticketed tonight, *conditional* on having been ticketed on this street last night?

DEFINITION OF CONDITIONAL PROBABILITY

There is a very handy definition of conditional probability. We first state it, and then illustrate how it works.

> When $Pr(B) > 0$
> $Pr(A/B) = Pr(A\&B)/Pr(B)$

$Pr(B)$ must be a positive number, because we cannot divide by zero. But why is the rest of this definition sensible? Some examples will suggest why.

CONDITIONAL DICE

Think of a fair die. We say the outcome of a toss is **even** if it falls 2, 4, or 6 face up.

Here is conditional probability:

$Pr(6/even)$

In ordinary English:

The probability that we roll a 6, on condition that we rolled an even number.
The conditional probability of sixes, given evens.

With a fair die, we roll 2, 4, and 6 equally often. So 6 comes up a third of the time that we get an even outcome.

$Pr(6/even) = 1/3$.

This fits our definition, because,

Pr(6 & even) = Pr(6) = 1/6.
Pr(even) = 1/2.
Pr(6/even) = (1/6)/(1/2) = 1/3.

OVERLAPS

Now ask a more complicated question, which involves *overlapping* outcomes. Let M mean that the die either falls 1 up or falls with a prime number up (2, 3, 5). Thus M happens when the die falls 1, 2, 3, or 5 uppermost. What is

Pr(even/M)?

The only prime even number is 2. There are 4 ways to throw M (1, 2, 3, 5). Hence, if the die is fair,

Pr(even/M) = 1/4.

This fits our definition, because

Pr(even & M) = 1/6.
Pr(M) = 4/6.
Pr(even/M) = (1/6)/(4/6) = 1/4.

WELL-SHUFFLED CARDS

Think of a well-shuffled standard pack of 52 cards, from which the dealer deals the top card. He tells you that it is *either* red, *or* clubs. But not which. Call this information RvC.

Clubs are black. There are 13 clubs in the pack, and 26 other cards that are red. We were told that the first card is RvC. What is the probability that it is an ace? What is Pr(A/RvC)? A & (RvC) is equivalent to ace of clubs, or a red ace, diamonds or hearts. For a total of 3. Hence 3 cards out of the 39 RvC cards are aces.

Hence the conditional probability is:

Pr[A/(RvC)] = 1/13.

This agrees with our definition:

Pr[A & (RvC)] = 3/52.
Pr(RvC) = 39/52.
$$Pr[(A/(RvC)] = \frac{Pr[A \ \& \ (RvC)]}{Pr(RvC)} = 3/39 = 1/13.$$

URNS

Imagine two urns, each containing red and green balls. Urn A has 80% red balls, 20% green, and Urn B has 60% green, 40% red. You pick an urn at random. Is it A or B? Let's draw balls from the urn and use this information to guess which urn it is. After each draw, the ball drawn *is replaced*. Hence for any draw, the probability of getting red from urn A is 0.8, and from urn B, the probability of getting red is 0.4.

Pr(R/A) = 0.8
Pr(R/B) = 0.4
Pr(A) = Pr(B) = 0.5

You draw a red ball. If you are like *Alert Learner*, that may lead you to suspect that this is urn A (which has more red balls than green ones). That is just a hunch. Let's be more exact.

We want to find Pr(A/R), which is [Pr(A&R)]/[Pr(R)].

You can get a red ball from either urn A or urn B. You get a red ball either when the event A&R happens, or when the event B&R happens. Event R is thus identical to (A&R)v(B&R).

The two alternatives (A&R) and (B&R) are mutually exclusive, so we can add up the probabilities.

Pr(R) = Pr(A&R) + Pr(B&R) [1]

The probability of getting urn B is 0.5; the probability of getting a red ball from it is 0.4, so that the probability of both happening is

Pr(B&R) = Pr(R&B) = Pr(R/B)Pr(B) = 0.4 × 0.5 = 0.2.

Likewise,

Pr(A&R) = 0.8 × 0.5 = 0.4.

Putting these into formula [1] above,

Pr(R) = Pr(A&R) + Pr(B&R) = 0.4 + 0.2 = 0.6.
Hence Pr(A/R) = Pr(A&R)/Pr(R) = (0.4)/(0.6) = 2/3.

DRAWING THE CALCULATION TO CHECK IT

You may find it helpful to visualize the calculation as a branching tree. We start out with our coin and the two urns. How can we get to a red ball? There are two routes. We can toss a heads (probability 0.5), giving us urn A. Then we can draw a red ball (probability 0.8). That is the route shown here on the top branch.

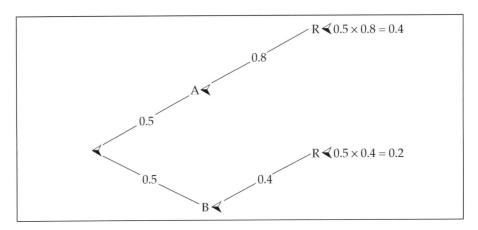

We can also get an R by tossing tails, going to urn B, and then drawing a red ball, as shown on the bottom branch.

We get to R on one of the two branches. So the total probability of ending up with R is the sum of the probabilities at the end of each branch. Here it is 0.4 + 0.2 = 0.6.

The probability of getting to an R following an A branch is 0.4.

Thus that part of the probability that gets you to R by A, namely Pr(A/R), is .4/.6 = 2/3.

MODELS

All our examples up to now have been dice, cards, urns. Now we turn to more interesting cases, more like real life. In each we make a model of a situation, and say that the real-life story is modeled by a standard ball-and-urn example.

SHOCK ABSORBERS

An automobile plant contracted to buy shock absorbers from two local suppliers, Bolt & Co. and Acme Inc. Bolt supplies 40% and Acme 60%. All shocks are subject to quality control. The ones that pass are called reliable.

Of Acme's shocks, 96% test reliable. But Bolt has been having some problems on the line, and recently only 72% of Bolt's shock absorbers have tested reliable.

What is the probability that a randomly chosen shock absorber will test reliable?

Intuitive guess: the probability will be lower than 0.96, because Acme's product is diluted by a proportion of shock absorbers from Bolt. The probability must be between 0.96 and 0.72, and nearer to 0.96. But by how much?

Solution

Let A = The shock chosen at random was made by Acme.
Let B = The shock chosen at random was made by Bolt.
Let R = The shock chosen at random is reliable.

$Pr(A) = 0.6$ $Pr(R/A) = 0.96$ So, $Pr(R\&A) = 0.576$.
$Pr(B) = 0.4$ $Pr(R/B) = 0.72$ So, $Pr(R\&B) = 0.288$.
$R = (R\&A)v(R\&B)$

Answer: $Pr(R) = (.6\times.96) + (.4\times.72) = 0.576 + 0.288 = 0.864$.

We can ask a more interesting question.

What is the conditional probability that a randomly chosen shock absorber, which is tested and found to be reliable, is made by Bolt?

Intuitive guess: look at the numbers. The automobile plant buys more shocks from Acme than Bolt. And Bolt's shocks are much less reliable than Acme's. Both these pieces of evidence count against a reliable shock, chosen at random, being made by Bolt. We expect that the probability that the shock is from Bolt is less that 0.4. But by how much?

Solution

We require $Pr(B/R)$.

By definition, $Pr(B/R) = Pr(B\&R)/Pr(R) = 0.288/0.864 = 1/3$.

Actually, you may like to do this without any multiplying, because almost all the numbers cancel:

$$= \frac{0.4 \times 0.72}{(.4\times.72) + (.6\times.96)} = 1/3$$

Answer: $Pr(B/R) = 1/3$.

DRAWING TO CHECK

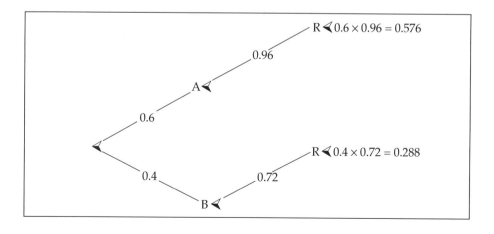

$Pr(R) = 0.576 + 0.288 = 0.864$. $Pr(B/R) = 1/3$.

WEIGHTLIFTERS

You learn that a certain country has two teams of weightlifters, either of which it may send to an international competition. Of the members of one team (the Steroid team), 80% have been regularly using steroids, but only 20% of the members of the other team are regular users (the Cleaner team). The head coach flips a fair coin to decide which team will be sent.

One member of the competing team is tested at random. He has been using steroids.

What is the conditional probability that the team in competition is the Steroid team, given that a member was found by a urine test to be using steroids? That is, what is $Pr(S/U)$?

Solution

Let S = The coach sent the Steroid team.
Let C = The coach sent the Cleaner team.
Let U = A member selected at random uses steroids.

$Pr(S) = 0.5$	$Pr(U/S) = 0.8$	$Pr(U\&S) = 0.4$
$Pr(C) = 0.5$	$Pr(U/C) = 0.2$	$Pr(U\&C) = 0.1$
$U = (U\&S)v(U\&C)$	$Pr(U) = 0.4 + 0.1 = 0.5$	

$Pr(S/U) = [Pr(S\&U)]/[Pr(U)] = 0.4/0.5 = 0.8$

Answer: Pr(Steroid team/selected member uses steroids) = 0.8.

So the fact that we randomly selected a team member who uses steroids, is pretty good evidence that this is the Steroid team.

TWO IN A ROW: WITH REPLACEMENT

Back to the urns on page 51. Suppose you pick an urn at random, and make two draws, *with replacement*. You get a red, and then a red again. What is $P(A/R_1\&R_2)$?

Let R_1 be the event that the first ball drawn is red, and R_2 the event that the second ball drawn is red. Then you can work out $P(A/R_1\&R_2)$ as:

$$\frac{Pr(A\&R_1\&R_2)}{Pr(R_1\&R_2)}$$

Now we know $Pr(A\&R_1\&R_2) = Pr(R_2/A\&R_1)Pr(A\&R_1) = 0.8 \times 0.4 = 0.32$.
Likewise, $Pr(B\&R_1\&R_2) = 0.08$.
$Pr(R_1\&R_2) = Pr(A\&R_1\&R_2) + Pr(B\&R_1\&R_2) = 0.32 + 0.08 = 0.4$
$Pr(A/R_1\&R_2) = 0.32/0.4 = 4/5 = 0.8$

Conditional probability of urn A, given that we:
  draw one red ball, is 2/3
  draw a second ball after replacement, also red, is 0.8

Thus a second red ball "increases the conditional probability" that this is urn A. The extra red ball may be taken as more *evidence*.

This suggests how we *learn by experience* by obtaining more evidence.

THE GAMBLER'S FALLACY ONCE AGAIN

Fallacious Gambler thought that he could "learn from experience" when he saw that a fair (unbiased, independent trials) roulette wheel came up 12 blacks in a row. That is, he thought that:

Pr(red on 13th trial/12 blacks in a row) > ½.

But if trials are independent, this probability is

$$\frac{\text{Pr(BBBBBBBBBBBBR)}}{\text{Pr(BBBBBBBBBBBB)}} = \frac{(\frac{1}{2})^{13}}{(\frac{1}{2})^{12}} = \frac{1}{2}.$$

This is a new way to understand the gambler's fallacy.

TWO WEIGHTLIFTERS: WITHOUT REPLACEMENT

Back to the weightlifters. Suppose we test two weightlifters chosen at random from a team that the coach selected by tossing a fair coin. We think: if both weightlifters test positive, that is pretty strong evidence that this is the Steroid team. Probability confirms this hunch.

We are sampling the team without replacement. So say there are **ten** members to a team. We randomly test two members.

Let S   = The coach sent the Steroid team.
Let C   = The coach sent the Cleaner team.
Let U_1 = The first member selected at random uses steroids.
Let U_2 = The second member selected at random uses steroids.

If we have the Steroid team, the probability that the first person tested uses steroids is 0.8 (on page 54 we had Pr(U/S) = 0.8). What is the probability of selecting two users?

There is a 4/5 probability of selecting one user. After the first person is selected, and turns out to be a user, there are 9 team members left, 7 of whom use steroids. So there is a 7/9 probability of getting a user for the next test. Hence the probability that the first two persons chosen from the Steroid team use steroids is $4/5 \times 7/9 = 28/45$.

Likewise, the probability that the first two persons chosen from the Cleaner team use steroids is $1/5 \times 1/9 = 1/45$.

The probability that the coach sent the Steroid team, when both team members selected at random are users, is,

$Pr(S\&U_1\&U_2) = 0.5(28/45) = 28/90.$

Likewise, $Pr(C\&U_1\&U_2) = 0.5(1/45) = 1/90.$

$Pr(U_1\&U_2) = Pr(S\&U_1\&U_2) + Pr(C\&U_1\&U_2) = 29/90.$

$$Pr(S/U_1\&U_2) = \frac{Pr(S\&U_1\&U_2)}{Pr(U_1\&U_2)} = 28/29 > 0.96$$

Conditional probability that this is the Steroid team, given that we randomly selected:
one weightlifter who was a user, is 0.8
a second weightlifter who was also a user, is > 0.96

Getting two members who use steroids seems to be powerful *evidence* that the coach picked the Steroid team.

EXERCISES

1 *Phony precision about tennis.* In real life, the newspaper story about tennis quoted Ivan as stating a probability not of "40%" but:

   The probability that Stefan will beat Boris in the semifinals is only 37.325%.

   Can you make any sense out of this precise fraction?

2 *Heat lamps.* Three percent of production batches of *Tropicana* heat lamps fall below quality standards. Six percent of the batches of *Florida* heat lamps are below quality standards. A hardware store buys 40% of its heat lamps from *Tropicana*, and 60% from *Florida*.
   (a) What is the probability that a lamp taken at random in the store is made by *Tropicana* and is below quality standards?
   (b) What is the probability that a lamp taken at random in the store is below quality standards?
   (c) What is the probability that a lamp from this store, and found to be below quality standards, is made by *Tropicana*?

3 *The Triangle.* An unhealthy triangular-shaped region in an old industrial city once had a lot of chemical industry. Two percent of the children in the city live in the triangle. Fourteen percent of these test positive for excessive presence of toxic metals in the tissues. The rate of positive tests for children in the city, not living in the triangle, is only 1%.
   (a) What is the probability that a child who lives in the city, and who is chosen at random, both lives in the Triangle and tests positive?
   (b) What is the probability that a child living in the city, chosen at random, tests positive?
   (c) What is the probability that a child chosen at random, who tests positive, lives in the Triangle?

4 *Taxicabs.* Draw a tree diagram for the taxicab problem, Odd Question 5.

5 *Laplace's trick question.* Look back at Laplace's question (page 44). An experiment consists of tossing a coin to select an urn, then drawing a ball, noting its color, replacing it, and drawing another ball and noting its color. Find, Pr(second ball drawn is red/first ball drawn is red).

6 *Understanding the question.* On page 45 we ended Chapter 4 with a way to understand Laplace's trick question. How does your answer to question 6 help with understanding Laplace's question?

KEY WORDS FOR REVIEW

Categorical

Conditional

Definition of conditional probability

Calculating conditional probabilities

Models

Learning from experience

6   The Basic Rules of Probability

This chapter summarizes the rules you have been using for adding and multiplying probabilities, and for using conditional probability. It also gives a pictorial way to understand the rules.

The rules that follow are informal versions of standard axioms for elementary probability theory.

ASSUMPTIONS

The rules stated here take some things for granted:

- The rules are for finite groups of propositions (or events).
- If A and B are propositions (or events), then so are AvB, A&B, and ~A.
- Elementary deductive logic (or elementary set theory) is taken for granted.
- If A and B are *logically equivalent*, then Pr(A) = Pr(B). [Or, in set theory, if A and B are events which are provably the same sets of events, Pr(A) = Pr(B).]

NORMALITY

The probability of any proposition or event A lies between 0 and 1.

(1) $0 \leq Pr(A) \leq 1$

Why the name "normality"? A measure is said to be *normalized* if it is put on a scale between 0 and 1.

CERTAINTY

An event that is sure to happen has probability 1. A proposition that is certainly true has probability 1.

(2)   Pr(certain proposition) = 1
         Pr(sure event) = 1

Often the Greek letter Ω is used to represent certainty: $\Pr(\Omega) = 1$.

ADDITIVITY

If two events or propositions A and B are mutually exclusive (disjoint, incompatible), the probability that one or the other happens (or is true) is the sum of their probabilities.

(3)   If A and B are mutually exclusive, then
         $\Pr(A v B) = \Pr(A) + \Pr(B)$.

OVERLAP

When A and B are not mutually exclusive, we have to subtract the probability of their overlap. In a moment we will *deduce* this from rules (1)–(3).

(4) $\Pr(A v B) = \Pr(A) + \Pr(B) - \Pr(A\&B)$

CONDITIONAL PROBABILITY

The only basic rules are (1)–(3). Now comes a *definition*.

(5)   If $\Pr(B) > 0$, then $\Pr(A/B) = \dfrac{\Pr(A\&B)}{\Pr(B)}$

MULTIPLICATION

The definition of conditional probability implies that:

(6)   If $\Pr(B) > 0$, $\Pr(A\&B) = \Pr(A/B)\Pr(B)$.

TOTAL PROBABILITY

Another consequence of the definition of conditional probability:

(7)   If $0 < \Pr(B) < 1$, $\Pr(A) = \Pr(B)\Pr(A/B) + \Pr(\sim B)\Pr(A/\sim B)$.

In practice this is a very useful rule. What is the probability that you will get a grade of A in this course? Maybe there are just two possibilities: you study hard, or you do not study hard. Then:

Pr(A) = Pr(study hard)Pr(A/study hard) + Pr(don't study)Pr(A/don't study).

Try putting in some numbers that describe yourself.

LOGICAL CONSEQUENCE

When B logically entails A, then

$$Pr(B) \leq Pr(A).$$

This is because, when B entails A, B is logically equivalent to A&B. Since

$$Pr(A) = Pr(A\&B) + Pr(A\&\sim B) = Pr(B) + Pr(A\&\sim B),$$

Pr(A) will be bigger than Pr(B) except when $Pr(A\&\sim B) = 0$.

STATISTICAL INDEPENDENCE

Thus far we have been very informal when talking about independence. Now we state a *definition* of one concept, often called statistical independence.

(8) If $0 < Pr(A)$ and $0 < Pr(B)$, then,
A and B are statistically independent if and only if:
$Pr(A/B) = Pr(A)$.

PROOF OF THE RULE FOR OVERLAP

(4) $Pr(AvB) = Pr(A) + Pr(B) - Pr(A\&B)$.

This rule follows from rules (1)–(3), and the logical assumption on page 58, that logically equivalent propositions have the same probability.

AvB is logically equivalent to: $(A\&B)$ v $(A\&\sim B)$ v $(\sim A\&B)$ (*)

Why? Those familiar with "truth tables" can check it out. But you can see it directly. A is logically equivalent to $(A\&B)$ v $(A\&\sim B)$. B is logically equivalent to $(A\&B)$ v $(\sim A\&B)$.

Now the three components $(A\&B)$, $(A\&\sim B)$, and $(\sim A\&B)$ are mutually exclusive. (Why?) Hence we can add their probabilities, using (*).

$Pr(AvB) = Pr(A\&B) + Pr(A\&\sim B) + Pr(\sim A\&B)$ (**)
A is logically equivalent to $[(A\&B)v(A\&\sim B)]$, and
B is logically equivalent to $[(A\&B)v(\sim A\&B)]$.

So,

$Pr(A) = Pr(A\&B) + Pr(A\&\sim B)$.
$Pr(B) = Pr(A\&B) + Pr(\sim A\&B)$.

Since it makes no difference to add and then subtract something in (**):

$Pr(AvB) = Pr(A\&B) + Pr(A\&\sim B) + Pr(\sim A\&B) + Pr(A\&B) - Pr(A\&B)$

Hence,

$Pr(AvB) = Pr(A) + Pr(B) - Pr(A\&B).$

CONDITIONALIZING THE RULES

It is easy to check that the basic rules (1)–(3), and (5), the definition of conditional probability, all hold in conditional form. That is, the rules hold if we replace $Pr(A)$, $Pr(B)$, $Pr(A/B)$, and so on, by $Pr(A/E)$, $Pr(B/E)$, $P(A/B\&E)$, and so on.

Normality

(1C) $0 \leq Pr(A/E) \leq 1$

Certainty

We need to check that for E, such that $Pr(E) > 0$,

(2C) $Pr([\text{sure event}]/E) = 1.$

Now E is logically equivalent to the occurrence of E with something that is sure to happen. Hence,

$Pr([\text{sure event}] \& E) = Pr(E).$
$Pr([\text{sure event}/E]) = [Pr(E)]/[Pr(E)] = 1.$

Additivity

Let $Pr(E) > 0$. If A and B are mutually exclusive, then

$Pr[(AvB)/E] = Pr[(AvB)\&E]/Pr(E) = Pr(A\&E)/Pr(E) + Pr(B\&E)/Pr(E).$
(3C) $Pr[(AvB)/E] = Pr(A/E) + Pr(B/E).$

Conditional probability

This is the only case you should examine carefully. The conditionalized form of (5) is:

(5C)   If $Pr(E) > 0$ and $Pr(B/E) > 0$, then
$$Pr[A/(B\&E)] = \frac{Pr[(A\&B)/E]}{Pr(B/E)}.$$

We prove this starting from (5),

$$Pr[A/(B\&E)] = \frac{Pr(A\&B\&E)}{Pr(B\&E)}.$$

The numerator (on top of the fraction) is $Pr(A\&B\&E) = Pr[(A\&B)/E] \times Pr(E)$.
The denominator (bottom of the fraction) is $Pr(B\&E) = Pr(B/E) \times Pr(E)$.
Dividing the numerator by the denominator, we get (5C).

Many philosophers and inductive logicians take conditional probability, rather than categorical probability, as the primitive idea. Their basic rules are, then, versions of (1C), (2C), (3C), and (5C). Formally, the end results are in all essential respects identical to our approach that begins with categorical probability and then defines conditional probability. But when we start to ask about various meanings of these rules, we find that a conditional probability approach sometimes makes more sense.

STATISTICAL INDEPENDENCE AGAIN

Our first intuitive explanation of independence (page 25) said that trials on a chance setup are **independent** if and only if the probabilities of the outcomes of a trial are not influenced by the outcomes of previous trials. But this left open what "influenced" really means. We also spoke of *randomness*, of trials having no *memory*, and of *the impossibility of a gambling system*. These are all valuable metaphors.

The idea of conditional probability makes one exact definition possible. The probability of A should be no different from the probability of A given B, $Pr(A/B)$.

Naturally, independence should be a symmetric relation: A is independent of B if and only if B is independent of A.

In other words, when $0 < Pr(A)$ and $0 < Pr(B)$, we expect that:

If $Pr(A/B) = Pr(A)$, then $Pr(B/A) = Pr(B)$ (and vice versa).

This is proved from definition (8) on page 60.

Suppose that $Pr(A/B) = Pr(A)$.
By (5), $Pr(A) = [Pr(A\&B)]/[Pr(B)]$.
And so $Pr(B) = [Pr(A\&B)]/[Pr(A)]$.
So, since A&B is logically equivalent to B&A,
$Pr(B) = Pr(B\&A)/Pr(A) = Pr(B/A)$.

MULTIPLE INDEPENDENCE

Definition (8) defines the statistical independence of a pair of propositions. That is called "pairwise" independence. But a whole group of events or propositions could be mutually independent. This idea is easily defined.

It follows from (6) and (8) that when A and B are statistically independent:

$Pr(A\&B) = Pr(A)Pr(B)$

(See exercise 3.) This can be generalized to the statistical independence of any number of events. For example A, B, and C are statistically independent if and only if A, B, and C are pairwise independent, and

$Pr(A\&B\&C) = Pr(A)Pr(B)Pr(C)$.

VENN DIAGRAMS

John Venn (1824–1923) was an English logician who in 1866 published the first systematic theory of probabilities explained in terms of relative frequencies. Most people remember him only for "Venn diagrams" in deductive logic. Venn diagrams are used to represent *deductive* arguments involving the quantifiers *all*, *some*, and *no*.

You can also use Venn diagrams to represent probability relations. These drawings help some people who think spatially or pictorially.

Imagine that you have eight musicians:

Four of them are singers, with no other musical abilities.
Three of them can whistle but cannot sing.
One can both whistle and sing.

A Venn diagram can picture this group, using a set of circles. One circle is used for each class. Circles overlap when the classes overlap. Our diagram looks like this:

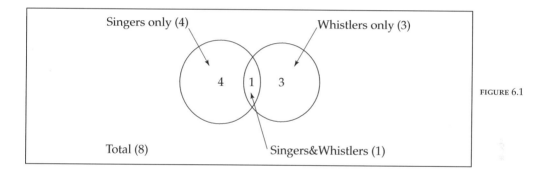

FIGURE 6.1

The circle representing the singers contains five units (four singers plus one singer&whistler), while the circle representing the whistlers has four units (three whistlers plus one singer&whistler). The overlapping region has an area of one unit, since only one of the eight people fits into both categories. We will think of the area of each segment as proportional to the number of people in that segment.

Now say we are interested in the probability of selecting, at random, a singer from the group of eight people. Since there are five singers in the group of eight people, the answer is 5/8.

What is the probability that a singer is chosen, on condition that the person chosen is also a whistler? Since you know the person selected is a whistler, this limits the group to the whistlers' circle. It contains four people. Only one of the four is in the singers' circle. Hence only one of the four possible choices is a singer. Hence, the probability that a singer is chosen, given that the singer is also a whistler, is 1/4.

Now let us generalize the example. Put our 8 musicians in a room with 12 nonmusical people, resulting in a group of 20 people. Imagine we were interested in these two events:

Event A = a singer is selected at random from the whole group.
Event B = a whistler is selected at random from the whole group.

Here is a Venn diagram of the situation, where the entire box represents the room full of twenty people.

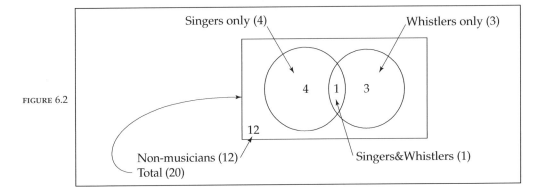

FIGURE 6.2

Notice the major change from the previous diagram: Figure 6.2 now has its circles enclosed in a rectangle. By convention, the area of the rectangle is set to 1. The areas of each of the circles correspond to the probability of occurrence of an event of the type that it represents: the area of circle A is 5/20, or 0.25, since there are 5 singers among 20 people. Likewise, the area of circle B is 4/20, or 0.2. The area of the region of overlap between A & B is 1/20, or 0.05.

These drawings can be used to illustrate the basic rules of probability.

(1) *Normality*: $0 \leq \Pr(A) \leq 1$.

This corresponds to the rectangle having an area of 1 unit: since all circles must lie within the rectangle, no circle, and hence no event can have a probability of greater than 1.

(2) *Certainty*: $\Pr(\text{sure event}) = 1$. $\Pr(\text{certain proposition}) = 1$.

With Venn diagrams, an event that is sure to happen, or a proposition that is certain, corresponds to a "circle" that fills the entire rectangle, which by convention has unit area 1.

(3) *Additivity*: If A and B are mutually exclusive, then:

$\Pr(A \vee B) = \Pr(A) + \Pr(B)$.

If two groups are mutually exclusive they do not overlap, and the area covering members of either group is just the sum of the areas of each.

(4) *Overlap*:

To calculate the probability of AvB, determine how much of the rectangle is covered by circles A and B. This will be all the area in A, plus the area that appears *only* in B. The area only in B is the areas in B, less the area of overlap with A.

$$Pr(AvB) = Pr(A) + Pr(B) - Pr(A\&B)$$

(5) *Conditional*:

Given that event B has happened, what is the probability that event A will also happen? Look at Figure 6.2. If B has happened, you know that the person selected is a whistler. So we want the proportion of the area of B, that includes A. That is, the area of A&B divided by the area of B.

$$Pr(A/B) = Pr(A\&B) \div Pr(B), \text{ so long as } Pr(B) > 0.$$

So, in our numerical example, $Pr(A/B) = 1/4$.
Conversely, $Pr(B/A) = Pr(A \& B)/Pr(A) = 1/5 = 0.2$.

ODD QUESTION 2

Recall the Odd Question about Pia:

2. Pia is thirty-one years old, single, outspoken, and smart. She was a philoso-phy major. When a student, she was an ardent supporter of Native American rights, and she picketed a department store that had no facilities for nursing mothers. Rank the following statements in order of probability from 1 (most probable) to 6 (least probable). (Ties are allowed.)

    _____(a) Pia is an active feminist.
    _____(b) Pia is a bank teller.
    _____(c) Pia works in a small bookstore.
    _____(d) Pia is a bank teller and an active feminist.
    _____(e) Pia is a bank teller and an active feminist who takes yoga classes.
    _____(f) Pia works in a small bookstore and is an active feminist who takes yoga classes.

This is a famous example, first studied empirically by the psychologists Amos Tversky and Daniel Kahneman. They found that very many people think that, given the whole story:

The most probable description is (f) Pia works in a small bookstore and is an active feminist who takes yoga classes.

In fact, they rank the possibilities something like this, from most probable to least probable:

(f), (e), (d), (a), (c), (b).

But just look at the logical consequence rule on page 60. Since, for example, (f) logically entails (a) and (b), (a) and (b) must be more probable than (f).

In general:

$$Pr(A\&B) \leq Pr(B).$$

It follows that the probability rankings given by many people, with (f) most probable, are completely wrong. There are many ways of ranking (a)–(f), but any ranking should obey these inequalities:

$Pr(a) \geq Pr(d) \geq Pr(e).$
$Pr(b) \geq Pr(d) \geq Pr(e).$
$Pr(a) \geq Pr(f).$
$Pr(c) \geq Pr(f).$

ARE PEOPLE STUPID?

Some readers of Tversky and Kahneman conclude that we human beings are irrational, because so many of us come up with the wrong probability orderings. But perhaps people are merely *careless*!

Perhaps most of us do not attend closely to the exact wording of the question, "Which of statements (a)–(f) are more **probable**, that is have the **highest probability**."

Instead we think, "Which is the most useful, instructive, and likely to be true thing to say about Pia?"

When we are asked a question, most of us want to be informative, useful, or interesting. We don't necessarily want simply to say what is most probable, in the strict sense of having the highest probability.

For example, suppose I ask you whether you think the rate of inflation next year will be (a) less than 3%, (b) between 3% and 4%, or (c) greater than 4%.

You could reply, (a)-or-(b)-or-(c). You would certainly be right! That would be the answer with the highest probability. But it would be totally uninformative.

You could reply, (b)-or-(c). That is more probable than simply (b), or simply (c), assuming that both are possible (thanks to additivity). But that is a less interesting and less useful answer than (c), or (b), by itself.

Perhaps what many people do, when they look at Odd Question 2, is to form a character analysis of Pia, and then make an interesting guess about what she is doing nowadays.

If that is what is happening, then people who said it was most probable that Pia works in a small bookstore and is an active feminist who takes yoga classes, are not **irrational**.

They are just answering the wrong question—but maybe answering a more useful question than the one that was asked.

AXIOMS: HUYGENS

Probability can be axiomatized in many ways. The first axioms, or basic rules, were published in 1657 by the Dutch physicist Christiaan Huygens (1629–1695), famous for his wave theory of light. Strictly speaking, Huygens did not use the idea of probability at all. Instead, he used the idea of the fair price of something like a lottery ticket, or what we today would call the expected value of an event or proposition. We can still do that today. In fact, almost all approaches take probability as the idea to be axiomatized. But a few authors still take expected value as the primitive idea, in terms of which they define probability.

AXIOMS: KOLMOGOROV

The definitive axioms for probability theory were published in 1933 by the immensely influential Russian mathematician A. N. Kolmogorov (1903–1987). This theory is much more developed than our basic rules, for it applies to infinite sets and employs the full differential and integral calculus, as part of what is called measure theory.

EXERCISES

1   *Venn Diagrams.*

> Let L: A person contracts a lung disease.
> Let S: That person smokes.

Write each of the following probabilities using the Pr notation, and then explain it using a Venn diagram.
(a) The probability that a person either smokes or contracts lung disease (or both).
(b) The probability that a person contracts lung disease, given that he or she smokes.
(c) The probability that a person smokes, given that she or he contracts lung disease.

2   *Total probability.* Prove from the basic rules that $\Pr(A) + \Pr(\sim A) = 1$.

3   *Multiplying.* Prove from the definition of statistical independence that if $0 < \Pr(A)$, and $0 < \Pr(B)$, and A and B are statistically independent,

$$\Pr(A\&B) = \Pr(A)\Pr(B).$$

4   *Conventions.* In Chapter 4, page 40, we said that the rules for normality and certainty are just conventions. Can you think of any other plausible conventions for representing probability by numbers?

5   *Terrorists.* This is a story about a philosopher, the late Max Black.
    One of Black's students was to go overseas to do some research on Kant. She was afraid that a terrorist would put a bomb on the plane. Black could not convince her that the risk was negligible. So he argued as follows:

> BLACK: Well, at least you agree that it is almost impossible that *two* people should take bombs on your plane?
> STUDENT: Sure.
> BLACK: Then you should take a bomb on the plane. The risk that there would be another bomb on your plane is negligible.

What's the joke?

KEY WORDS FOR REVIEW

Normality	Conditional probability	Total probability
Certainty	Venn diagrams	Logical consequence
Additivity	Multiplication	Statistical independence

7 Bayes' Rule

One of the most useful consequences of the basic rules helps us understand how to make use of new evidence. Bayes' Rule is one key to "learning from experience."

Chapter 5 ended with several examples of the same form: urns, shock absorbers, weightlifters. The numbers were changed a bit, but the problems in each case were identical.

For example, on page 51 there were two urns A and B, each containing a known proportion of red and green balls. An urn was picked at random. So we knew:

Pr(A) and Pr(B).

Then there was another event R, such as drawing a red ball from an urn. The probability of getting red from urn A was 0.8. The probability of getting red from urn B was 0.4. So we knew:

Pr(R/A) and Pr(R/B).

Then we asked, what is the probability that the urn drawn was A, *conditional* on drawing a red ball? We asked for:

Pr(A/R) = ? Pr(B/R) = ?

Chapter 5 solved these problems directly from the definition of conditional probability. There is an easy rule for solving problems like that. It is called *Bayes' Rule*.

In the urn problem we ask which of two *hypotheses* is true: Urn A is selected, or Urn B is selected. In general we will represent hypotheses by the letter H.

We perform an *experiment* or get some *evidence*: we draw at random and observe a red ball. In general we represent evidence by the letter E.

Let's start with the simplest case, where there are only two hypotheses, H and ~H. By definition these are **mutually exclusive,** and **exhaustive.**

Let E be a proposition such that $Pr(E) > 0$. Then:

$$Pr(H/E) = \frac{Pr(H)Pr(E/H)}{Pr(H)Pr(E/H) + Pr(\sim H)Pr(E/\sim H)}$$

This is called *Bayes' Rule* for the case of two hypotheses.

PROOF OF BAYES' RULE

$$Pr(H\&E) = Pr(E\&H)$$
$$\frac{Pr(H\&E)Pr(E)}{Pr(E)} = \frac{Pr(E\&H)Pr(H)}{Pr(H)}$$

Using the definition of conditional probability,

$$Pr(H/E)Pr(E) = Pr(E/H)Pr(H).$$
$$Pr(H/E) = \frac{Pr(H)Pr(E/H)}{Pr(E)}$$

Since H and (~H) are mutually exclusive and exhaustive, then, by the rule of total probability on page 59,

$$Pr(E) = Pr(H)Pr(E/H) + Pr(\sim H)Pr(E/\sim H).$$

Which gives us Bayes' Rule:

$$(1) \quad Pr(H/E) = \frac{Pr(H)Pr(E/H)}{Pr(H)Pr(E/H) + Pr(\sim H)Pr(E/\sim H)}$$

GENERALIZATION

The same formula holds for any number of *mutually exclusive* and *jointly exhaustive* hypotheses:

$H_1, H_2, H_3, H_4, \ldots, H_k$, such that for each i, $Pr(H_i) > 0$.

Mutually exclusive means that only one of the hypotheses can be true. *Jointly exhaustive* means that at least one must be true.

By extending the above argument, if $Pr(E) > 0$, and for every i, $Pr(H_i) > 0$, we get for any hypothesis H_k,

$$(2) \quad Pr(H_j/E) = \frac{Pr(H_j) \ Pr(E/H_j)}{\Sigma[Pr(H_i) \ Pr(E/H_i)]}$$

Here the Σ (the Greek capital letter sigma, or S in Greek) stands for the *sum* of the terms with subscript i. Add all the terms $[Pr(H_i)Pr(E/H_i)]$ for i =1, i = 2, up to i = k.

Formula (1) and its generalization (2) are known as **Bayes' Rule**.

The rule is just a way to combine a couple of basic rules, namely conditional and total probability. Bayes' Rule is trivial, but it is very tidy. It has a major role in some theories about inductive logic, explained in Chapters 13–15 and 21.

URNS

Here is the urn problem from page 51:

Imagine two urns, each containing red and green balls. Urn A has 80% red balls, 20% green, and Urn B has 60% green, 40% red. You pick an urn at random, and then can draw balls from the urn in order to guess which urn it is. After each draw, the ball drawn *is replaced*. Hence for any draw, the probability of getting red from urn A is 0.8, and from urn B it is 0.4.

$$Pr(R/A) = 0.8 \qquad Pr(R/B) = 0.4 \qquad Pr(A) = Pr(B) = 0.5$$

You draw a red ball. What is P(A/R)?

Solution by Bayes' Rule:

$$Pr(A/R) = \frac{Pr(A)Pr(R/A)}{Pr(A)Pr(R/A) + Pr(B)Pr(R/B)}$$

$$= (0.5 \times 0.8)/[(0.5 \times 0.8) + (0.5 \times 0.4)] = 2/3.$$

This is the same answer as was obtained on page 51.

SPIDERS

A tarantula is a large, fierce-looking, and somewhat poisonous tropical spider.

Once upon a time, 3% of consignments of bananas from Honduras were found to have tarantulas on them, and 6% of the consignments from Guatemala had tarantulas.

40% of the consignments came from Honduras. 60% came from Guatemala.

A tarantula was found on a randomly selected lot of bananas. What is the probability that this lot came from Guatemala?

Solution

Let G = The lot came from Guatemala. $\Pr(G) = 0.6$.

Let H = The lot came from Honduras. $\Pr(H) = 0.4$.

Let T = The lot had a tarantula on it. $\Pr(T/G) = 0.06$. $\Pr(T/H) = 0.03$.

$$\Pr(G/T) = \frac{\Pr(G)\Pr(T/G)}{\Pr(G)\Pr(T/G) + \Pr(H)\Pr(T/H)}$$

Answer: $\Pr(G/T) = (.6 \times .06) / [(.6 \times .06) + (.4 \times .03)] = 3/4$

TAXICABS: ODD QUESTION 5

Here is Odd Question 5.

> You have been called to jury duty in a town where there are two taxi companies, Green Cabs Ltd. and Blue Taxi Inc. Blue Taxi uses cars painted blue; Green Cabs uses green cars.
>
> Green Cabs dominates the market, with 85% of the taxis on the road.
>
> On a misty winter night a taxi sideswiped another car and drove off. A witness says it was a blue cab.
>
> The witness is tested under conditions like those on the night of the accident, and 80% of the time she correctly reports the color of the cab that is seen. That is, regardless of whether she is shown a blue or a green cab in misty evening light, she gets the color right 80% of the time.
>
> You conclude, on the basis of this information:
>
> _____(a) The probability that the sideswiper was blue is 0.8.
> _____(b) It is more likely that the sideswiper was blue, but the probability is less than 0.8.
> _____(c) It is just as probable that the sideswiper was green as that it was blue.
> _____(d) It is more likely than not that the sideswiper was green.

This question, like Odd Question 2, was invented by Amos Tversky and Daniel Kahneman. They have done very extensive psychological testing on this question, and found that many people think that (a) or (b) is correct. Very few think that (d) is correct. Yet (d) is, in the natural probability model, the right answer! Here is how Bayes' Rule answers the question.

Solution

Let G = A taxi selected at random is green. $\Pr(G) = 0.85$.

Let B = A taxi selected at random is blue. $\Pr(B) = 0.15$.

Let W_b = The witness states that the taxi is blue.

$\Pr(W_b/B) = 0.8$.

Moreover, $\Pr(W_b/G) = 0.2$, because the witness gives a *wrong* answer 20% of the time, so the probability that she says "blue" when the cab was green is 20%.

We require $\Pr(B/W_b)$ and $\Pr(G/W_b)$.

$$Pr(B/W_b) = \frac{Pr(B)Pr(W_b/B)}{Pr(B)Pr(W_b/B) + Pr(G)Pr(W_b/G)}$$

$$Pr(B/W_b) = (.15 \times .8) / [(.15 \times .8) + (.85 \times .2)] = 12/29 \approx 0.41$$

Answer:

$Pr(B/W_b) \approx 0.41.$

$Pr(G/W_b) \approx 1 - 0.41 = 0.59.$

It is more likely that the sideswiper was green.

BASE RATES

Why do so few people feel, intuitively, that (d) is the right answer? Tversky and Kahneman argue that people tend to ignore the *base rate* or background information. We focus on the fact that the witness is right 80% of the time. We ignore the fact that most of the cabs in town are green.

Suppose that we made a great many experiments with the witness, randomly selecting cabs and showing them to her on a misty night. If 100 cabs were picked at random, then we'd expect something like this:

The witness sees about 85 green cabs. She correctly identifies 80% of these as green: about 68.

She incorrectly identifies 20% as blue: about 17.

She sees about 15 blue cabs. She correctly identifies 80% of these as blue: about 12.

She incorrectly identifies 20% as green: about 3.

So the witness identifies about 29 cabs as blue, but only 12 of these are blue! In fact, the more we think of the problem as one about frequencies, the clearer the Bayesian answer becomes.

Some critics say that the taxicab problem does not show that we make mistakes easily. The question is asked in the wrong way. If we had been asked just about frequencies, say the critics, we would have given pretty much the right answer straightaway!

RELIABILITY

Our witness was pretty reliable: right 80% of the time. How can a reliable witness not be trustworthy? Because of the base rates. We tend to confuse two different ideas of "reliability."

Idea 1: $Pr(W_b/B)$: How reliable is she at identifying a cab as blue, given that it is in fact blue? This is a characteristic of the witness and her perceptual acumen.

Idea 2: $Pr(B/W_b)$: How well can what the witness said be relied on, given that she said the cab is blue? This is a characteristic of the witness **and** the base rate.

FALSE POSITIVES

Base rates are very striking with medical diagnoses. Suppose I am tested for a terrible disease. I am told that the test is 99% right. If I have the disease, the test says YES with probability 99%. If I do not have the disease, it says NO with probability 99%.

I am tested for the disease. The test says YES. I am terrified.

But suppose the disease is very rare. In the general population, only one person in 10,000 has this disease.

Then among one million people, only 100 have the disease.

In testing a million people at random, our excellent test will answer YES for about 1% of the population, that is, 10,000 people. But as we see by a simple calculation in the next section, *at most 100 of these people actually have the disease*! I am relieved, unless I am in a population especially at risk.

I was terrified by a result YES, plus the test "reliability" (*Idea 1*):

Pr(YES/I'm sick).

But I am relieved once I find out about the "reliability" of a test result (*Idea 2*):

Pr(I'm sick/YES).

A test result of YES, when the correct answer is NO, is called a *false positive*. In our example, about 9,900 of the YES results were false positives.

Thus even a very "reliable" test may be quite misleading, if the base rate for the disease is very low. Exactly this argument was used against universal testing for the HIV virus in the entire population. Even a quite reliable test would give far too many false positives. Even a reliable test can be trusted only when applied to a population "at risk," that is, where the base rate for the disease is substantial.

PROBABILITY OF A FALSE POSITIVE

The result of testing an individual for a condition D is *positive* when according to the test the individual has the condition D.

The result of testing an individual for a condition D is a *false positive* when the individual does not have condition D, and yet the test result is nevertheless positive.

How much can we rely on a test result? This is *Idea 2* about reliability. The probability of a false positive is a good indicator of the extent to which you should rely on (or doubt) a test result.

Let D be the hypothesis that an individual has condition D.
Let Y be YES, a positive test result for an individual.
A false positive occurs when an individual does not have condition D, even though the test result is Y.
The probability of a false positive is Pr($\sim$D/Y).

In our example of the rare disease:

The base rate is $\Pr(D) = 1/10,000$. Hence $\Pr(\sim D) = 9,999/10,000$.
The test's "reliability" (*Idea 1*) is $\Pr(Y/D) = 0.99$.
And $\Pr(Y/\sim D) = 0.01$.

Applying Bayes' Rule,

$$\Pr(-D/Y) = \frac{\Pr(-D)\Pr(Y/-D)}{\Pr(\sim D)\Pr(Y/\sim D) + \Pr(D)\Pr(Y/D)} = 9999/(9999 + 99) \approx 0.99.$$

STREP THROAT: ODD QUESTION 6

6. You are a physician. You think it is quite likely that one of your patients has strep throat, but you aren't sure. You take some swabs from the throat and send them to a lab for testing. The test is (like nearly all lab tests) not perfect.

> If the patient has strep throat, then 70% of the time the lab says YES. But 30% of the time it says NO.
> If the patient does **not** have strep throat, then 90% of the time the lab says NO. But 10% of the time it says YES.

You send five successive swabs to the lab, from the same patient. You get back these results, in order:

YES, NO, YES, NO, YES

You conclude:
_____(a) These results are worthless.
_____(b) It is likely that the patient does **not** have strep throat.
_____(c) It is **slightly** more likely than not, that the patient **does** have strep throat.
_____(d) It is **very much more** likely than not, that the patient **does** have strep throat.

In my experience almost no one finds the correct answer very obvious. It looks as if the yes-no-yes-no-yes does not add up to much. In fact, it is very good evidence that your patient has strep throat.

Let S = the patient has strep throat.
Let ~S = the patient does not have strep throat.
Let Y = a test result is positive.
Let N = a test result is negative

You think it likely that the patient has strep throat. Let us, to get a sense of the problem, put a number to this, a probability of 90%, that the patient has strep throat. $\Pr(S) = 0.9$.

Solution

We know the conditional probabilities, and we assume that test outcomes are independent.

$Pr(Y/S) = 0.7$ $Pr(N/S) = 0.3$
$Pr(Y/\sim S) = 0.1$ $Pr(N/\sim S) = 0.9$

We need to find $Pr(S/YNYNY)$.

$Pr(YNYNY/S) = 0.7 \times 0.3 \times 0.7 \times 0.3 \times 0.7 = 0.03087$
$Pr(YNYNY/\sim S) = 0.1 \times 0.9 \times 0.1 \times 0.9 \times 0.1 = 0.00081$

$$Pr(S/YNYNY) = \frac{Pr(S)Pr(YNYNY/S)}{Pr(S)Pr(YNYNY/S) + Pr(\sim S)Pr(YNYNY/\sim S)}$$

$$Pr(S/YNYNY) = \frac{0.9 \times 0.03087}{(0.9 \times 0.03087) + (0.1 \times 0.00081)} = 0.997$$

Or you can do the calculation with the original figures, most of which cancel, to give $Pr(S/YNYNY) = 343/344$. Starting with a prior assumption that $Pr(S) = 0.9$, we have found that $Pr(S/YNYNY)$ is almost 1!

Answer: So (d) is correct: *It is very much more* likely than not, that the patient *does* have strep throat.

SHEER IGNORANCE

But you are not a physician. You cannot read the signs well. You might just as well toss a coin to decide whether your friend has strep throat. You would model your ignorance as tossing a coin:

$Pr(S) = 0.5.$

Then you learn of the test results. Should they impress you, or are they meaningless? You require $Pr(S/YNYNY)$.

Solution

Using the same formula as before, but with $Pr(S) = 0.5$,
$Pr(S/YNYNY) = (.5 \times .03087)/[(.5 \times .03087) + (.5 \times .00081)] \approx 0.974$.
Or, exactly, $343/352$.

Answer: This result shows once again that the test results YNYNY are *powerful* evidence that your friend has strep throat.

REV. THOMAS BAYES

Bayes' Rule is named after Thomas Bayes (1702–1761), an English minister who was interested in probability and induction. He probably disagreed strongly with the Scottish philosopher David Hume about evidence. Chapter 21 explains how one might evade Hume's philosophical problem about induction by using Bayesian ideas.

Bayes wrote an essay that was published in 1763 (after his death). It contains the solution to a sophisticated problem like the examples given above. He imagines that a ball is thrown onto a billiard table. The table is "so made and leveled" that a ball is as likely to land on any spot as on any other. A line is drawn through the ball, parallel to the ends of the table. This divides the table into two parts, A and B, with A at a distance of a inches from one end.

Now suppose you do not know the value of a. The ball has been thrown behind your back, and removed by another player.

Then the ball is thrown n times. You are told that on k tosses the ball falls in segment A of the table, and in $n-k$ tosses it falls in segment B. Can you make a guess, on the basis of this information, about the value of a? Obviously, if most of the balls fell in A, then a must cover most of the length of the table; if it is about 50:50 A and B, then a should be about half the length of the table.

Thomas Bayes shows how to solve this problem exactly, finding, for any distance x, and any interval ε, the probability that the unknown a lies between $(x-\varepsilon)$ and $(x+\varepsilon)$.

The idea he used is the same as in our examples, but the mathematics is hard. What is now called *Bayes' Rule* (or, misleadingly, Bayes' Theorem) is a trivial simplification of Bayes' work. In fact, as we saw in Chapter 4, all the work we do with Bayes' Rule can be done from first principles, starting with the definition of conditional probability.

EXERCISES

1 *Lamps and triangles.* Use Bayes' Rule to solve 2(c), and 3(c) in the exercises for Chapter 5, page 56.

2 *Double dipping.*

> Contents of urn A: 60 red, 40 green balls.
> Contents of urn B: 10 red, 90 green balls.

An urn is chosen by flipping a fair coin.
(a) Two balls are drawn from this urn with replacement. Both are red. What is the probability that we have urn A?
(b) Two balls are drawn from this urn without replacement. Both are red. What is the probability that we have urn A?

3 *Tests.* A professor gives a true-false examination consisting of thirty T-F questions. The questions whose answers are "true" are randomly distributed among the thirty questions. The professor thinks that ¾ of the class are serious, and have correctly mastered the material, and that the probability of a correct answer on any question from such students is 75%. The remaining students will answer at random. She glances at a couple of questions from a test picked haphazardly. Both questions are answered correctly. What is the probability that this is the test of a serious student?

4   *Weightlifters.* Recall the coach that sent one of two teams for competition (page 54 above). Each team has ten members. Eight members of the Steroid team (S) use steroids (U). Two members of the Cleaner team (C) use steroids. The coach chooses which team to send for competition by tossing a fair coin.

One athletics committee tests for steroids in the urine of only one randomly chosen member of the team that has been sent. The test is 100% effective. If this team member is a user, the team is rejected.
   (a) What would be a false positive rejection of the entire team?
   (b) What is the probability of a false positive?
   (c) Another committee is more rigorous. It randomly chooses two different members. What is the probability of a false positive?

5   *Three hypotheses.* (a) State Bayes' Rule for the conditional probability $\Pr(F/E)$ with three mutually exclusive and exhaustive hypotheses, F, G, H. (b) Prove it.

6   *Computer crashes.* A small company has just bought three software packages to solve an accounting problem. They are called Fog, Golem, and Hotshot. On first trials, Fog crashes 10% of the time, Golem 20% of the time, and Hotshot 30% of the time.

Of ten employees, six are assigned Fog, three are assigned Golem, and one is assigned Hotshot. Sophia was assigned a program at random. It crashed on the first trial. What is the probability that she was assigned Hotshot?

7   *Deterring burglars.* This example is based on a letter that a sociologist wrote to the daily newspaper. He thinks that it is a good idea for people to have handguns at home, in order to deter burglars. He states the following (amazing) information:

> The rate with which a home in the United States is burgled at least once per year is 10%. The rate for Canada is 40%, and for Great Britain is 60%. These rates have been stable for the past decade.

Don't believe everything a professor says, especially when he writes to the newspaper! Suppose, however, that the information is correct as stated, and that:

> Jenny Park, Larry Chen, and Ali Sami were trainee investment bankers for a multinational company. During the last calendar year Jenny had a home in the United States, Larry in Great Britain, and Ali in Canada.

One of the trainees is picked at random. This person was burgled last year. What is the probability that this person was Ali?

KEY WORDS FOR REVIEW

Bayes' Rule
Base rates
False positives

8 Expected Value

Inductive logic is risky. We need it when we are uncertain. Not just uncertain about what will happen, or what is true, but also when we are uncertain about what to do. Decisions need more than probability. They are based on the value of possible outcomes of our actions. The technical name for value is **utility**. This chapter shows how to combine probability and utility. But it ends with a famous paradox.

ACTS

Should you open a small business?

Should you take an umbrella?

Should you buy a Lotto ticket?

Should you move in with someone you love?

In each case you settle on an *act*. Doing nothing at all counts as an act.

Acts have *consequences*.

You go broke (or maybe found a great company).

You stay dry when everyone else is sopping wet (or you mislay your umbrella).

You waste a dollar (or perhaps win a fortune).

You live happily ever after (or split up a week later).

You do absolutely nothing active at all: that counts as an act, too.

Some consequences are desirable. Some are not. Suppose you can represent the cost or benefit of a possible consequence by a number—so many dollars, perhaps. Call that number the *utility* of the consequence.

Suppose you can also represent the *probability* of each possible consequence of an act by a number.

In making a decision, we want to assess the relative merits of each possible act. There is a simple way to combine probabilities and utilities in order to evaluate possible acts: multiply! That is,

> *Multiply (the probability by the utility of each consequence of an act) and then add the results for each possible consequence of the act.*

The result of this calculation is called the **expected value** of the act.

NOTATION

Acts: denoted by **bold capital letters** (e.g., A).
Consequences: denoted by capital letters, (e.g., C).
The utility of a possible consequence C: U(C).
The probability of C happening, if act A is taken: $Pr(C/A)$ (a conditional probability).
The expected value of A: $Exp(A)$.

JUST TWO POSSIBLE CONSEQUENCES

Act: A.
Consequences: C_1, C_2.
Utilities: $U(C_1)$, $U(C_2)$.
Probabilities: $Pr(C_1/A)$, $Pr(C_2/A)$.

Definition:

Expected value of A = $Exp(A) = [Pr(C_1/A)][U(C_1)] + [Pr(C_2/A)][U(C_2)]$.

When it is perfectly clear that we are talking about the consequences of a specific act A, it is easier to write:

$Exp(A) = [Pr(C_1)][U(C_1)] + [Pr(C_2)][U(C_2)]$.

The expected value of an act is the *sum* of the *products*
(utilities $\times$ probabilities).

A FREE RIDE

Your aunt offers you a free lottery ticket for your birthday, but says you don't have to take it. The two possible acts are: accept, and do not accept.

The expected value of not accepting is just 0. What is the expected value of accepting? Suppose the lottery has 100 tickets, with a prize of $90 for the one ticket that is drawn. If you accept the ticket, there are two possible consequences:

Consequence 1: Your ticket is drawn.
Utility of Consequence 1: $90.
Probability of Consequence 1: 0.01.

Consequence 2: Your ticket is not drawn.
Utility of Consequence 2: 0.
Probability of Consequence 2: 0.99.

Expected value of accepting the ticket:

$$\text{Exp}(A) = (0.01)(\$90) + (0.99)(0) = 90\text{¢}.$$

Expected value of not accepting it: 0.

FAIR'S FAIR

Now suppose your aunt is stingy. She offers to sell you the ticket. "It cost me a dollar!" she says. You are nice to your aunt, and consider paying her $1 for the ticket. Call this act of buying the ticket act B. What is the expected value of B?

$$\text{Exp}(B) = [(0.01)(\$90 - \$1)] + [(0.99)(-\$1)] = -10\text{¢}.$$

This suggests that somehow you would be at a disadvantage if you bought the ticket from her for $1. What would be a fair price, so that neither of you was taking advantage of the other?

Consider a third possible act, C, in which you pay your aunt 90¢ for the ticket.

$$\text{Exp}(C) = 0 \text{ when the agreed price of a ticket is } 90\text{¢}.$$

That makes 90¢ seem like a fair price.

You should look at it from your aunt's point of view, too. She has an asset, a lottery ticket. She is considering the act D, selling the ticket to you for 90¢. Here she loses her asset, but is 90¢ richer. If x stands for what she thinks is the fair price for the ticket, then the expectation of act D, in which she sells the ticket, should be:

$$\text{Exp (D)} = 90\text{¢} - x = 0.$$

So the fair price for her, too, would be 90¢. Other arguments lead to the same conclusion. Here are two of them.

FAIR PRICE ARGUMENT 1

Suppose the lottery is run every day of the week, and every day your aunt offers to sell you a ticket in the day's game. In each game, one ticket out of 100 is drawn, and if you hold the winning ticket, you get $90. If you were to play every day for years, you would expect your average winning to be 90¢ per game. If you paid less than 90 per ticket, you would be getting a bargain. In the long run, you would be taking advantage of your aunt. If you paid more, she would be taking advantage of you. So in terms of a long run of plays, 90¢ is once again the fair price.

FAIR PRICE ARGUMENT 2

Suppose you bought each and every one of the 100 tickets in the lottery for 90¢. Then you would pay $90. You would also win $90, for you would be sure to own the winning ticket. So you would break even. That sounds fair, and suggests that 90¢ is the fair price for a ticket.

Now imagine that one hundred people each bought one ticket, so that all the tickets were sold. Between them, they stand to gain a total of $90. The lottery is so made that there is a complete symmetry between all the players. Any gambler knows as much as any other. Perhaps each believes the lottery itself is unbiased; at any rate, they do not know it is biased in any particular way. Hence each purchaser should pay the same amount for a ticket as every other one. Altogether they should not pay more than $90, or the lottery owner would have an advantage. It is only fair that each should pay the same amount for a ticket. Hence they should each pay 90¢ a ticket.

GENERALIZING

Now consider any finite number of mutually exclusive consequences of act A:

Consequences: $C_1, C_2, \ldots, C_n$.
Utilities: $U(C_1), U(C_2), \ldots, U(C_n)$.
Probabilities: $Pr(C_1), Pr(C_2), \ldots, Pr(C_n)$.

Definition:

$$Exp(A) = [Pr(C_1)U(C_1)] + [Pr(C_2)U(C_2)] + \ldots + [Pr(C_n)U(C_n)].$$

In words, the expected value is the *sum* of the *products* of the *probabilities* times the *utilities*.

$$Exp(A) = \Sigma\, [Pr(C_i)U(C_i)]$$

Expected value can be thought of as a *weighted average*. An ordinary average of, say, four quantities a, b, c, d, is $(a + b + c + d)/4$. But suppose we wish to give different *weights* to the four quantities, weighting them in the ratios $x:y:z:w$. We could do this by averaging x times a, y times b, and so forth.

The weighted average of a, b, c, d is thus $(xa + yb + zc + wd)/4$.

TWO TICKETS

What would be the expected value of holding two tickets in our little lottery? Only one can win the $90.

Let A be the act of accepting two free tickets, each with a 1/100 chance of winning $90.

$\text{Exp}(A) = 2[(0.01) \times (\$90)] = \$1.80$

A RAFFLE

Imagine a raffle of 100 tickets, each with a 1/100 probability of being drawn. The first ticket drawn will give a prize of $90. The second ticket drawn gives a prize of $9. None of the rest give you any gain or loss at all.

What is the expected value of A: accepting one free ticket in the raffle? There is a 1/100 chance that your ticket is the first one drawn, and likewise a 1/100 chance that it is the second one drawn. (The chance that your ticket is the second one drawn is **not** 1/99. Why not? Think of a simpler case. Suppose there were only two tickets. Then you would have a ½ chance of getting $90. Your chance of getting $9 is also ½—**not** $1/(2-1) = 1$.)

$\text{Exp}(A) = [(1/100) \times \$90] + [(1/100) \times \$9] = 99\cent$

What is the expected value of B: buying one ticket in the raffle for $1?

$\text{Exp}(B) = [(1/100)(\$89)] + [(1/100)(\$8)] + [(98/100)(-\$1)] = -1\cent$

The *fair price* for a ticket in this raffle is 99¢. A dollar is too much, but 99¢ is just right.

STREET LIFE

My friend Martin is an illegal street vendor at a major city intersection. His sales on a typical day came to $300. The fine for illegal vending is $100.

Martin works the street Tuesdays through Saturdays and has found that he is ticketed about twice a week (but not regularly—there are runs when he is ticketed every day, and periods when he is left in peace). The chance of being ticketed on any given day is, he finds, 40%. He is never ticketed more than once a day, and there is no pattern of police harassment—ticketing seems to be random.

What is the expected value of a day's work?

Let W be the act of going to work on any given day.

Assumptions:

(1) The cost of the merchandise that he sells for $300 is only $100, so there is a $200 profit.

(2) The fine is $100.

(3) The probability of being ticketed on any given day is 0.4. The probability of being ticketed twice in one day is 0.

I SELF-EMPLOYED

Martin wants to keep on the good side of the law, so although he will go on vending, he will pay every ticket so as not to be in contempt. The expected value of a day's work is, then,

$$Exp(W) = (0.6)(\$200) + (0.4)(\$200 - \$100) = \$160.$$

Here we have reasoned that there is a 60% chance of getting the full $200 (no fine), and a 40% chance of getting $100, the net profit after paying a fine. We could think of this differently. He is sure to get $200, but has a 40% chance of paying out $100 in a fine:

$$Exp(W) = (\$200) - (0.4)(\$100) = \$160.$$

In exercise 3 (page 95) we work out the expected value when Martin knows that the law is poorly enforced, and also knows that if he goes to court, the case will probably not proceed because the policeman who charged him will probably not show up.

II EMPLOYED, HONEST BOSS

A different situation: Martin works for a big fish in the street-vending world. *Big Fish* promises to pay all of Martin's fines. He charges Martin $50 a day for the use of his cart. Martin can sell only goods bought from *Big Fish*. If *Big Fish* honors his promise to look after the legal work and pay the fines, what is the expected value of a day's work? That's easy, because Martin has traded a probability for a certainty.

$$Exp(W) = \$150$$

In this case, Martin runs no risk, but his expected net income is less than in risky situation (I).

EXPECTED TIME OF TRAVEL

Time is not money, but it is a value. The definition of expected value applies to any set of values for which we have probabilities.

You have a job interview in Ottawa, Canada, in midwinter. Your prospective employer will pay your travel expenses. There are two ways to go: train, or plane from the airport.

A bad storm is predicted with probability 0.2.

The storm will not affect the time required to get from your home to the departure point, or from the arrival point to your place of interview. These times are:

Train: to the train station, 30 minutes; scheduled departure 10 minutes later.
Train: station to interview, 20 minutes.

Plane: to airport, 80 minutes; scheduled departure one hour later.
Plane: airport to interview, 40 minutes.

If there is no storm:

Train time is five hours.
Plane time is one hour.

If there is a storm:

Train time is seven hours.
Plane is grounded for ten hours before take-off.

What are the expected total times in transit by train or plane?

Solution
Let T and P be the acts of taking the train or the plane.
$Exp(T) = 1 + (.8)(5 \text{ hours}) + (.2)(7 \text{ hours}) = 6.4 \text{ hours} = 6 \text{ hours}, 24 \text{ minutes}$
$Exp(P) = 3 + (.8)(1 \text{ hour}) + .2(11 \text{ hours}) = 6 \text{ hours}$

Should you decide to take the plane, since the expected time of travel is shorter? *It depends on your values, your overall utilities.*
If your only utility is taking as little time as possible, then you might prefer the airplane trip. But you could have other utilities.
If you took the plane and you had a storm, you might miss the interview—*disaster*, no job. But if the interviewer would not blame you, and would give you a new appointment if there were a storm, you might prefer the airplane.
If waiting makes you nervous, then ten hours in an airport might drive you crazy, and you would fail the interview. So you take the train, even though the expected travel time is longer.

ROULETTE

At Las Vegas, and at most casinos in North America, a standard roulette wheel has 18 reds, 18 blacks, and 2 zeros. A simple bet of $1 on red pays back $2 if and only if the wheel stops at a red segment. What is the expected value of act R, bet on red? There is an 18/38, or 9/19 chance of winning $2, and a certainty of paying out $1:

$Exp(R) = (9/19)(\$2) - \$1 \approx -5\cent.$

At Monte Carlo, and at most casinos in Europe, a standard roulette wheel has 18 reds, 18 blacks, but only 1 zero. A simple bet of $1 on red pays back $2 if and only if the wheel stops at a red segment. What is the expected value of such a bet?

$$\text{Exp}(R) = (18/37)(\$2) - \$1 \approx -3\cancel{c}$$

LOTTO

Lotto 6/49 has become the most common form of state-run gambling in most parts of the world. You pay $1. You choose 6 different numbers from 1 through 49. The Lotto Corporation draws 6 numbers at random from 1 through 49. If your 6 numbers match the drawn numbers, you win an enormous prize. The system of payoffs varies slightly from place to place, but here is one widespread system:

> The lottery company takes off 55% of the sum invested for a given draw. Some of this pays for administration; the rest of the 55% is given to charity, and 45% is paid out in prizes.
> Every ticket with exactly three matching numbers gets exactly $10.
> Every ticket with exactly four matching numbers gets $100.
> Of the remaining prize money, 15% is divided evenly among tickets with exactly five matching numbers.
> The remainder is divided evenly among tickets with all numbers matching.
> If there are no 6-matches (or 5-matches), the sum allotted to them is credited to the total for the next lottery. That is why the big prize can be $2 million for one week, and $17 million a few weeks later.

Many lotteries have so-called bonus systems, but these do not affect the actual total amount of money paid back in prizes. A rake-off of 55% is perhaps the worst used in North America, but in general such public lotteries pay back only about half the gross receipts. Hence you can think of public lotteries as a kind of voluntary taxation.

Lotteries like Lotto 6/49 were introduced, for just this purpose, in Italian city-states early in the sixteenth century. (See our cover illustration for a painting of around 1535, with *Chance* holding lottery tickets.) The longest running lottery is in Spain. Although it entered the game late, in December 1763, there has been a regular Lotto running since March 4th, 1812, when a lottery was organized to raise money for the defense of a city being besieged by Napoleon. In Spain the great Christmas lottery is a national event, and every village buys blocks of tickets. This *Navidad* (nativity of Christ) lottery is the world's biggest. Just before Christmas about *one billion dollars* worth of tickets are sold, and that is for only one of many Spanish lotteries held throughout the year. (Comparison: total world sales of government-run lottery tickets is about $80 billion.) The *Navidad* returns 70% of the price of the tickets to the gamblers. By comparison, the best return on lottery tickets in North America may be in Iowa, which returns 53%. Our figure of 45% comes from Ontario.

EXPECTED VALUE OF LOTTO 6/49

What is the expected value of the act of buying, at random, an arbitrary Lotto 6/49 ticket? Since in the long run 45¢ in every dollar is paid back in prizes, the expected value is (45¢ − $1.00) = −55¢. If N is the number of tickets sold between one lottery in which the grand prize is awarded, and the next such lottery, the total payout is $0.45N.

Every standard gamble based on an artificial randomizer has a VERY much higher expected value than Lotto 6/49 (and similar lotteries available to the gambling public). And, as we shall see in a moment, that is not the end of the bad news for Lotto players.

The expected value of buying an arbitrary Lotto 6/49 ticket in Ontario is −55¢. Or: The fair price for a single ticket chosen at random is 45¢. The percentage retained, in the long run, by a gambling house is called the *house edge*. The edge in Lotto 6/49, using the payback rule stated, is 55%.

You cannot, however, compute the expected value of a ticket in an individual lottery. On week 1, say, the prize is $1,800,000. If no one wins the big prize for four weeks, then on week 5, the big prize, if won, might be $17,000,000. You cannot do a good job of calculating, in advance, the expected value of buying a ticket on week 1 as opposed to week 5, because that depends on the number of tickets sold.

It seems that nearly everyone would prefer a ticket in the week 5 lottery. Certainly sales increase dramatically when a big prize is advertised. But maybe "nearly everyone" is wrong.

The number of tickets in the draw depends on the advertised size of the big prize, for more people are tempted to bet for $17,000,000 than for $1,800,000. This does not affect the low prizes (3 or 4 matches) but increases the probability that more than one person will pick the numbers for a large prize. If 2 people won the big prize, each would get only $8,500,000. If 17 won, they would get only $1,000,000.

ACTUAL PROBABILITIES

The actual probabilities of winning in Lotto 6/49 are:

Chance of 6 matches: about 1 in 14 million (1 in 13,983,816).
Chance of exactly 5 matches: about 1 in 54,000 (258 in 13,983,816).
Chance of exactly 4 matches: about 1 in 1,032.
Chance of exactly 3 matches: about 1 in 56.

What do these odds mean? If you bought 100 tickets a week (for $100 a week), you would have a 50:50 chance of winning the big prize in the next 2,700 years.

With a house edge of 55%, Lotto 6/49 gives the gambler far, far less expected value per dollar than any casino bet.

Gambling houses have many gambles based on artificial randomizers: blackjack, bingo, several kinds of poker, roulette, craps. Old-fashioned gamblers like complicated rules. For example, *craps* is a fast-moving dice game played on a classy table with a complex betting layout. The house edge in craps depends on the type of bet. Many bets in craps have a house edge of only 1.4%. The house edge in Lotto is 55%. Even in the *Navidad* the edge is 30%. Nevertheless, you can gamble only twice a week at Lotto 6/49, or once a year at the *Navidad*. If you spend an hour at the craps table, and bet on every roll, you will lose a lot, because the game goes so fast that you make a lot of bets, which add up—add up for the house, that is.

The staple randomizer for mass-consumption gambling almost everywhere in North America is the slot machine, once a mechanical device of spinning wheels, now a video game. The house edge can be fixed anytime by the house. In the past, in Las Vegas or Atlantic City, the house edge has usually been about 3%, with some houses advertising an edge of only 2%. Although the edge in craps is better for the gambler, you can make more bets per hour with a slot machine, so your losses may well be worse than with the slots.

ACTUAL WINNINGS

We said that the fair price of a Lotto 6/49 ticket is 45¢. But it is not always so simple. It depends on where you live, and the expected value in money may differ for different people, even if the lotteries they play use exactly the same rules.

This is because there are more rules in this world than lottery rules. There are income taxes.

In Canada, citizens do not pay income tax on lottery winnings. So if Canadians gamble on their national lotteries, the expected value of a $1 ticket is, indeed, −55¢. Spaniards do not pay income tax on lottery winnings. So the expected value for a Spaniard with a 100-peseta ticket is −30 pesetas.

United States taxpayers, however, do pay income tax on lottery winnings. For really huge prizes, like $17 million, the tax bite will be very large. So the actual net expected value of a lottery for an American buying the most favorable lottery ticket—in Iowa—appears to be even worse than −47¢. But matters are even more complicated. U.S. tax law allows gamblers to deduct their bets and lottery tickets as "investments." (That is not allowed in Spain or Canada.) So although the real cost of a $1 ticket is $1 for a poor American who pays zero income tax, it is only 72¢ for a rich American paying a 28% (marginal) rate of tax.

To compound the problem, American lotteries divide up huge winnings into twenty annual installments, so that the income tax liability can be lessened. This means that even before taxes you get less than your full huge prize, because you do not have access to the money now, and do not get an allowance for inflation or a maximum rate of interest on the money that is tied up. If you win two million dollars, the lottery management need only invest one million dollars in guaranteed returns in order to pay you two million over twenty years.

The payoff rules quoted earlier are for Ontario. There the house edge is 55%. The Iowa state lottery returns 47%, so the edge appears to be less than in Ontario. But in fact, for the large payoffs the Iowa lottery is paying out much less than a corresponding prize in Ontario—it need set aside only $1 million when someone "wins" $2 million. So the house edge in Iowa is actually much more favorable to the lottery than the house edge in Ontario.

The point of these observations is only to introduce a reality check. It sounds neat and tidy to say the expected value, for repeated purchase of a ticket in every lottery, is exactly −55¢ in Ontario and −47¢ in Iowa. Real life is seldom as tidy as a simple calculation.

INCREDIBLE ODDS: ONLY 5,500 TICKETS CAN BE SOLD!

A national ballet company runs a posh lottery. There are only 5,500 tickets. Each ticket costs $100. The prizes are drawn over the course of eight months, the first drawing being held in November and the last in June. Tickets are on sale October through May. The prizes are:

$2,500 cash. Drawing date: November 24.
$7,500 Bang & Olufsen luxury TV/VCR. Drawing date: January 7.
$10,000 in Visa travelers checks. Drawing date: March 4.
$6,600 trip for two to Thailand. Drawing date: May 18.
"Mercedes Benz 300SL—the stunning new model with a value of $100,000."
   Draw date: June 1.

So drawing is with replacement. The organizers do not expect to sell all the tickets before the first drawing. But suppose you bought a ticket before November 24, and all 5,500 tickets had been sold then. What would be the expected value of that act?

$$Exp(A) = [(1/5500)(\$2500 + \$7,500 + \$10,000 + \$6,600 + \$100,000)] - \$100$$
$$= -\$77$$

Or, to put the matter another way, you could think of the fair price for a ballet lottery ticket as being about $23.

WHICH LOTTERY WOULD YOU PREFER?

Disregarding taxes and so forth, the fair price for one hundred $1 tickets in Lotto 6/49 is $45.

The fair price for a $100 ticket in the ballet lottery is about $23.

It looks as if Lotto 6/49 is almost twice as good as the ballet lottery. Why does the ballet say "incredible odds"? Shouldn't Lotto 6/49 sue for false advertising, because its expected value is better?

No, because the lotteries can be compared in different ways.

One of every 1100 tickets in the ballet lottery carries a sizable prize. So, as the organizers put it, the "odds" are "incredible"—or at any rate, there is a non-negligible chance of winning a big prize. By contrast, the chance of winning the biggest prize in Lotto 6/49 is negligible.

So if what you want is a "reasonable chance" at a "fairly good" prize, you might choose an act of lower expected value over an act which gave you a minute chance on an absolutely enormous prize that would change your life.

CHEAP THRILLS

Is it stupid for a poor person to buy lottery tickets? Maybe not. You don't just buy a chance on a big prize. You buy a thrill, a hope, or a fantasy. One consequence of buying a lottery ticket is having an agreeable fantasy. The poorer you are, the more you may need such fantasies just to carry on. You could say that such fantasies are "worth more" to the poor person than to someone with a comfortable job and good prospects. So maybe it is not so stupid to buy a lottery ticket with little chance of winning.

Suppose you are very poor and, unlike university students, have no prospects of a comfortable life. You value having some hope in your life at $2.50. Then a $1 lottery ticket is a bargain. The expected value of buying a ticket (on this assumption) is +$1.95

Thus, contrary to what many more prosperous people say, it is *not* obviously irrational for poor people to spend some of their not-so-spare cash in a kind of voluntary taxation. But it is a miserable world, where that is the only way that many people can put a little hope into their lives.

MARTINGALES

Martin likes to gamble, but he does not like to take risks. "I've got a guaranteed winning strategy," he says. "I know an honest bookmaker, *Mr. Gale*, and an honest banker who checks up on his assets to make sure that *Mr. Gale* can cover all his bets." So what is your strategy, we ask.

> "*Mr. Gale* tosses a fair coin. You can bet any amount of money on heads (say), starting at $10. If you bet $N on heads, and win, he gives you 2($N), so your net profit on that bet is $N. Otherwise, he keeps your stake of $N, that is his profit.
>
> "I bet $10 to start with. If I lose, I bet $20, so that if I win, I will recoup my losses ($10) and make a profit ($10). If I lose again, I am now out of pocket $30, so I bet $40 on the next toss. I keep on doing that—after a run of n losses, I bet $2^n(\$10)$.
>
> "Sooner or later heads will turn up with a fair coin, so I am bound to win $10. How about that?"

"But pretty soon you will be betting a lot of money," we remark. "What if *Mr. Gale* cannot cover your bet?" *Martin* has a good answer:

> "The banker makes sure that he deposits all his winnings in the bank until I stop playing. Since all I will get back, when I finally win, is what he has won from me so far, plus $10, I know he can cover my losses."

Then we have a harder question for Martin: "But sooner or later you will go broke! After a run of 10 tails, you will have to bet $10,240 to win $10. And you will already have lost $10 + $20 +40 +$80 + . . . So if the coin falls 10 tails in a row, you will have to risk a total of $20,480. And things get worse! If the coin falls tails 15 times in a row, you need to have started with a capital of $655,360 to keep on playing for a measly $10 profit. Sooner or later you will run out of money."

What is true is that Martin will make a little money from time to time until he runs out of money.

Martin's scheme against *Mr. Gale* has a long history. It is an example of what is called a "martingale." The name has been around for 200 years, but no one seems to know where it came from.

THE ST. PETERSBURG GAME

We conclude by going from poverty to unlimited riches. Imagine a fair coin, tossed in a sturdy chance setup.

The coin is tossed once. If it falls heads, you receive a prize of $2, and the game stops.

If not, it is tossed again. If it falls heads on the second toss, you get $4, and the game stops.

If not, it is tossed again. If it falls heads on the third toss, you get $8, and the game stops. And so on.

The game stops after the first head is thrown. If the first head is thrown at the nth toss, the prize is $\$(2)^n$.

STRANGE EXPECTATIONS

Suppose you are offered a chance to play this game, but an entry fee will be charged. What is the fair price? Call it x.

> Let S be the act of paying x to play this game.
> Let N be the event that the game stops at the nth toss.
> $U(N) = 2^n$
> $Pr(N) = (1/2)^n$

If x is the fair price, then,

Exp(S) − x should be 0. That means that $x = \Sigma\,[(1/2^n(2^n)]$.
For $n = 1$, we have $1/2 \times (\$2) = \$1$.
For $n = 2$, we have $1/4 \times (\$4) = \$1$.
For any n, we have $1/2^n \times (\$2^n) = \$1$.

So the fair price is $\$1 + \$1 + \$1 + \$1 + \ldots$.

That means that the fair price should be infinite, or at any rate, that there is no upper bound on the fair price.

To put it another way, no matter what price you pay to enter the game, the expected value of entering is infinite, or at least has no upper bound.

PARADOX

The word "paradox" has several meanings. Logicians use the word in this way:

> An argument that apparently derives self-contradictory or absurd conclusions by reasoning from apparently acceptable premises.

The strange expected value of the St. Petersburg game seems to lead to a paradox.

The absurd conclusion is that the fair price for playing this game is as high as you please. This is absurd, and everyone knows it. Would you accept a chance to play this game for all your present cash and future lifetime income? Of course not.

Think for a while. How much would *you* pay to enter this game?

Write your answer here: _____

Note that it must be worth at least $2 to enter the game, for you should get at least $2 back, it seems, assuming the game does sometime come to an end.

Not very many people will go above five or six dollars.

What is wrong with the argument leading to the St. Petersburg paradox? Here are some possible answers.

SOLUTION 1: ANY FINITE PRICE *IS* A BARGAIN!

There is no paradox. There really is no upper bound to the expected utility of a chance in this game. Of course, most of the time the game ends after a few tosses, and the prize is small. But no matter how large a prize you think of, there is some chance of winning it. At any price, this is a better bet than Lotto 6/49.

Retort: No one in their right mind would pay much to enter this game.

SOLUTION 2: THE GAME IS IMPOSSIBLE

A real coin would wear out; more importantly, any real bank would go broke after forty or so tosses.

Retort: True enough, but we are here considering an ideal game. It at least makes sense to ask, in our imagination, about the fair price for entering this game. And even if you do think that the game is going to end after 40 tosses, thanks to bankruptcy or whatever, with no pay-off if the coin falls tails 41 times in a row, would you pay even $50 to enter this game? Why not? No bank would go broke paying you back after 6 tosses, which is all you need to make a profit for an investment of $50.

SOLUTION 3: NO EXPECTED VALUE IS DEFINED

We have been careless in defining expected value. An expected value is defined as a sum of the products (probabilities times utilities). The sum is defined only when it has an upper bound. Hence the expected value of playing the St. Petersburg game is not defined.

> Retort: This excludes the embarrassing game, but why? This is "monster-barring." You have trimmed your definition because you encountered a monster, but you give no explanation of why the definition should be limited like this.

SOLUTION 4: DIMINISHING MARGINAL UTILITY

A dollar is worth a lot to a poor person, but not to a rich one. With small sums we can conveniently use the fiction that every dollar is worth as much as every other dollar. So that to someone with a bank account of $14, an extra dollar is worth as much as it is to someone who has $35 under the mattress. An extra dollar to a millionaire is not, however, worth as much as it is to a poor student.

The **marginal utility** of a quantity Q given quantity R is the utility of adding Q to a person's fortune, if they already have R. And if we are comparing winning R to winning Q+R, the additional value of winning Q is not Q but the marginal utility of winning Q, given R.

Technical note for those familiar with natural logarithms: a common simple curve for diminishing marginal utility of money is $U(\$x) = \$(\log x)$.

In the St. Petersburg game, you get twice as many dollars if you win at the $(n+1)$st toss as you do if you win at the nth toss. But that does not mean that you get twice as much value or utility. The marginal utility of twice $\$2^n$, given $\$2^n$, is less than $\$(2^{n+1}) - \$2^n$. This is a case of **diminishing marginal utility**.

> Retort: The idea of diminishing utility is very important in economics, but it does not satisfactorily relieve the paradox at the extremes, such as in the St. Petersburg game. When you start doing the details, and make plausible allowance for diminishing marginal utility, the entry price of the game is still far higher than anyone in real life would want to risk.
>
> One trouble is that if you are going to play the game only once you are unlikely to want to spend even $20, in which case you have to make the utilities diminish very, very fast, far more than is realistic. And if you are able to play many times before you win, you have to have a large capital, in which case the utility of what you expect to win is not worth it anyway.

SOLUTION 5: LOW CHANCES

Recall the difference between the ballet lottery and Lotto 6/49. Some prosperous people would rather gamble $100 on the ballet lottery, than buy one hundred $1 tickets for Lotto 6/49. This is because there is a larger probability ("1 in 5,500") of winning a significant prize with the ballet lottery. Perhaps the sheer improbability of winning a lot from a St. Petersburg game is part of what makes it so unattractive.

DANIEL BERNOULLI

The St. Petersburg problem has been puzzling probability theorists for a long time. It was investigated by Daniel Bernoulli (1700–1782), a member of a famous Swiss family of mathematicians (in fact, his brother Nicholas passed the problem on to him). He did most of his work employed in St. Petersburg, then the capital of Russia. Daniel was a nephew of an even more famous contributor to probability, Jacques Bernoulli (1654–1705), one of whose theorems is the topic of Chapter 16.

Daniel Bernoulli used his paradox to develop the concept of diminishing marginal utility, a central idea for modern economics. He proposed a utility function for money in such a way that the marginal utility of very large winnings was very small. Hence he obtained a finite expected value for the St. Petersburg game.

Some people invent paradoxes for fun. "They only do it to annoy, because they know it teases." But paradoxes can be useful. They force us to focus on some unclarity in our thought. The best reaction to a paradox is to invent a genuinely new and deep idea. Daniel Bernoulli developed the idea of diminishing marginal utility.

LOGIC, OR THE ART OF THINKING

Modern probability ideas began around 1660. The first axioms, due to Christiaan Huygens, were published in Dutch in 1657. Nowadays a few books on deductive logic end with some chapters on probability and inductive logic. They follow an example set in 1662, a book published in French with the title *Logic, or The Art of Thinking*. These chapters were strongly influenced by Blaise Pascal (1623–1662, see page 124). The chapters make plain that decisions, and indeed hope and fear themselves, depend on two things: what you believe, and what you want (or do not want). They depend on *probability* and *utility*.

> Many people are exceedingly frightened when they hear thunder. . . . If it is only the danger of dying by lightning that causes them this unusual apprehension, it is easy to show that this is unreasonable. For out of two million people, at most there is one that dies this way. We could even say that there is hardly a violent death that is less common. Our fear of death ought to be

proportional not only to the magnitude of the harm, but also to the probability of the event. Just as there is hardly any kind of death more rare than being struck by lightning, there is also hardly any that ought to cause less fear.

Thus from the very beginning of probability theory people have been aware that there are two factors to risk: the gravity of the consequences, and the probability or likelihood that they will occur.

We are afraid of lightning. *Logic, or The Art of Thinking*, makes the same observation about hopes. Don't just think of the $17 million big prize in Lotto 6/49! Remember that the probability of your ticket winning is about one in 14 million (see page 87). It is just when we forget about probability that we are attracted to lotteries.

Is it not highly advantageous, people say, to win $20,000 for one dollar? Each person thinks he will be the happy person who will win the jackpot. No one reflects that if the jackpot is, for example, $20,000, it may be 30,000 times more probable for each individual to lose rather than win it.

The flaw in this reasoning is that in order to decide what we ought to do to obtain some good or avoid some harm, it is necessary to consider not only the good or harm in itself, but also the probability that it will or will not occur.

Decision theory begins with these sentences, published in 1662.

EXERCISES

1   *Winter travel.* Once in midwinter a severe snowstorm was predicted for our city. My son Oliver had to go far out in the suburbs for a one-day job. I said that he should take public transportation, much of which ran underground to the job location and would not be disrupted by the weather. He said that he should borrow the car. Was it likely we disagreed about probabilities, utilities, or both?

2   *Gimmicks.* An advertiser's gimmick tells you to tear a coupon off the back of a package and mail it to a contest address. If you are the lucky winner, you get a prize worth $10,000. For every 40,000 coupons sent in, one will be drawn. Say the cost of mailing (postage, envelope, etc.) is 45¢. What is the expected value of the act M: mail the coupon?

3   *Street vendor: fines not enforced.* The conditions are the same as in our first story about Martin, the street vendor (page 83), except that Martin knows that the law is poorly administered. He will pay only if he is charged in court, and the policeman who issued the ticket shows up in court that day. The chance of that happening, for any given ticket, is only 20%. What is the expected value of a day's work?

4   *Street vendor with a bad boss.* The same as the second story about the street vendor, except that the boss, *Big Fish*, is unreliable, and will do anything he can to take advantage of anyone he can. Martin does not trust *Fish*, and knows that the

probability that *Fish* will pay a given fine before it goes to court is only 75%. So 25% of the time Martin's tickets go to court. But as in question 3, there is only a 20% chance of an unpaid ticket ending up in court with an actual fine. What is the expected value of a day's work?

5   *The best of possible worlds.* We have now described four arrangements, two in the text, (I) Self-employed and (II) Honest boss, and two as exercise (3) (Fines not enforced) and exercise (4) (Bad boss). Which is the worst situation for Martin? Which is the best?

6   *Insurance.* William's only valuable possessions are a used car, worth $5,400, and his grandfather's gold pocket watch, which he keeps unlocked in his boarding house. It is worth $600.

The probability of his car being stolen in the course of one year is 1/900. But there are so many untrustworthy strangers dropping in at the boarding house, that the probability of his watch being stolen is 1/30.

Assume that the two types of theft are statistically independent.

(a) What is the probability that both watch and car are stolen? Watch and not car? Car and not watch? Probability of no loss either way?

An insurance company offers William theft insurance on both items for $60, with a deductible of 10% (it pays him only 90% of the true value of a stolen item).

Let I be the act of buying insurance. Let D be the act of declining to buy insurance.

(b) What are the possible consequences of D? Determine Exp(D).

(c) What are the possible consequences of I? Determine Exp(I).

(d) Should William insure or not?

Suppose that William has a note in the car telling where the watch is, so that we expect that someone who steals the car is more likely to steal the watch too: Pr(watch stolen/car stolen) > Pr(watch stolen).

(e) Are the two types of theft still statistically independent?

(f) Now explain, qualitatively, how such nonindependence would affect Exp (I).

7   *Doubling up.* Some gamblers think that they have a nifty way of winning money. *Slick Jim* likes to go to the horse races. He enjoys the scene. He does not want to get rich, but at least he wants to cover the price of admission, which in our town is $10. So he bets enough on the first race to win $10. He is betting on a favorite, so he has to put up $7. If he loses, he bets enough to win $17. Next race he bets on a long shot, and he puts up $3. If he loses that race, he bets enough to win $20. And so on. If he loses on every race this Saturday, he is out of pocket, say, $164. So next Saturday he has to bet enough to win $164 + $10. What is wrong with this strategy?

8   *The Moscow Game.* In Moscow they play a game different from the St. Petersburg game. The rules are just the same, but play stops at 40 tosses of tails. At that point the house takes all the bets.

(a) If you play this game for stake S, what is the probability that you will lose your stake without winning anything?

(b) Is there an upper bound to the expected value in the Moscow game?

(c) What is the fair price for entering the Moscow game?

(d) What is the probability that on any one play of the Moscow game, you will make a profit, if you pay the fair price?

(e) A somewhat shady new Russian banking company mysteriously named MMM is bankrolling the Moscow game. Thanks to recent speculation in spot oil futures, it has a capital of a billion dollars ($1,000 million). Estimate how many tails must turn up in a row before the bank goes bankrupt. (This is not quite such an imaginary story. MMM was indeed a real post-Soviet speculative outfit involved in many deals that have not been clarified to this day.)

KEY WORDS FOR REVIEW

Acts	Fair price	Diminishing marginal
Consequences	Expected time	utility
Utility	Lotteries	
Expected value	St. Petersburg paradox	

9 Maximizing Expected Value

How do you choose among possible acts? The most common decision rule is an obvious one. Perform the action with the highest expected value. There are, however, a few more paradoxes connected with this simple rule.

RISKY DECISIONS

Logic analyzes reasons and arguments. We can give reasons for our *beliefs*. We can also give reasons for our *actions* and our *decisions*. What is the best thing to do under the circumstances? Inductive logic analyzes risky arguments. It also helps with **decision theory**, the theory of making risky decisions.

Should I go out in a thunderstorm to fetch a book, even though I am scared of lightning? I go out in a thunderstorm because I *believe* I left a book outside. I *believe* it will get wet and be ruined. I also *believe* I will not be struck by lightning. But I also go outside because I *want* the book, among other things. Of course, my beliefs are not certainties—I am pretty confident I left the book there. I am pretty sure it will get wet if it is there. I know it is not probable that I will be hit by lightning.

Decisions depend on two kinds of thing:

- What we believe.
- What we want.

Sometimes we can represent our degrees of belief or confidence by *probabilities*. Sometimes we can represent what we want by dollar values, or at least by judgments of value, which we call *utilities*.

A decision is a decision to do something (or nothing). It is a decision to act (or not to act). **Acts** usually have a number of possible values and consequences. We have shown how to compute the expected value of an act. But we have not shown how to *use* this number.

DECISION THEORY

How can we decide what to do, when we have only probabilities to work with? This is one topic of *decision theory*. Expected value is a fundamental tool in making models of decisions.

Suppose that you have to choose among a set of acts. You know enough about the consequences of the acts, and the probabilities of their consequences, that you can compute the expected value of each act. Then one practical rule says you should *perform that act which has the highest expected value*. (Or, if several acts tie for maximum expected value, perform any one of those acts; there is nothing more to choose between them.)

EXPECTED VALUE RULE:
Act so as to maximize expected value.

RESERVATIONS

This rule should be treated cautiously.

The expected value of the act of buying one hundred tickets in Lotto 6/49 is twice the expected value of buying a $100 ticket in the ballet lottery—$45 compared to $23. (See pages 87–89). But many people think it sensible to prefer the ballet lottery over Lotto. This is because the chance of winning a fortune at Lotto is so very small, while the chance of winning a sizable prize in the ballet lottery is not quite negligible.

Suppose someone offers you one hundred Lotto 6/49 tickets at the fair price of $45, *on condition that you do not resell them at a profit*. You have two options:

Act B: Buy the tickets for $45.   Exp(B) = 0.
Act D: Decline the offer.   Exp(D) = 0.

The expected value of acts B and D is 0. So according to the expected value rule, you should be indifferent between them.

Now think of a couple of students, Garvin and Elena, who are young and don't need the kind of fantasy "hope" you can get from a lottery ticket that we mentioned on page 90. Both students are offered one hundred Lotto tickets for $45, on condition that they don't resell them.

GARVIN: That's a bargain! Here's $45!
ELENA: I want no part of it. Forty-five dollars in my purse is worth a lot more to me than a very risky gamble.

Both Garvin and Elena are violating the rule of expected value. Garvin is **risk-prone**. Elena is **risk-averse**.

These may be personality traits. Suppose we offered the two students the following choice: one hundred Lotto 6/49 tickets or one $100 ballet lottery ticket. We might guess that the risk-averse Elena would prefer the ballet, while Garvin would prefer Lotto.

The expected value rule is a rule of thumb. Some experts think that it is a standard of rationality. They are *expected-value-rule dogmatists*.

They say that a person who does not act according to the rule is *irrational*.

Expected-value-rule dogmatists seem rather arrogant. Few of us would feel that either Garvin or Elena is "irrational."

UTILES

Money value is only a gross measure of utility. There are other values than money. We want a measure of utility, not in dollars but in more general units called **utiles**. We can treat small quantities of money as if they were utiles. We can think of $2 as worth 2 utiles, but we should not think of 2 million dollars as worth 2 million utiles. That fits in with Daniel Bernoulli's idea of diminishing marginal utility (page 93). If $30 is worth 30 utiles, it does not follow that $30,000,000 is worth, in utiles, one million times as much. To solve the St. Petersburg paradox, Daniel Bernoulli thought that $30 million dollars was worth only about 600,000 utiles.

Garvin was willing to pay $45 for one hundred Lotto 6/49 tickets, while Elena preferred to keep her cash. Can we explain their behavior in terms of utility?

SAVING THE RULE?

We can assign utility values to things that don't really have dollar value. For example, perhaps risk has a negative utility for Elena and a positive utility for Garvin (he likes to take risks).

Thus in buying the lottery tickets for $45, Garvin reckons he is getting, say, 45 utiles plus 7 utiles for the pleasure of risk. So he is paying 45 utiles for 52 utiles, a bargain.

Elena hates taking risks. For her, risking money on lottery tickets has a negative utility of, say −19 utiles. If she bought the lottery tickets, she would get only 26 utiles at a cost of 45 utiles.

> *Expected-value-rule dogmatist*: Exactly so! Both Garvin and Elena turn out to be rational just because they maximize what is, for them, expected value in utiles. Garvin goes for the act whose expected value is a net +7 Garvin-utiles. Elena prefers the act whose expected value is zero Elena-utiles to one whose expected value is −19 Elena-utiles.

VOLATILITY

That idea of building risk aversion into utility does go some way toward saving the expected value rule. In daily practice, however, it seems somewhat artificial.

This is because risk aversion appears to be in a different dimension from utility. Take the case of trading stocks and bonds.

When honest stockbrokers sell investments to inexperienced clients, they ask:

- What are your investment goals? That is a question about the utility preferences of the clients.
- How much risk and volatility can you take? That is a quite distinct question.

In the stock market, no outsider can buy no-risk big-return investments. Hence a client has to bind a balance between two different kinds of considerations, the desire to avoid risk, and the desire to get rich. Garvin, young and ambitious, would like to buy penny stocks in diamond mines, which are probably worth nothing, could increase in value a hundredfold, and anyway go up and down every day. Elena's grandparents, who need to preserve their life savings, and may need to access their savings at any time for a health emergency, want good safe stocks or bonds that earn income but do not fluctuate much in value.

These are (at least) two dimensions of choice. They should not be collapsed into one abstract concept of utility.

INSURANCE

Insurance is based on risk aversion.

Recall question 6 of the previous chapter (page 96). William owned only two valuables, his car and his grandfather's gold watch. An insurance company made him an offer.

- Expected value of the act, "buy insurance": −$62.60.
- Expected value of the act, "decline the offer": −$26.00.

The act of highest expected value is "decline." But we can well imagine William buying insurance just because he is risk-averse. Insurance companies cater to risk aversion. In fact, if they charged really fair premiums, they would charge William $26 for the insurance. But then they would not make a profit. Insurance companies have been making very good profits for some three hundred years.

ACTUARIAL INSURANCE

Very roughly there are two kinds of insurance:

- Ordinary "actuarial" insurance.
- Extraordinary insurance.

"Actuary" is an old-fashioned word that has dropped out of use. According to one dictionary, it meant:

> An expert authority on rates of mortality and other details of fire, life and accident insurance.

"Actuarial" means insurance based on known or predicted rates of mortality, fire, and so forth.

Life insurance, automobile insurance, and home insurance are familiar examples of ordinary insurance. Insurance companies base their premiums on actuarial experience. Thus, in effect, they state frequency-type probabilities that a person of a certain age and health history will live another year, that a driver with a certain type of track record will drive without an accident for another year, and so on.

Insurance companies charge premiums so that the expected value, for a person taking out a policy, is negative. That means that on average the company will make a profit. It will pay out less each year than it receives in premiums.

Anyone who buys an ordinary insurance policy seems to be acting against the expected value rule.

> *Expected-value-rule dogmatist*: Not if we think about true utility rather than mere dollars! William could not afford to buy a new car, yet he needs a car for his job. So the real negative utility of having his car stolen, while uninsured, is a lot more than the loss of the dollar value of the car. And even if we can put a cash value on losing a job due to losing a car, that does not cover the hassle of trying to get a new job. As for his grandfather's gold watch, he could not replace that very watch. It has sentimental value—it is the last trace of family history, the last little bit of his grandfather that is still, in a way, alive. The insurance cannot cover the real loss, but at least it can diminish the pain. All these things have to be put into a real measure of utility and preference. When we do that, we find people do act so as to maximize expected value.

We have not explained how to define a person's utilities in an operational way. One important method first determines a person's:

- Actual assessments of probabilities.
- Actual preferences, in an experimental or real-life situation.

That gives a new meaning to the expected value rule. It ceases to be a practical rule for deciding what to do. Instead, it becomes a way of defining utilities. That is, the measure of a person's utilities, or value system, will be determined by their preferences and belief-type probabilities. We save the expected value rule by making it a definition.

EXTRAORDINARY INSURANCE

There is also extraordinary insurance, which is more like gambling, or taking bets.

Private companies that launch space rockets take out insurance. Space launches for practical purposes (TV satellites, etc.) are becoming increasingly common, and rockets are becoming commercial. But they are still uncommon enough, and variable enough, that there is not much actuarial experience for rockets. You hear about disasters only with rockets carrying people, but rockets carrying payloads crash or malfunction quite often.

The premiums for rocket launches have recently been as high as 25% of the value insured. This is a straight gamble between the rocket company and the insurance underwriters.

PARKING

You are staying overnight with friends. They live on a crowded city street, where curbside parking is restricted to residents with parking decals on their cars. You have driven a car, but there is no place nearby where you can park legally without paying. There is a nearby lot that charges $3 a night. It is the middle of winter, freezing cold. It is a half-hour walk to the nearest likely free spot.

> Your friends say: Just park on the street. It is patrolled about only once every ten days, so the probability of getting a ticket is only 0.1.

The fine is $20.00, and you always pay parking fines in order to renew your license. What is the expected value of parking illegally? It will be a negative value.

I: Park illegally.
L: Park in the lot.
T = You get a ticket.
P = You pay $3.
$Pr(T/I) = 0.1$.

If you valued *only* the cash loss (and discounted the inconvenience of getting a ticket), the utility of parking illegally would be $U(T) = -\$20$. The expected value of the act, park illegally, would be:

$$Exp(I) = (0.1)(-\$20) + (0.9)(\$0) = -\$2.$$

There are no uncertainties about parking in the lot. If you valued *only* the cash expense, the expected value of the act, park in the lot, $Exp(L) = -\$3$.

WHAT TO DO?

The expected value rule gives clear advice. Act so as to maximize expected utility. The highest utility you can expect is $-\$2$. So: *park illegally.*

That is not the end of the matter. Some people think it is wrong to break the law—any law. Other people might think the law is not so important, but it is wrong to harm other people, for example, by taking the parking place of a local resident.

Let us give a special name to a person who hangs onto the expected value rule: Utilitarian. Utilitarianism is a subtle and complicated moral philosophy. The expected value rule is only a simple-minded version. The most famous Utilitarian philosopher is John Stuart Mill (1806–1873), author of *On Liberty, Utilitarianism,* and a major feminist essay, *On the Subjection of Women.* His *System of Logic* is a fundamental study of inductive reasoning.

The most important Western moral philosophy opposed to Utilitarianism is associated with Immanuel Kant (1724–1804). His most famous book is called *The Critique of Pure Reason.* In later work on ethics, Kant emphasized among many other things the importance of *duty,* of fulfilling obligations, almost regardless of the utility of doing so.

PARTY TALK

After you have parked, you arrive at a party. Three guests, named *Uty, Duty,* and *Beauty,* discuss the parking problem.

> *Duty*: I wouldn't maximize utility, because I don't like breaking the law and I don't like inconveniencing other people.
>
> *Uty*: All you're saying is that being fined or paying for parking are not the only factors. In your scale of values, acts that involve breaking the law or inconveniencing strangers have negative utility. The utility (for you) of breaking the law and being a nuisance to others may be something like −$5. Hence your expected utility for illegal parking is:
>
> $$\text{Exp(I)} = (0.1)(-\$20-\$5) + (0.9)(\$0-\$5) = -\$7.$$
>
> Your "dutiful" decision is just another way to maximize expected value, because you prefer a utility of −$3 (cost of parking lot) to an expected utility of −$7 (for illegal parking).
>
> *Duty*: But that just doesn't represent how I feel about things!
>
> *Uty*: Well, think about it. If you were really fixed on never breaking the law, then maybe for you the utility of breaking the law is −$10,000. You'd still park illegally to save a life, wouldn't you?
>
> *Beauty*: *Duty* does break the law. She was arrested last summer for blockading a road into a wilderness area to keep the loggers out.
>
> *Duty*: That is because it is my higher duty to save the wilderness from greedy logging companies and corrupt politicians!
>
> *Uty*: So, we work out how much you value that . . .
>
> *Duty*: I don't like measuring my serious values by dollar bills.
>
> *Uty*: That's just a manner of speaking. Money is only a measure of the value for which we would exchange various things, including even our sense of honor. We are really talking about utiles.

RISK AVERSION

> *Beauty*: I don't have *Duty*'s moral scruples. But I wouldn't maximize expectation either. It's all very well to say that the expected value of parking

illegally is only −$2, while the cost of using the lot is −$3. The fact is, however, that there is a 10% risk of a $20 fine, and I simply can't afford $20. If I get ticketed, the money I have been saving for my Saturday night out is gone! I'd rather pay to park.

Uty: So? You attach more value to $20 than twenty times $1. If the value of a single dollar is 1 utile, then the value of $20 to you right now is more than 20 utiles. Later on in life, when you own a franchised chain of beauty parlors, this won't be so, and you'll be out parking illegally like all the other fat cats. Utiles measure your real value right now.

Beauty: But you can't calculate with these utiles!

Uty: Yes, you can. Let's assume for the moment that we can add utiles, and then use your own preferences to figure out how much you value having $20 on Saturday night.

You prefer the lot to parking on the street. That means you have a bigger negative expected utility for parking illegally than of paying the $3 user fee. Let's say that −$3 is equivalent to −3 utiles. What must be your utility for getting a ticket?

$$\text{Exp}(I) = (0.1)(U(T)) + (.09)(\$0) < -3 \text{ utiles.}$$

Hence $U(T) < -30$ utiles. That shows how much you are afraid of getting ticketed.

Beauty: This is entirely artificial!

Duty: Right. We don't weigh off duties to keep the law and respect others against any kind of pretend numerical values that you call utiles.

Beauty: That's your problem, not mine. But it is silly to say that I value $20 more than twenty times $1. As far as I'm concerned, $20 is worth twenty times $1. The simple truth is not that I value $20 at more than twenty times $1, but that *I don't like taking risks*.

Uty: We can measure that, too.

Beauty: No, you can't; that has nothing to do with my scale of values; it is just a feature of my nervous character. I am just **risk-averse**.

IDEAL MODELS

The expected value rule does not factor in such attitudes as risk aversion (unless we try to build them into utilities). That is a criticism of, or limitation of, the rule. Do not confuse a criticism like that with a case where the rule is wrongly applied.

For example, in calculating expected values we begin with a set of *mutually exclusive* and *exhaustive* possible consequences of an act that is under consideration: $C_1, C_2, \ldots, C_n$.

Any splitting up of the consequences like that is an idealization or simplification. Most acts have indefinitely many consequences, reaching far into the future. A person might make a disastrous decision by not fully analyzing the consequences. Here is a true story.

Albert bought a lottery ticket and won millions. A few days earlier he had moved out on his wife. He tried to keep all the money for himself, but put it in the hands of his new girlfriend for safekeeping. The wife sued for half the money. The girlfriend went to Argentina with the money and was never seen again. When Albert was in the headlines, several other old girlfriends talked to reporters and called him a rat. His creditors moved in and extracted what money Albert had not given to his new girlfriend. Albert got drunk and crashed his car, injured an innocent bystander, and went to jail. A court awarded half the winnings to his wife. Albert is now in jail, owing millions to his wife, which he has no hope of paying because his ex-girlfriend took his money.

When Albert bought the winning ticket, we would have visualized a partition into four consequences: C_1 (win millions), C_2 (win a sizable prize), C_3 (win a small prize), C_4 (win nothing).

In real life, we see that Albert's C_1 broke into a whole lot of possible consequences: (girlfriend stayed loyal/absconded to Argentina), (not much press publicity/all too much), and so on.

The fact that Albert did not foresee the consequences of his action is not a criticism of the expected value rule. It is a criticism of Albert for not examining the possible consequences of his act more closely.

DISAGREEMENTS

We disagree about what to do for all sorts of reasons. We may disagree about *the probability of the consequences*. We may also disagree about the *utilities*: how *dangerous or desirable* the consequences are.

Often there is a disagreement about both probability and utility. Decision theory cannot settle such disagreements. But at least it can analyze the disagreement, so that both parties can see what they are arguing about. Here is a typical news story which appeared before the Galileo space probe was sent off:

GROUPS PROTEST USE OF PLUTONIUM ON GALILEO

The nearly 50 pounds of plutonium that will produce electricity on the Galileo [space] probe make this space shuttle launching the most disputed ever.

The Energy Department has done about 100 tests over a decade to check the safety of the plutonium units, subjecting them to a variety of conditions they might encounter in a shuttle accident.

The tests, the Energy Department says, show the units are highly resistant to damage.

The nub of the controversy is how resistant. NASA has said the highest probability of launch-area release of plutonium due to a shuttle accident is less than 1 in 2500. The antinuclear groups disagree, saying the odds are as great as 1 in 430.

The two sides also disagree on the medical effects of a plutonium release. The groups estimate that it could cause thousands of fatal cancers. But the space agency says so little plutonium would be released that there would be no additional cancer deaths.

NASA's health-effects estimate is much more optimistic than that of a federal interagency panel that evaluated Galileo. It reported that a launching pad accident could release enough plutonium to cause 80 cancer deaths eventually. The panel said that if the probe reentered the atmosphere as it swung by the earth, up to 2000 cancer deaths could be caused by released plutonium.

Steven Aftergood, a senior research analyst with the Washington-based Federation of American Scientists, said the real issue was how much risk was acceptable. "My own judgement is that the risk is small," he said, "and the scientific payoff is large."

THE PROBABILITIES

The space probe goes so far from the sun that it cannot use solar energy. The only reliable long-term source of energy is a small plutonium nuclear reactor. The risk is that there will be an accident to the shuttle launching the probe, or some other disaster in or near the Earth's atmosphere, releasing plutonium, one of the most lethal substances in the universe.

Interested parties divide into two groups, whom we'll call *Explorers* and *Safety-first*. *Explorers* include NASA and the U.S. Department of Energy, while *Safety-first* groups are environmentalist and antinuclear. They disagree about the probabilities. *Explorers* say that the probability of an accident is 1/2500. *Safety-first* people say that the probability of an accident is 1/430.

What kinds of probabilities are these? There is only one Galileo space probe. There is either a major accident, or there is not. *Explorers* are not, however, just saying, "this is what I believe." They are saying something more like, "this is what we, the concerned scientific community, judge in the light of the best available evidence." Given the available evidence, it is reasonable to believe, to degree 2499/2500, that there will be no accident. The *Safety-first* advocates are not merely saying that they have different beliefs from *Explorers*. They are saying that *Explorers* are wrong, have mistaken beliefs.

THE CONSEQUENCES

If you inhale a particle of plutonium you will be poisoned by it. You will get cancer if you don't die of something else first. Unlike many poisons, plutonium has, relative to human beings, a long half-life. Once in the atmosphere, it does not go away.

Explorers say that even if there were an accident, the number of deaths by cancer would not increase. This is because they have baked the plutonium into ceramic blocks like oven dishes, that do not vaporize or otherwise get into the atmosphere. If there were an accident, the consequences would be disagreeable—lost time, effort, and resources, not to mention a bad press and reduced funding for future projects. But that, they suppose, is about the worst that could happen.

The *Safety-first* people instead follow the guidelines of a panel that said that if there were an accident, 2,000 people could get cancer.

Explorers think that if the launch is a success, there will be an exhilarating exploration of the universe, bringing new knowledge and much excitement. The *Safety-first* groups also respect scientific research, but have different evaluations of the whole set of consequences.

Finally, the reporters consult a judicious person, Dr Aftergood. He seems to put all these conclusions into the balance, and says, "The risks are small, and the scientific pay-off is large." (But do we really know who *Dr Aftergood* is? Is the Federation of American Scientists maybe just a group of *Explorers*, and not neutral?)

THE DANGER

How dangerous is the space probe? The answer depends on two things: the probabilities of the various possible outcomes, and the costs of the consequences. We can represent the two different assessments as follows:

Explorers assessment

	Probability	Consequence
Accident	1/2500	Disagreeable
No Accident	2499/2500	Explore!

No matter what utility you assign to the consequences, you can see why *Explorers* think the Galileo space probe is a terrific idea.

Safety-first assessment

	Probability	Consequence
Accident	1/430	>2000 deaths
No Accident	429/430	Small*

* "Small," for a *Safety-first* person, means "small, relative to the potential danger to human beings."

No matter what utility you assign to the consequences, you can see why a *Safety-first* person might think that the Galileo space probe is a terrible idea.

Who is right? Inductive logic cannot answer. It can say only this: given the probabilities and utilities assigned by *Explorers*, then the probe should go ahead. Given the probabilities and utilities assigned by the *Safety-first* group, then the probe should be terminated.

THE ALLAIS PARADOX

We conclude with another paradox. Like many paradoxes, it is artificial. The point is to clarify our ideas about maximizing expected value.

Number 100 cards consecutively from 1 to 100. The cards are shuffled, and a card is drawn. The possible outcomes are grouped as three mutually exclusive possibilities.

L: A "low" card is drawn, numbered below 90 (probability 0.89).
N: Card 90 is drawn (probability 0.01).
H: A "high" card is drawn, numbered 91 or higher (probability 0.1).

ALLAIS' FIRST GAMBLE

At no cost to yourself, you are offered one of the two following options.

A: $500,000 if a high card (H) or card N is drawn (probability 0.11). Otherwise, nothing happens (probability 0.89).
B: $2,500,000 if a high card (H) is drawn (probability 0.1). Otherwise, nothing happens (probability 0.9).

Would you perform act A (choose A), or act B (choose B)?
    Answer here: _____
Experiments show that most people choose B. A 10% chance of getting $2,500,000 is preferred to an 11% chance of getting $500,000. Somehow, in the minds of most people, a smallish (10%) chance of getting a great deal, seems better than a slightly better chance of getting a whole lot less.

ALLAIS' SECOND GAMBLE

Now consider two other options.

F: You get an outright gift of $500,000 (free!).
G: $2,500,000 if a high card (H) is drawn (probability 0.1).
    $500,000 if a low card (L) is drawn (probability 0.89).
    Otherwise, nothing happens (probability 0.01).

Would you perform act F (choose F), or act G (choose G)?
    Answer here: _____
Experiments show that a great many people choose F. Many of us would rather have a risk-free half-million dollars, than a 10% chance of a lot more, but a real chance of getting nothing. We would rather become very rich for sure, than risk getting nothing.

APPLYING THE RULE

What does the rule for maximizing expected value say about the two gambles? It is happy with A and B. Most people apparently prefer B. And that is the gamble with the highest expected value.

  Exp(A) = $55,000   Exp(B) = $250,000

The rule does not, however, agree with popular opinion in the case of the gift F.

Exp(F) = \$500,000
Exp(G) = (0.89)(\$500,000) + (0.1)(\$2,500,000) = \$695,000
So, Exp(G) > Exp(F).

As we see in exercise 10, the numbers in this argument do not matter much.

RISK AVERSION?

What does the Allais paradox show? Suppose that experimenters are right in their findings, that most people prefer act B out of the first gamble, and act F out of the second gamble. What does this mean? Statisticians and philosophers have given very different answers. Here are two of them.

- The Allais paradox shows that almost everyone is a little bit risk-averse. Even people who will gamble, who will take risks, and who will park illegally despite the fines, finally find a point where they stop risking. They would rather have a sure thing that they want, say a million dollars, than a middle-sized (10%) chance of more, with a small but real (1%) chance of nothing.
- The Allais paradox shows that you have to think. Even if you first prefer F, once you think about the second gamble, and reflect on the expected value, you will discover that you really prefer G.

L. J. SAVAGE AND MAURICE ALLAIS

The Allais paradox is artificial. But there is a story about it.

After World War II, the great advocate of personal probability and maximizing personal expected value was the American mathematician and statistician L. J. Savage (1917–1971). He did more for the Bayesian approach to inductive inference described in Chapters 13–15 than anyone else (see page 184).

When he advanced his ideas, some statisticians were very suspicious of his approach. There was even a bit of national antagonism. For example, a group of French mathematicians thought that there was something mechanical, unthinking, and terribly "American" about having a blind rule to compute your free choices.

The French mathematician Maurice Allais produced his paradox to argue that human beings do not automatically act so as to maximize expected value. Our hopes and fears and expectations are too complex to put into a single mindless calculating machine.

SAVAGE'S REACTION

Savage records his own reactions when Allais presented him with the paradox.

When the two situations were first presented, I immediately expressed preference for F as opposed to G and for B as opposed to A, and I still feel an intuitive attraction for those preferences. But I have accepted the following way of looking at things.

One way in which A, B, F, and G could be realized is by a lottery with a hundred numbered tickets [we have already done that above] according to this schedule:

Prizes in units of $100,000 in a lottery

	Ticket number		
	1–89	90	91–100
Option F	5	5	5
Option G	5	0	25
Option A	0	5	5
Option B	0	0	25

After drawing this table, Savage continued,

Now, if one of the tickets number 1 through 89 is drawn, it will not matter [in either pair of choices] which option I choose. I therefore focus on the possibility that one of the tickets numbered from 90 through 100 will be drawn, in which case the two gambles [choose F or G, choose A or B] are exactly parallel.

So, of course, looking at things this way, Savage chose act G over F, and act B over A, and said:

It seems to me that in reversing my preferences between Options F and G, I have corrected an error.

EXERCISES

1 *Locking.* You have just bought an old bicycle for $80. You can either buy an unbreakable Kryptonite lock for $20 or a cheap chain and lock for $8. You reckon no one would bother stealing your bike if it is locked with Kryptonite—too much work. But there is a 10% chance of the cheap chain being snipped, and your bike being stolen. If the bike is stolen, you won't bother to replace it. If we have listed all the relevant values, and you act so as to maximize expectation, which lock do you buy?

2 *Inconvenience.* Suppose you buy the Kryptonite lock, explaining "because I don't want the inconvenience of losing my old clunker." If you are a utility maximizer, you are putting some value on inconvenience. At least how much?

3 *Repeated losses.* Suppose that you maximized expected dollar value and bought the cheap lock. But your bike was stolen. You decide to buy a new bike, but

accept that all the information given in (1) still holds. You curse having bought a cheap lock. Is it now rational for you to buy the Kryptonite lock?

4 *Planning ahead.* In question 3 you decided to buy the new bike after your first bike was stolen. Would it make any difference to your decision in question 1, if you already planned to buy another $80 bike if your first one was stolen? Suppose you really work this out, and see that if you bought a second bike you would still, in line with question 3, buy a cheap lock for $8, and not a Kryptonite lock for $20.

5 *Be wise the first time?* But suppose you know yourself well enough to know that if your first bike were stolen, the second time you would buy the Kryptonite lock rather than the cheap one. What act maximizes expected value now?

6 *No insurance.* A brilliant but rather self-centered bachelor probability theorist drove for years without any automobile insurance whatsoever. (This is still legal in some American jurisdictions.) When he married and began to raise a family he took out ample automobile insurance. Explain his actions.

7 *Uty and Duty.* Explain why *Uty* might agree with the brilliant bachelor, while *Duty* would criticize him.

8 *Atoms and coal.* The nuclear power industry urges that nuclear power is quite safe; it causes far fewer deaths than coal-mining; it causes far less environmental harm than acid rain resulting from burning coal to generate electricity. (And so on.) Advocates of fossil fuels contend that nuclear power is in the long run incredibly costly—allow for dismantling old plants and storing terrible poisons, not to mention the risk of horrendous accidents. (And so on.)
Discuss this example in two ways.
(a) As illustrating how the two sides differ about their probabilities and utilities.
(b) As illustrating how the two sides have different attitudes toward risk aversion.

9 *The longest bridge.* The longest bridge over part of the ocean—eight miles long (thirteen kilometers), and arching to a height over the Atlantic greater than the height of a twenty-story building—was being built between New Brunswick and Prince Edward Island. Each spring gigantic ice floes break up through this channel, and not everyone believed this bridge would be safe. A newspaper reported:

> The primary concern is how the bridge's 44 pillars will affect the island's microclimate by preventing "ice-out"—the day when the strait flows clear. A delay which would cool the water and air might severely interfere with the scallop and lobster fisheries, and also with the potato harvest [the island provides about 20% of the french fries for some of the fast food chains around the continent].
>
> The 1990 environmental panel, reporting before construction began, set as its threshold a delay of only two days in ice-out every 100 years. More apocalyptically, there are concerns that ice floes could knock out a pillar. Pillars are cemented, not bolted, to the strait floor. Critics and long-time strait watchers say that computerized studies of probability are not the same as possibility.

Write a brief statement expressing either the opinion of "critics and long-time strait watchers," or the opinion of the consultants who say that the bridge is safe and will do no significant ecological harm.

Your statement should try for a clear—but not necessarily numerical—estimate of probabilities and utilities. If you are a critic, you should, among other things, explain what (if anything) is meant by "computerized studies of probability are not the same as possibility." If you are a consultant, you should, among other things, rebut this remark.

10 *Allais.* The Allais paradox uses money. Can we use something like Daniel Bernoulli's diminishing marginal utility to beat the paradox? Or use some other way of fiddling with the utilities and probabilities?

KEY WORDS FOR REVIEW

Decision theory	Risk aversion
Expected value rule	Insurance
Utiles	Assessing risks
Utilitarianism	Allais paradox

10 Decision under Uncertainty

Sometimes a decision problem can be solved without using probabilities or expected value at all. These are situations in which one strategy dominates all others, no matter what happens in the actual world. This is called **dominance**. It is illustrated by a very famous argument for acting as if you believed in God. Variations on that argument lead to other decision rules.

The expected value rule can be used only when some probabilities are available. Sometimes we are so ignorant that we are not inclined to talk even of the probabilities of different alternatives. That is the extreme end of uncertainty. Yet there may still be more or less reasonable decisions.

DOMINANCE

It was a dark and foggy night when Peter made his first trip to Holland, the homeland of his parents. His parents gave him enough money to rent a car to see the family, but after that he was practically broke. He was planning to stay with his distant relatives. So he was driving along a road, somewhat lost, when he came to an overhead signpost. Unfortunately, a garbage bag had blown over the front of the sign, obscuring the first three letters of each town. What he saw was:

█AVENHAGE ↑
█TERDAM →

Peter figured the topmost town must be " 's Gravenhage" (in English, "The Hague," where the World Court is located). But the second town might be "Amsterdam" or "Rotterdam." What should he do? Go straight ahead, or turn right?

Easy. Peter had no family in The Hague, and he had relatives in both Amsterdam and Rotterdam. So he turned right.

That is obvious, but let us draw a table to see why.

Actions:

R: Go right (and end up in Amsterdam or Rotterdam).
S: Go straight ahead (and end up in The Hague).

The possible states of affairs were,

A: TERDAM in full was "Amsterdam."
T: TERDAM in full was "Rotterdam."

He did not know whether "■■TERDAM" pointed to Rotterdam or to Amsterdam, but either way, the strategy of turning right had positive utility (find some distant relatives who will look after Peter). The strategy of going straight had negative utility (a dark and stormy night in a strange town with no place to stay). Putting rough-and-ready measures on the utilities:

$$U(R, A) = 2 \qquad U(S, A) = -3$$
$$U(R, T) = 2 \qquad U(S, T) = -3$$

	A	T
R	+2	+2
S	-3	-3

Self-evidently, R is better than S in either possible state of affairs. We say that R *dominates* S.

THREE RULES

The very first attempt to study decision under uncertainty is bizarre. It is nevertheless a handy introduction to the three decision rules to be studied in this chapter:

(1) Dominance rule.
(2) Expected value rule (as in Chapter 9).
(3) Dominant expected value rule.

The arguments below try out (1). When that is criticized, they move to (2). When that is criticized, they move to (3).

PASCAL'S WAGER

We have come across Blaise Pascal at the end of Chapter 8. He contributed the very first chapters on inductive logic to be put into a logic textbook.

Pascal thought carefully about an extreme case of decision under uncertainty. It is a religious argument. It is not so much about the *existence* of God, as about whether one should *act* so as to come to *believe* in God.

The argument is for people who are completely unmoved by the usual arguments for the existence of God. They think that revelation and testimony, found in the Bible or the Koran, are completely untrustworthy. They find that arguments from natural religion—the world is well organized, so there must have been a Designer who made it—lead nowhere. Yet for some such people, the religion of their community and culture—not any religion, but the religion that is around them—has a certain pull. They don't think there is any decent evidence for that religion, and yet, well, they're worried.

Such people are in a state of extreme uncertainty. The existence of God is a real possibility for them. Yet they find no evidence one way or the other.

Such people can decide to join a religious community, and gradually acquire the beliefs of that community. Or they can have nothing to do with religion.

Pascal's decision problem: should one act so as to come to believe in God?

We use Pascal's thought here, not because it is a compelling argument, but as an example of inductive logic and decision theory. It is good as an example, because Pascal distinguishes the three rules (1), (2), and (3).

A PSYCHOLOGICAL THEORY

Pascal held a psychological theory about fundamental beliefs. If you live with a group of people committed to a certain way of life, and wholeheartedly engage in their activities, you will come to share their basic life principles and prejudices.

Many of you will know this from your own experiences, even if you have broken away from your family traditions. Children brought up in a family of atheists, or observant Buddhists, Jews, Marxists, Muslims, Protestants, and so on, tend to have the same religious or political attitudes as the family, until, perhaps, the teenage breakaway.

Pascal held that if you became a truly observant member of a religious community, then you would gradually acquire its faith, even if you joined in a rather cynical mood. He thought that faith is catching.

He is very frank about this. For his place and time, the community to join was Roman Catholic. If you live with Catholics and, as he scathingly put it, mindlessly follow a life of holy water and sacraments, then you will find that you become a believer.

LIVE POSSIBILITIES

Some possibilities are real options for us, while others we cannot seriously consider. Some people can seriously consider astrology as a method of foretelling the future. I cannot. To use a good phrase due to the American pragmatist philosopher William James (1842–1910), astrology is not a *live* possibility for me. But it is a live possibility for many people in many parts of the world today.

In Pascal's day, the religion for most French people was Roman Catholicism. Even when Pascal himself adopted a rather puritanical form of faith, very similar in many respects to militant Protestantism, his group remained within the Roman Catholic Church (which strongly disapproved). When it came to religion, some form of Roman Catholic Christianity was the only live possibility. Atheism was also a live possibility: most of Pascal's gambling friends toyed with serious atheism.

Pascal's argument could, however, be used only by someone who felt that, in addition to atheism, there was only one live religious possibility. Buddhism, Islam, and Judaism, were not live possibilities for Pascal and his peers.

One of Pascal's critics said: "An imam could just as well reason this way." (An imam is a Muslim spiritual leader.) That's right, but not as a criticism of Pascal's logic. It is a criticism of his premise, that the only two possibilities are atheism and Roman Catholic faith.

A PARTITION

Thus Pascal's personal decision problem was not:

Should I act so as to come to believe in God?

It was instead the more specific:

Should I act so as to come to believe in God as described in Roman Catholic teachings current at the present time?

For Pascal there were two mutually exclusive and exhaustive possibilities:

God (as described by Roman Catholics) exists.
Such a God does not exist.

These two form a **partition** of possible states of affairs. A partition is a set of possibilities such that one of them must be true (exhaustive), but only one can be true (mutually exclusive).

Pascal abbreviated his partition as: (*God exists, God does not exist*).

DECISION PROBLEMS

In Chapter 8, we distinguished acts, consequences, and the utility of consequences. But if we really know very little, we may step further back, and consider just the live possibilities that interest us.

A **partition** of possible states of affairs is a set of exhaustive and mutually exclusive possible states of the universe. There are innumerable ways of partitioning states of affairs. A problem has to be set up so that there is a natural partition relevant to the problem.

A decision problem under uncertainty has these ingredients:

- A *partition* of possible states of affairs.
- The *possible acts* that the agent can undertake.
- The *utilities* of the *consequences* of each possible act, in each possible state of affairs in the partition.

Let U(A,X) be the utility of performing act A when X is the state of affairs. A decision problem is then naturally presented in a table, like this one for two possible states of affairs X and Y, and two possible acts A and B:

	X	Y
A	U(A,X)	U(A,Y)
B	U(B,X)	U(B,Y)

PASCAL'S PARTITION

For Pascal the acts under consideration are:

A: Act as an atheist: carry on gambling, drinking to excess, having promiscuous sex, studying mathematical physics, running a pickpocket ring, managing a bank, or whatever you enjoy most.

B: Act as a believer: act so as to come to believe that God exists. Join the church, live with believers, engage in the rituals, follow the commandments, aspire to have pious attitudes, and so on.

For Pascal the partition of states of affairs is abbreviated as (G, N), where:

G = God exists (where the God in question is as described in current Roman Catholic teaching).
N = God does not exist.

FIRST UTILITY ASSIGNMENT

We require the *utilities* of the *consequences* of each *act* in each *state of affairs* in the *partition*.

In Pascal's partition, if there is a God, then atheists who have had the opportunity to become believers, but refuse, end up going to Hell. So U(A,G) is infinitely bad, "minus infinity," so to speak. We write this:

$$U(A,G) = -\infty$$

Compared to infinite utilities, the utility of being an atheist in a secular world might just as well be set at zero.

$$U(A,N) = 0$$

In Pascal's partition, if there is a God, then those who believe in that God and live a virtuous life are rewarded with heavenly bliss, of infinite value.

$U(B,G) = +\infty$

Compared to infinite bliss, $U(B,N)$ might just as well be set at zero.

$U(B,N) = 0$

FIRST DECISION TABLE

These assignments are best presented in a table, called a decision table.

	G	N
A	$-\infty$	0
B	$+\infty$	0

In state G, when God exists, act B is definitely (infinitely) better than act A. In state N, there is nothing to choose between them. In this structure of acts, beliefs, and utilities:

- In at least one possible state of affairs (namely G), B has higher utility than A.
- In no possible state of affairs does B have lower utility than A.

A "possible" state of affairs X is one which, for all we know, may be true. We have no compelling reason, in our current state of knowledge, for thinking that X is false.

In these circumstances, B is said to *dominate* A. It seems "self-evident" that when one act dominates another, you should perform the dominant act. There is *no way* that any other act in the decision problem could give you better results than a dominant act.

FIRST WAGER: DOMINANCE

> If in at least one state of affairs one act has more utility than every other act, and if in no state of affairs does it have less utility, then this act *dominates* the others.

The **dominance rule** says, in effect: if one act dominates the others, do it.

If the consequences of two acts have the same utilities in every state of affairs in a partition, then there is nothing to choose between them. You can decide which to perform by tossing a coin, if you want.

Pascal's *first* argument concludes: perform act B—act so as to come to believe in God—because it is the dominant act.

THE DOMINANCE RULE

The dominance rule requires what now seems to be a rather obvious restriction, irrelevant to Pascal's first wager. For a moment let us fast-forward. Tomer is a young student heavily addicted to smoking. He is not considering his religion but whether to quit smoking or not. Q = He quits. S = He continues smoking.

He simplifies his decision problem to a partition into two states of affairs:

Y: He dies young, before age sixty-five.
O: He dies old, age sixty-five or older.

Tomer makes a rough assessment of his utilities:

$$U(S,Y) = 0 \qquad U(S,O) = 100$$
$$U(Q,Y) = -5 \qquad U(Q,O) = 95$$

Or, in a table:

	Y	O
Q	−5	95
S	0	100

Smoking dominates. So according to the dominance rule as sketched, Tomer ought to continue smoking. That strikes most physicians as a bad rule, no matter how pleased Tomer is.

In fact, Tomer's friend Peggy consults a medical statistician, who informs her that a male of Tomer's age is much more likely to die young if he continues smoking, rather than quitting now. Putting together some 147 published statistical analyses, our statistician tells Peggy that:

$$Pr(Y/S) = 0.36 \qquad Pr(O/S) = 0.64$$
$$Pr(Y/Q) = 0.15 \qquad Pr(O/Q) = 0.85$$

Given this data, the dominance rule offers advice that is *inconsistent* with the advice offered by the expected value rule. For Q is the act of greatest expected value.

$$Exp(S) = (0.36)(0) + (0.64)(100) = 64$$
$$Exp(Q) = (0.15)(-5) + (0.85)(95) = 80$$

Hence the expected value rule advises Tomer to quit.

The trouble with the sketched dominance rule is that a person's life expectancy is *not independent* of whether the person decides to quit or not.

This is because the decision itself makes a difference to the possible states of affairs in the partition, Y and O. If Tomer quits, he is more likely to live to a ripe old age. If he continues to smoke, he is less likely to do so.

To fix this difficulty, we have to add a restriction to make the dominance rule sensible.

DOMINANCE RULE:
If no act in the set of acts has any causal influence on the states of affairs in the partition, then if one act dominates, do it.

Notice that probabilities do not enter into the idea of dominance itself. But they do matter to whether you can use dominance to make a reasonable decision. Now back to probabilities—and Pascal.

SECOND UTILITY ASSIGNMENT

The agnostic does not care for Pascal's first argument. Pascal, you are wrong (he argues). My life as a Parisian man-about-town is not worth zero, as you have it in your table. So, maybe I am risking something after all.

U(A,N) is the value of being a cheerful party-going atheist, with no God around to watch. All fun and no guilt. So we should represent U(A,N) by some positive finite value "+". (Or use any finite positive number you want).

Likewise, if the agnostic becomes a believer but there is no God, the reward is a dreary life with a bunch of believers with stupid practices and false beliefs. That is a definite negative. We should represent U(B,N) by "−". (Or use any finite negative number you want).

	G	N
A	$-\infty$	+
B	$+\infty$	−

In this new utility assignment, B no longer dominates. It has a bigger payoff than A in state of affairs G, and a lower payoff than A in state of affairs N.

SECOND WAGER: USE A PROBABILITY

Pascal responds to the agnostic's new utilities by bringing in probabilities, and using the *expected value rule*. In his metaphorical words: "A game is on at an infinite distance. Is the outcome heads or tails?" So he is modeling the question, "Is there a God?" by tossing a coin where we cannot now tell the outcome. Or he is simply proposing to the agnostic a personal probability of ½ for "God exists," and equally ½ for "God does not exist."

Then we can compute expected values for A and B. Let the size of "+" and "−" be as big as you please. So long as they are finite, we still have:

$$Exp(A) = -\infty$$
$$Exp(B) = +\infty$$

Pascal's *second* argument concludes: Perform act B—act so as to come to believe in God—because it is the act of highest expected value.

THIRD WAGER: USE A RANGE OF PROBABILITIES

The agnostic is still unhappy. Why, he asks, are you so confident that the odds are 50:50? It is really very unlikely that God exists. I don't have much confidence in this stuff about Heaven and Hell!

Pascal replies: you admit that it is possible that God exists? "Yes." That is, there is a nonzero probability that God exists, and that the stories about Heaven and Hell are true? "Yes."

Well, says Pascal, let us consider all admissible assignments of probability. The expected value of B is given by the formula:

$$Exp(B) = Pr(G)U(B,G) + Pr(N)U(B,N).$$

You agreed that $Pr(G) > 0$. However tiny the personal probability that you assign to G, God's existence, U(B,G) is infinite. Hence Exp(B) is still infinite.

$$Exp(B) = \infty$$

You agreed that $Pr(N) < 1$. No matter how large a probability you assign to N, and no matter how great a finite utility you assign to act A in state of affairs N, U(A,N) is still finite. Since:

$$Exp(A) = Pr(G)U(A,G) + Pr(N)U(A,N).$$
$$Exp(A) = -\infty.$$

Thus whatever probabilities we assign to G and N, so long as we do not rule out either possibility entirely, and whatever utilities we assign in event N, so long as they are finite, the expected value of B infinitely exceeds that of A. This is an argument of *dominating expected value*.

DOMINATING EXPECTED VALUE RULE

A decision problem consists of:

◆ The **acts** that the agent can undertake.
◆ A **partition** of possible states of affairs.
◆ The **utilities** of the **consequences** of each possible act, in each possible state of affairs in the partition.

Pascal has added a fourth, and rather unusual, ingredient to the decision problem.

◆ A class of **admissible** probability assignments to the states of affairs in the partition.

This introduces not the simple utilities of acting in various states of affairs, but the expected values of acting.

The definition of dominance can be extended:

If in every admissible probability distribution, one act has greater expected value than every other act, then this act **dominates** the others in **expected value.**

DOMINANT EXPECTED VALUE RULE
If one act dominates the others in expected value, DO IT!

Pascal's *third* argument concludes: Perform act B—act so as to come to believe in God—because it dominates in expected value.

CRITICISMS

Very few people today are impressed by Pascal's wagers. But decision theorists have long been using the arguments he invented almost 350 years ago.

We may worry about using *infinite* utilities. Recall that these may be the problem with the St. Petersburg paradox (page 91).

Otherwise, Pascal's *logic* is sound. The trouble is that his starting points no longer apply for most of us. They are no longer "live possibilities."

You might be skeptical of his psychological theory (that belief is catching). Yet Pascal may have had more insight into the human heart than most mathematicians.

Where we must part company with Pascal is with his partition. There are many more possibilities than Roman Catholicism. For example: some types of strict Calvinism in which it is predetermined exactly who goes to Heaven—regardless of their deeds.

It is easy for you to invent imaginary theologies in which God is diabolical, and condemns all Roman Catholics to hellfire. If that were, for you, a live possibility, then Pascal's wager definitely would not work!

RECOMBINANT DNA

We have come to take molecular biology for granted. But when the first recombinant DNA experiments began in the 1970s, some scientists were gravely concerned that we could now manufacture organisms against which we have no resistance whatsoever.

We might, for instance, produce a strain of something like anthrax which swept across all the farm animals in the world, wiping them out. We might develop an infection that killed all wheat. We might create a new and ghastly plague, easily transmitted, and against which the human body has no resistance.

In 1974 there was a conference of the world's leading molecular biologists in Asilomar, California, which urged strong restraints and controls on recombinant DNA research. Some even urged that *we must not engage in this research*. The argument had the form of Pascal's wager.

There are, the scientists said, essentially two acts open to us, research and no-research. And there are two important possibilities, a life-destroying disaster, and no disaster.

They used a form of Pascal's wager to conclude that the no-research option dominates the research option.

BLAISE PASCAL

Blaise Pascal (1623–1662) was a gifted French mathematician. Among other things, he invented a calculating machine, a forerunner of the digital computer. That is why one of the first modern computing language was named PASCAL. Pascal's correspondence with Fermat (of Fermat's Last Theorem) is often said to have started probability theory. When he was a young man about Paris, he was (it is said) a serious gambler, not the least of his vices. Later he became fed up with his Parisian life and became an ascetic, deeply concerned with problems of morality, religion, and faith. He is regarded as one of the first great Christian existentialist philosophers. His collected *Thoughts* (*Pensées*) consists of a lot of short reflections on morals and faith. The argument now known as Pascal's wager is only one among his many brief but often moving thoughts about the human condition, morals, spirituality, and religion. One of Pascal's famous sayings is:

The heart has its reasons that reason cannot know.

What does that mean? Perhaps it means that a real person can have reasons that cannot be studied by decision theory, a discipline that Pascal himself invented.

<u>**EXERCISES**</u>

Three students are considering two career options:

C: Take a degree in computer science.
P: Take a degree in philosophy.

They think that there are just two real possibilities about the future:

B: Bad times are ahead, and they will get worse.
G: Good times are ahead, and they will get better.

They all believe that in state of affairs B, computer scientists will get jobs, but philosophers will not.

They also believe that in state of affairs G, computer scientists and philosophers will get jobs, but computer scientists will earn more.

1 *Mercenary Sarah.* Sarah considers nothing but her income when she thinks of a job.

Assign plausible utilities for Sarah in a decision table, so that one act dominates. What does she decide to do? By what decision rule?

2 *Dreamer Peony.* Peony hates computer science, even though she is good at logic, and would be well able to earn a living as a computer scientist. She would like to be a philosopher. But she also wants to be able to support herself comfortably.

Assign plausible utilities for Peony in a decision table.

Are the utilities enough for her to decide what to do? What else might she need? If she needs more input, give it to her.

What does she decide to do? By what decision rule?

3 *Idealist Maria.* Same problem for Maria, who would rather be on welfare and think about philosophical problems, than work as a computer scientist.

4 *Criticizing Pascal.* An argument from dominance can be criticized on three grounds:
(a) The partition is wrong.
(b) Some acts influence the states of affairs in the partition.
(c) The utilities are wrong.

From a present-day perspective, how would you criticize Pascal's argument from dominance, and why?

5 *Study-or-not.* Discuss this argument. James is considering whether to study hard for the next test. He considers two acts, S = Study hard and R = Review the notes casually. He thinks three grades are possible for him, A, B, and C. Since he would rather not study hard, but put his time elsewhere, his decision table matrix is:

	A	B	C
R	++++	++	0
S	+++	+	--

He sees that the casual review dominates and decides not to study hard. Is this a good argument?

6 *Twenty-first-century gloom.* Bill Joy, a major innovator in software technology, did his bit for the new millenium by issuing a warning:

- Scientific breakthroughs in redesigning living matter have, he said, "set the stage for new man-made plagues that could literally wipe out the natural world."
- Developments in robotics "are laying the groundwork for a robot species of intelligent robots that can create evolved copies of themselves."
- Nanotechnology can be used to make smart machines that are microscopically small.

■ *"All three could easily replicate themselves creating a cascade effect that could sweep through the physical world. . . . It is no exaggeration to say we are on the cusp of the further perfection of extreme evil."*

"The cusp of the further perfection of extreme evil"? Jill Kiljoy has no idea what *that* means, but it sounds like very, very bad news. So she tries to construct an argument from dominance to show that we should stop work on robotics, genetic engineering, and nanotechnology, now.

Present Jill K.'s argument briefly and precisely, with utility assignments and a simple partition of possibilities. Include a decision table. Then present general criticisms of the argument.

KEY WORDS FOR REVIEW

Decision under uncertainty	Dominance
Pascal's wager	Causal influence
Partition	Dominance rule
Live possibilities	Dominant expected value rule

11 What Do You Mean?

The idea of probability leads in two different directions: **belief** and **frequency**. Probability makes us think of the degree to which we can be confident of something uncertain, given what we know or can find out. Probability also makes us think of the relative frequency with which some outcome occurs on repeated trials on a chance setup.

Thus far we have used both ideas almost interchangeably, because the basic rules for calculating with each are virtually identical. But now we have to distinguish between them, because the philosophical and practical uses of these two ideas are very different. The distinction is essential for the rest of this book (and for all clear thinking about probability).

We have been doing all these calculations about probabilities, and have not said a word about what we mean by "probability" itself. Now we are going to set things right. Up to now it has not mattered a great deal what we mean by the word. From now on it will make all the difference.

This chapter is an example of one kind of philosophy, often called analytic philosophy. We will try to come to grips with different concepts associated with the idea of probability. Many students find this chapter the hardest one of all. Not surprising! The distinctions that we have to make have bedeviled probability theorists—including some of the very best—for more than 200 years. Debates between experts who take the frequency approach, and those who take the belief approach, continue to be acrimonious. *In this chapter and the next one, you will have to make up your own mind about where you stand on these issues.*

A BIASED COIN

In ordinary language we use the word "probability" in different ways. We say things like this:

(1) This coin is biased toward heads. The probability of getting heads is about 0.6.

We take for granted that (1) is a statement about the coin. It implicitly refers to some method of tossing in a definite chance setup. Here are five remarks about (1):

a   Statement (1) is either true or false, regardless of what we know about the coin. If (1) is true, it is because of how the world is, especially how the coin and tossing device are.

b   If (1) is true, we suppose that the coin is asymmetrical. (Or maybe there is something unusual about the tossing device.)

c   We imagine that someone could explain (1) by facts drawn from the geometry of the coin, or the laws of physics.

d   We could do experiments to test (1). We conduct many trials on the chance setup, and observe the relative frequency of heads. If we get 63 heads irregularly distributed in 100 tosses, we are ready to accept (1) as true. But if we get only 37 heads, we are very dubious about (1).

e   In short: (1) states a fact about how the world is, and we can collect evidence to see whether (1) is true or false.

Notice that we could say very much the same thing about radioactive decay. If you put a Geiger counter next to a small piece of radium, you hear clicks every time a product of radioactive decay passes through the detector. Holding the counter four feet away from the source, you will notice a random sequence of clicks. This is a chance setup, and you might find out that:

The probability of getting a click in any given three-second interval is 0.6.

a   This statement is true or false, regardless of what we know about the radium and the detector.

c   We imagine that someone could explain it by facts drawn from the way the counter is made, facts about the sample of radium, and the laws of physics.

d   We could do experiments to test the statement. We observe the relative frequency of 3-second periods in which there are clicks.

e   In short: the statement states a fact about how the world is, and we can collect evidence to see whether it is true or false.

More sophisticated statements about the half-life of radium, for example, are to be understood in the same way.

THE EXTINCT DINOSAURS

We also say things like this:

(2) It is probable that the dinosaurs were made extinct by a giant asteroid hitting the Earth.

We can add details and precision to (2), as in this conversation from the TV program "The Science of Yesterday":

> Science journalist *Betty Glossop*: There is a lot of new evidence about a layer of iridium deposits in many parts of the Earth. Geologists have identified them as contemporary with the extinction of the dinosaurs.
> The interviewer *Joe Penchant*: What's that got to do with it?
> *Betty*: Iridium is an uncommon element that is the most corrosion-resistant substance found in nature. We have identified an asteroid crater rich in iridium, presumably from the asteroid. We think that it produced a gigantic cloud of dust, including iridium, that covered the earth. Plants needed for vegetarian dinosaurs, and for the prey of carnivorous ones, simply didn't grow well and the dinosaurs starved to death.
> *Joe*: So how probable is it, in the light of all this new information, that it was an asteroid that killed off the dinosaurs?
> (3) *Betty*: Taking all the evidence into consideration, the probability is about 90%.

The word "probability" seems to be used differently in (1) and (3). In (3), *Betty Glossop* is talking about the probability of a *proposition*, namely:

(4) The dinosaurs were made extinct by a giant asteroid hitting the Earth.

Let us first of all look just at (3), where *Betty* refers to her evidence about iridium and so on. Let's make some contrasts, item by item, between (3) and points a–e about (1), the biased coin. Read the following statements, and the previous one, very carefully. See if you agree with every single statement.

First, review exactly what (1), (2), (3), and (4) are. Notice that (4) is not a probability-statement at all. Notice that only (3) mentions evidence.

DINOSAURS AND PROBABILITY

a Statements (1) and (4) [but not (3)] are similar in one respect. Statement (4), like (1), is either true or false, regardless of what we know about the dinosaurs. If (4) is true, it is because of how the world is, especially what happened at the end of the dinosaur era. If (3) is true, it is not true because of "how the world is," but because of how well the evidence supports statement (4).

b If (3) is true, it is because of inductive logic, not because of how the world is.

c The evidence *mentioned* in (3) will go back to laws of physics (iridium), geology (the asteroid), geophysics, climatology, and biology. But these special sciences do not explain why (3) is true. Statement (3) states a relation between the evidence provided by these special sciences, and statement (4), about dinosaurs.

d We can do experiments to test the claims about iridium and so on. But we cannot do experiments to test (3). Notice that the tests of (1) may involve repeated tosses of the coin. But *it makes no sense at all* to talk about repeatedly testing (3).

e   In short: statement (3) makes a claim about how the evidence supports statement (4).

ON NOT MENTIONING EVIDENCE

We have bypassed (2), which is like (3), but does not mention the evidence. To make (2) look more like (1) and (3), we will put a number on that "probable":

(2.1) The probability that the dinosaurs were made extinct by a giant asteroid hitting the Earth is very high—about 0.9.

Statement (2.1) is different from (3), because it does not mention evidence. But in some ways it is like (3). Point d is one way they are alike:

d   We can do experiments to test the claims about iridium and so on, which might lead someone to assert (2.1). But we cannot do experiments to test (2.1). Notice that the tests of (1) may involve repeated tosses of the coin. But *it makes no sense at all* to talk about repeatedly testing (2.1).

Unfortunately, there are at least two ways to understand (2.1). We may think that (2.1) is "really" just short for (3). When people say that so and so is probable, they mean that relative to the available evidence, so and so is probable. We will call this the *interpersonal/evidential* way to understand (2.1). We will call the other way to understand (2.1) the *personal* way.

INTERPERSONAL/EVIDENTIAL

On this way of understanding (2.1), it is short for:

(2.2) Relative to the available evidence, the probability that the dinosaurs were made extinct by a giant asteroid hitting the Earth is very high—about 0.9.

We could say of someone who long-windedly states (2.2):

◆ She is taking for granted that any *reasonable* person who thought about the evidence, would find it very *reasonable to think that* an asteroid wiped out the dinosaurs.
◆ She thinks that it is *rational* to be pretty *confident* that the asteroids caused the extinction of the dinosaurs.
◆ She thinks that to say (2.1) is to mean something like (2.2)—or *Betty Glossop*'s less long-winded (3).
◆ She thinks that (2.2) is *interpersonal*—because it is about what it is reasonable for any reasonable person to believe. And since the degree of belief should depend on the available *evidence*, we call this *interpersonal/evidential*.

◆ Since she thinks that (2.2) is interpersonal, and about rational degrees of belief, she thinks that (2.2) is "objective."

SUBJECTIVE/OBJECTIVE—NOT

If you read a lot about probability, you will often read about "objective" and "subjective" probabilities. These are terrible terms, loaded with ideology. "I'm objective, you're subjective, he is prejudiced." How often have you heard this sort of conversation?

JAMES: That's just your subjective opinion.
MARY: Nonsense, it is an objective fact.

How often have *you* talked just like that?

Don't get into that rut, in probability or in the rest of your life. *James* and *Mary* are not arguing, they are just slinging mud at each other.

But do notice that both (1), about the bias and the die, and (2.2) or (3), can be called "objective"—although for quite different reasons. Statement (1) is called "objective" because it is a statement about how the world is. Statement (2.2) is called "objective" because of a supposed logical relation between the evidence and a proposition [namely, (4)].

PERSONAL DEGREE OF BELIEF

There is another way to understand (2). When someone says (2), they may mean only something about themselves, something like:

(2.3) I personally am very confident that the dinosaurs were made extinct by a giant asteroid hitting the Earth.

Or even this way to understand (2.1):

(2.4) If I had to make a bet on it, I would bet 9 to 1 that the dinosaurs were made extinct by a giant asteroid hitting the Earth.

TIME TO THINK ABOUT YOURSELF

What do *you* mean, when you say things like (2), "It is probable that the dinosaurs were made extinct by a giant asteroid hitting the Earth"?

What do you mean when you say things like:

It will probably rain today.
It is probable that I will flunk my geology test; I just can't tell those stupid rock samples one from the other.
The probability that there was a second gunman involved in the John F. Kennedy assassination is negligible.

In all probability, we are going through a period of extreme global warming due to burning fossil fuels, aerosols, methane produced by manure from beef cattle grown so we can kill and eat them, and so on.

Despite all the propaganda, the global warming hypothesis is not at all probable; we are just going through a routine climatic cycle.

It is very probable that the company my father works for will be downsized after the takeover, and he will be out of a job.

BELIEF-TYPE

Statement (4) was a proposition about dinosaur extinction; (2)–(2.2) and (3) are about how *credible* (believable) (4) is. They are about the degree to which someone *believes*, or *should believe*, (4). They are about how *confident* one can or should be, in the light of that evidence.

The use of the words "probable" and "probability" in (2)–(2.2) and (3) is related to ideas such as:

belief   confidence
credibility   evidence

We need a name for this family of uses of probability words. Philosophers have used a lot of different names. The easiest to remember is:

BELIEF-TYPE PROBABILITY

This is not the end of the matter. We just saw that belief-type probabilities can be thought of in at least two ways: *interpersonal/evidential* and *personal*.

FREQUENCY-TYPE

Now look at (1) again:

(1) The probability of getting heads with this coin is 0.6.

The truth of this statement seems to have nothing to do with what we believe. We seem to be making a completely factual statement about a material object, namely the coin (and the device for tossing it). We could be simply wrong, whether we know it or not. This might be a fair coin, and we may simply have been misled by the small number of times we tossed it. We are talking about a physical property of the coin, which can be investigated by experiment.

What is this physical property? We may be saying something like:

- In repeated tossing, the *relative frequency* of heads settles down to a stable proportion, 6/10.
- The coin has a *tendency* to come down heads far more often than tails.
- It has a *propensity* or *disposition* to favor heads.
- Or we are saying something more basic about the asymmetry of the coin and tossing device. We may be referring to the *geometry* and *physics* of the coin, which cause it to come down more often heads than tails.

The use of the word "probability" in (1) is related to ideas such as

frequency	disposition
tendency	symmetry
propensity	

We need a name for this family of uses of probability words. Philosophers have used a lot of different names. The easiest to remember is:

FREQUENCY-TYPE PROBABILITY

OTHER NAMES

You won't believe the number of names that philosophers have given to these two groups of uses of the word "probability." In case you look at other books, here is a little dictionary.

- *Subjective/objective*. The oldest pair of words for the belief-type and frequency-type distinction is "subjective" (belief-type) and "objective" (frequency-type). **Objection**: why say that the long statement (3), referring to the available evidence about the iridium layer and so forth, is "subjective"? Many scientists would claim that it is an "objective" assessment of the evidence.
- *It's all Greek to me*. Belief-type probabilities have been called "epistemic"— from *episteme*, a Greek word for knowledge. Frequency-type probabilities have been called "aleatory," from *alea*, a Latin word for games of chance, which provide clear examples of frequency-type probabilities. **Objection**: these words have never caught on. And it is much easier for most of us to remember plain English words rather than fancy Greek and Latin ones.
- *Number 1 and number 2*. The philosopher and logician Rudolf Carnap (1891–1970) called belief-type probability "probability$_1$," and frequency-type probability "probability$_2$." **Objection**: Carnap's proposal never caught on. And it is hard to remember which is number 1 and which is number 2.

Many other labels for the two groups of probability ideas have been used, but that is enough for now. Now let us look at some of our own examples earlier in the book. Where did we implicitly think of frequency-type probability? Where did we implicitly think of belief-type probability?

SHOCKS

Page 52 gave some data about two suppliers of shock absorbers, Bolt & Co. and Acme Inc. We began with the information that:

> Bolt supplies 40% of the shock absorbers for a manufacturer, and Acme 60%. We took the probability of a randomly selected shock absorber being made by Bolt to be 0.4.
> Of Acme's shocks, 96% test reliable. But Bolt has been having some problems on the line, and recently only 72% of Bolt's shock absorbers have tested reliable.

We asked:

> What is the probability that a randomly chosen shock absorber will test reliable? The probability worked out to be 0.864.
> What is the conditional probability that a randomly chosen shock absorber, which is tested and found to be reliable, is made by Bolt? The answer was $\frac{1}{3}$.

Here it is natural to take a frequency perspective.

We are talking about a mass-produced product from an assembly line. We observe the relative frequency of defective and reliable products from the two lines, one at Bolt, one at Acme. These frequencies must reflect a difference between the two companies.

STREP THROAT

Page 75 discussed Odd Question 6, about strep throat. You were asked to imagine that you were a physician examining a patient, and sending swabs to the lab for testing. We said,

> You think it likely that the patient has strep throat. Let us, to get a sense of the problem, put a number to this, the probability is 90% that the patient has strep throat. $Pr(S) = 0.9$.

You, as physician, were asked to reach a conclusion on the basis of seemingly inconsistent reports from the lab: 3 positive tests and 2 negative ones. You concluded,

> It is very much more likely than not, that the patient does have strep throat. The probability that the patient has strep throat, given the data, is 343/344, or 0.997.

Then we moved to another case, called "sheer ignorance." We said that the ignorant person might say,

> It is 50–50 whether this patient has strep throat.
> The probability that the patient has strep throat is 0.5.
> That is, $\Pr(S) = 0.5$.
> You computed your probability of strep throat, in the light of the news from the lab, as the rather surprising 343/352, or 0.974.

In this example we do have some frequency data, namely the probability of false positives in the lab test. Nevertheless, we are plainly talking about the beliefs of the physician or the ignorant amateur, both before and after getting the lab results.

In this case it is natural to take a belief perspective.

Notice that the problem about shock absorbers and the problem about strep throat can be solved in exactly the same way, using Bayes' Rule. The formal, logical, arithmetical problem is the same, but the meaning is somewhat different.

STATING THAT, AND REASONS FOR

Frequency-type probability statements state *how the world is*. They state, for example, a physical property about a coin and tossing device, or the production practices of Acme and Bolt.

Belief-type probability statements express a person's confidence in a belief, or state the credibility of a conjecture or proposition in the light of evidence.

Beware of a confusion that troubles a lot of students.

If I state a matter of fact, you expect me to believe what I state. You expect me to have some reasons for thinking my belief is true. You expect me to be able to give you my reasons.

So some students think: every statement about how the world is, states reasons and beliefs. NO!

A statement about how the world is, is a statement made (we hope) because a person has some beliefs and some reasons for them. But what it *says* is not, "I have reasons for my belief that *p*." What it says is, "This is how the world is: *p*."

Distinguish:

◆ What a person says (what a proposition states).
◆ The reasons that a person may have, for stating or believing some proposition.

Actually, people often do not have reasons for what they say. Sometimes they do not even believe what they say. A person may say "how the world is" in many different circumstances. The person may:

◆ Have excellent reasons.
◆ Merely hope the statement is true but have no reasons.

◆ Be lying—believe that the proposition is false, have reasons for thinking so, but want to misinform someone.

THE SINGLE CASE

Frequency-type probabilities usually are about items of some kind that occur in a sequence: spins of a wheel, shock absorbers produced by a manufacturer.

It does not make sense to speak of the "frequency" of a single event. A patient either has, or has not, got strep throat. In the taxicab problem, Odd Question 5, either a blue cab sideswiped another car, or a green cab did it. As stated, these problems involve a single event, a single car, a single patient, a single case.

Such probabilities cannot literally be understood as a frequency. They cannot be understood as tendencies or propensities either.

In the taxicab story, the *witness* has a tendency or propensity or disposition to make a correct identification of cab color on a misty night. She gets things right 80% of the time. That is a frequency. But there is not a tendency on the part of the *sideswiper* to be green or blue. It was green. Or it was blue.

> If someone speaks of the probability of a single event, then they must be taking the belief perspective.

Sounds simple, but beware. *Dean* tosses a coin, and it falls on the table in front of me. Before *Dean* or anyone else has a chance to observe the outcome, he slams a book down on top of the coin.

> DEAN: What is the probability that the coin under the book is heads up?
> BEANO: 60%
> DEAN: You mean that the probability is 0.6, that the coin under the book is heads up?
> BEANO: Yes.
> DEAN: Why do you say that?
> BEANO: I thought you were tossing that biased coin you discussed in (1) at the start of this chapter. I thought that this coin is biased towards heads, and the probability of getting heads is about 0.6.

In this case, *Beano* is making a belief-type statement about *this* toss of *this* coin, a single case. He has a *reason* for this belief-type statement, namely a frequency-type statement about the coin.

SWITCHING BACK AND FORTH

We use one word, "probability," from both a frequency and a belief perspective. That is no accident. We switch back and forth between the two perspectives. We computed that:

> The conditional probability is 1/3 that a shock absorber is made by Bolt, if it has been tested at random and found to be reliable.

That is a statement about the production characteristics of shock absorbers bought by the automobile manufacturer. Tomorrow, *Rosie the Riveter*, the quality control engineer, tests a shock absorber at random from a batch of shocks. She finds that it is reliable.

What is the probability that *this* shock absorber was made by Bolt?

Rosie knows the answer: the probability is 1/3.

But this probability is about a single case. There is no frequency with which this shock, or this batch, is made by Bolt. It is, or it is not.

Rosie made a belief-type statement. Her reason for making it was her knowledge of the relative frequencies with which randomly selected shock absorbers, in this setup, are reliable.

So *Rosie* has switched from a frequency perspective to a belief perspective.

THE FREQUENCY PRINCIPLE

We switch perspectives by a rule of thumb, which has been called the *frequency principle*. It connects belief-type and frequency-type probabilities.

It is a rule about *knowledge* and *ignorance*. Suppose that:

◆ You *know* the frequency-type probability of an event on trials of some kind.
◆ You are *ignorant* of anything else about the outcome of a single trial of that kind.

Then you take the frequency-type probability as the belief-type probability of the single case.

We could call it a *know-almost-nothing-but-the-frequency* rule. Here is a very pedantic way to state the frequency principle:

If S is an individual event of type E,
and the *only* information about whether E occurred on a trial of a certain kind, on a certain chance setup, is that on trials of that kind on that setup the frequency-type probability $Pr(E) = p$,
then the belief-type probability of S is also p.

RELEVANT SUBSETS

The frequency principle is a rule of thumb. When is a frequency-type probability absolutely "all" that we know about the occurrence of an event? Only in artificial situations, as when we toss a fair coin and hide the result. Nevertheless, in real life we quite often have "something like" this situation.

Usually we have a lot of not-very-tidy information. The weather office took the smallest subset of weeks like the week just ended, and worked out the tendency of such weeks to be followed by precipitation.

When we implicitly use the frequency principle, we often make a judgment of relevance like that. Recall Tomer, the heavy smoker, from page 120. His friend Peggy was told by the statistician that:

> The probability of a male of about Tomer's age (and otherwise like Tomer) dying before age sixty-five, given that he smokes, is 0.36.

The statistician chose a *relevant subset* of males, chiefly by age, but also with a view to getting a trustworthy statement of frequency-type probabilities. Real-life application of the frequency principle requires a lot of judgment.

PROBABILITIES OF PROBABILITIES

Back to the gambler's fallacy. *Alert Learner* (page 31) noticed that the wheel had stopped at black on twelve spins in a row. She suspected bias. After doing some more experiments on the wheel, suppose she concludes that the wheel is heavily biased toward black:

> $0.91 \leqslant \Pr(B) \leqslant 0.93$.

She intends this to be understood as a statement about the properties of the wheel. Because of the way in which the wheel is made and spun, it stops at black about 92% of the time.

This is a risky conclusion. *Alert Learner* may still feel confident enough to say,

> It is very probable that the probability of black is close to 0.92.

She might even try something more precise-sounding: "The probability that $0.91 \leqslant \Pr(B) \leqslant 0.93$ is at least 95%."

Apparently *Alert Learner* is expressing a belief-type probability of a frequency-type probability. How on earth can she do that? Easy. It is a matter of fact, whether the probability of getting black is between 0.91 and 0.93 or not. And we can discuss the probability of that being true. A probability (belief-type) of a probability (frequency-type).

EXERCISES

1   *Shock absorbers again.* (a) In the shock absorber example, Acme had a better record of reliability than Bolt. What might be the causes of this difference? (b) Why are causes relevant to the distinction between frequency-type and belief-type probabilities?

Classify each of the following statements in italics as frequency-type or belief-type. If you think that one or more could be understood as either frequency-type or belief-type, explain why.

2   *Influenza.* These are all quotations from a newspaper story.
   (a) *When a flu epidemic strikes, the probability that a person who was exposed will get sick is between 10% and 15%.*

(b) *The disease is likely to run its course in 5 to 7 days in healthy young people.*
(c) But *it is far more probable that the flu will last for weeks in an old person than in a healthy young person.*
(d) Making a vaccine is always a guessing game, because there is no way to predict what flu strains will appear. But researchers can get a good idea by detecting what strains start cropping up at the end of a previous year. *If a strain appears at the end of the season, there is a good probability that it will make the rounds next year.*
(e) *The probability that the flu vaccine prevents flu in a young healthy person is 70 to 90 percent,* Dr. Gunn said. *The probability is only 50 percent in people over 65.* But, he added, *the probability that it prevents death in an older person is 0.85.*

3   (a) *January 31, 1996*: (from a news story that day): China is determined to abolish the local legislature . . . *It is also probable that it will weaken Hong Kong statutes that protect civil liberties.*
(b) *February 1, 2006*: (from a news story to appear that day): Contrary to recent reports, *it is not probable that the breakaway southern province will choose Hong Kong as its capital city.*

4   *The Fed.* The speaker was the chairman of the Federal Reserve Board (the "Fed") that determines the U.S. money supply and basic interest rates. According to a newspaper story, the chairman said:
(a) *The probability of a recession is less than 50%, in contrast with growing fears of an economic downturn a year ago.*
(b) Recent Fed analysis of leading economic indicators put *the chances of a recession in the next 6 months even lower, at between 10 and 20 percent.*
(c) *I wouldn't bet the ranch on such statistical measures.*

5   *Clones* (from *Nature*, one of the major weekly science journals): Researchers have identified a gene linked with Marfan syndrome—which involves a wide variety of problems, eyesight defects, heart disease and abnormally long limb bones . . . Francesco Ramirez has now cloned the gene for fibrillin and mapped it to a segment of chromosome 15. After studying families with the disorder, he concluded that *the probability of exhibiting Marfan syndrome, given the defective gene, is over 0.7.*

KEY WORDS FOR REVIEW

Frequency	Interpersonal/evidential
Belief	Personal probability
Single case	Propensity
Frequency principle	Relevant subset

12 Theories about Probability

There have been two fundamentally different approaches to probability. One emphasizes the frequency idea. The other emphasizes the belief idea.

Some theorists say that only one of those two ideas really matters. We will call them *dogmatists*. In this book we are *eclectic*. Here are two definitions taken from a dictionary:

- Eclectic. Adjective. 1. (in art, philosophy, etc.) Selecting what seems best from various styles, doctrines, ideas, methods, etc.
- Dogmatic. Adjective. 1. Characterized by making authoritative or arrogant assertions or opinions, etc.

FREQUENCY DOGMATISTS

Some experts believe that all inductive reasoning should be analyzed in terms of frequency-type probabilities. This is a dogmatic philosophy, saying that inductive reasoning should rely on exactly one use of probability. Belief dogmatists often say that frequency-type probabilities "have no role in science."

BELIEF DOGMATISTS

Some experts believe that all inductive reasoning should be analyzed in terms of belief-type probabilities. This is a dogmatic philosophy, saying that inductive reasoning should rely on exactly one use of probability. Belief dogmatists often say that frequency-type probability "doesn't even make sense."

OUR ECLECTIC APPROACH

Chapters 16–19 and 22 use the frequency idea. Chapters 13–15 and 21 use the belief idea.

Luckily, most (but not all) data and arguments that a frequency dogmatist can analyze, a belief dogmatist can analyze too. And vice versa. Only in rather specialized situations do the two schools of thought draw really different inferences from the same data. They differ more about how to get data in the first place. They disagree about how to design experiments in order to get the most useful information.

Our eclectic approach values both families of ideas.

THE WEATHER

Weather forecasts come with probabilities:

(a) The probability of precipitation tomorrow is 30%.

What does that mean? Since the statement is about rain (or snow or hail) *tomorrow*, it is about a single case. Either it rains, or it does not. There is only one tomorrow. So this must be a belief-type probability.

If you ask the weather office what it means, you will hear something like this:

(b) We have compared the weather conditions for the past week with a very large data bank, and have selected all those weeks which in the relevant ways are like the week just ended. Of those weeks, 30% were followed by rain. The probability of rain the next day, after a week like last week, is 30%.

This is stated as a frequency-type probability. If the weather office means what it says, then it must be using the frequency principle to go from (b) to (a). Some meteorologists say that when their office issues forecast (a), it just *means* (b)—or better, it is a short form of (b). They say that they always mean frequency-type probabilities. They are *frequency dogmatists*.

Belief dogmatists suggest that the weather people don't know what they are talking about. Meteorologists ought never to mean frequencies. For they don't rely only on past frequencies of precipitation. They use all sorts of information, including (b), and make some judgment calls. But statement (a) is exactly what it seems. It is used to state the extent to which the weather people expect rain.

Luckily, most people don't know about such dogmatic infighting. No one, in daily life, is worried about what forecast (a) means.

FOUR THEORIES ABOUT PROBABILITY

Both kinds of dogmatist try to make their ideas as clear as possible. Hence there are quite a lot of what philosophers call "theories of probability." We will briefly describe two frequency-type theories, and two belief-type theories.

PERSONAL PROBABILITY

Recall the dinosaurs. Someone says, "The reign of the dinosaurs was brought to an end when a giant asteroid hit the Earth." We can say something quite impersonal about this claim:

It is probable that the reign of the dinosaurs was brought to an end when a giant asteroid hit the Earth.

That suggests that "anyone" who is well informed ought to make the same judgment. This *interpersonal* notion leads to anonymous assertions like:

One can be very confident that the dinosaurs were extinguished after a giant asteroid hit the Earth.

Then there are *personal* statements, which express the speaker's own personal confidence or degree of belief:

I am very confident that the dinosaurs were extinguished after a giant asteroid hit the Earth.

This leads to the idea of **personal probability**. It is a kind of belief-type probability. You might think that personal probability is totally "subjective" and of no value for inductive logic. In fact, it is a very powerful idea, developed in Chapters 13–15. People who want to be consistent must (we show) have personal probabilities that obey the basic rules of probability.

LOGICAL PROBABILITY

Personal probability is one rather extreme kind of belief-type probability. At the opposite extreme is **logical probability**. Here is a long probability statement about dinosaurs:

Relative to recent evidence about a layer of iridium deposits in many parts of the Earth, geologically identified as contemporary with the extinction of the dinosaurs, the probability is 90% that the reign of the dinosaurs was brought to an end when a giant asteroid hit the Earth.

One could also say:

Relative to the *available evidence*, it is *reasonable* to have a high *degree of belief* in the dinosaur/asteroid hypothesis.

This is a statement of a conditional probability. We called it *interpersonal/evidential*.
    Let H be the hypothesis about dinosaurs, and let E be the evidence. Then this statement is of the form,

$Pr(H/E) = 0.9.$

The theory of logical probability says statements like that express a *logical* relation between H and E, analogous to logical deducibility.
    Logical probabilities are supposed to be logical relations between evidence and an hypothesis. On this theory, it makes no sense to talk about the probability of H all by itself.
    According to the theory of logical probability, probability is always *relative to*

evidence. When we don't actually mention evidence, we are implicitly referring to some body of evidence.

Frequency dogmatists cannot abide this conclusion. One of the first explicit frequency theories about probability was due to John Venn (1834–1923), better known as the inventor of Venn diagrams (page 63). He said that

> The probability of an event is no more relative to something else than the area of a field is relative to something else.

THE PRINCIPLE OF INSUFFICIENT REASON

What if there is no relevant evidence at all? From the earliest days of numerical probabilities, people have been inclined to say that if there is no reason to choose among several alternatives, they should be treated as equally probable.

Example: Peter on a road in the Netherlands (page 114) does not know if the sign,

■■TERDAM →

indicates the way to Amsterdam or to Rotterdam. He sees no reason to choose among the alternatives. He does not know of any other major city ending in "terdam," so he says that the probability of each is 0.5.

Example: Mario Baguette is to meet his friend Sonia at the Metropolitan Airport. She is flying in from New York. She has told Mario that she is arriving between 3:00 and 4:00 in the afternoon. Five different airlines have flights from New York arriving during that hour—Alpha Air, Beta Blaster, Gamma Goways, Delta, and Eatemup Airlines. Mario can think of no reason to favor one over the others, so he says that the probability of each is 0.2. Alpha and Beta arrive at terminal 1, Gamma and Delta at terminal 2, and Eatemup arrives at terminal 3. Hence his expectation for Eatemup and terminal 3 is lowest, and he flips a coin to see whether he goes to terminal 1 or 2.

The advocate of logical probability says that when there is no evidence favoring one of n mutually exclusive and jointly exhaustive hypotheses, then one should assign them each probability $1/n$. This is called *the principle of insufficient reason*, or *the principle of indifference*.

TOO EASY BY HALF

The principle of insufficient reason sounds fine. But there are real problems. Would you say it is equally probable that a car is red or not red? Or that it is red or blue or green or some other color? The principle quickly leads to a lot of paradoxes.

BAYESIANS

We will see in Chapter 15 how both personal and logical probability theories make heavy use of Bayes' Rule. Belief dogmatists who make exclusive use of belief-type probabilities and place great emphasis on Bayes' Rule are often called Bayesians.

KEYNES AND RAMSEY

The idea of logical probability—which is always "relative to the evidence"—goes back at least 200 years, but the first systematic presentation of logical probability, as a logical relation, was by John Maynard Keynes (1883–1946). Keynes is the famous economist whose theories are sometimes credited with saving capitalism during the crisis of the Great Depression of 1929–1936. His *Treatise on Probability* (1921) was his first major work, submitted for a prize fellowship (something like a post-doc, but with no Ph.D.) at Cambridge University.

In 1926, a second young man at Cambridge, Frank Plumpton Ramsey (1903–1930), presented the first modern theory of personal probability (see page 000). He died during an operation when he was twenty-six, after having made fundamental contributions to economics, mathematical logic, probability theory, and philosophy.

Logicians, and especially Rudolf Carnap, have been very attracted to Keynes's logical probability. Nevertheless, a few simple words by Ramsey are impressive.

> The most "fundamental criticism of Mr. Keynes' views . . . is the obvious one that there really do not seem to be any such things as the probability relations he describes."

DE FINETTI AND SAVAGE

Two great figures in the history of personal probability are the Italian mathematician Bruno de Finetti and the American L. J. Savage. You will find out more about Savage on page 184. De Finetti pioneered his ideas, in Italian, at about the same time as Ramsey did in English. But Ramsey thought there was room, in his mental space, for a frequency-type concept of probability, especially in quantum mechanics. De Finetti was convinced that only a personal belief-type concept made sense. So was Savage. Both were belief dogmatists, who taught us an enormous amount about the idea of personal probability and what is now called Bayesian statistics.

LIMITING FREQUENCY

Belief-type probabilities split into logical probabilities at one extreme and personal probabilities at another. Something similar happens with frequency-type probabilities.

Thus far we have mentioned a family of ideas: frequency, long run, geometrical symmetry, physical property, tendency, propensity. How can these be made precise? One way is to emphasize relative frequency in the long run. What is a "long run"? Mathematicians immediately think of an idealization: an *infinite* sequence of trials.

The next idea that occurs to a mathematician is that of a *convergence* and *mathematical limit*. That leads to the idealization of an infinite sequence of trials in which the relative frequency of an outcome S *converges* to a *limit*.

But there is another requirement. Think of a sequence of tosses of a coin, in which heads and tails alternate:

H T H T H T....

The relative frequency certainly converges to ½, but we do not think of this as a probability, because the sequence is fully determinate. So we add a further clause to this definition of probability. It was mentioned earlier on page 28: *The impossibility of a gambling system*.

This theory about probability was first stated clearly by John Venn in 1866. It was systematically developed in 1928 by the Austrian-born applied mathematician (aerodynamics) and philosopher Richard von Mises (1883–1953), who became a professor at Harvard.

The idea of "the impossibility of a gambling system" has turned out to be very fruitful. It has led to fundamental new ideas about computational complexity, pioneered by A. N. Kolmogorov (see page 67). Roughly speaking, a sequence is now said to be random, relative to a class of ideal computer programs, if any program sufficient to generate the sequence is at least as long as the sequence itself.

PROPENSITY

The limiting frequency idea is one extreme frequency-type probability. It idealizes a series of actual results of trials on a chance setup. It emphasizes what can be seen to happen, rather than underlying causes or structures.

Stable relative frequencies exist only if a setup has some underlying physical or geometrical properties. And we can have that underlying structure even if in fact no actual trials are ever made.

A second extreme frequency-type idea emphasizes the tendency, disposition, or *propensity* of the chance setup. This seems particularly natural when we think of stochastic processes found in nature, such as radioactive decay. We are concerned less with the distribution of clicks on a Geiger counter, than with the basic physical processes.

The propensity account of probability was developed by the Austrian-born philosopher Karl Popper (1902–1994), who became a professor at the London School of Economics. Popper may have been the most influential philosopher of science of the twentieth century. We discuss his evasion of the problem of induction in Chapter 20. Popper believed that his propensity approach was important for understanding fundamental issues of quantum mechanics.

EXPECTED VALUES

We have spent so much space on kinds of probability, that we may be in danger of ignoring expected values and fair prices.

When expected values are explained in terms of probability, every ambiguity in the word "probability" shows up in "expected value." Thus there are personal expected values, logical expected values (conditional on evidence), propensity expected values, and so forth. And there are the usual debates between different theories. This anecdote will make the point.

THE OLD COKE MACHINE

Once upon a time a bottle of Coca-Cola cost only five cents. Coke machines would dispense a bottle for a nickel. Then the price went up to six cents. *Unhappy Sailor* remembered this to his dying day. (He told me this story himself, when I visited him at the U.S. Bureau of Standards, where he had become chief statistician.)

He visited a Pacific naval base where the machine had been fixed to allow for inflation. Each time you put a nickel in, there was a one-in-six chance that you got nothing. *Sailor* was ashore for one day only, and he wanted just one bottle of Coke. He lost the first time, and he had to pay another nickel to get his drink. "That's not fair!" said he.

The machine was equivalent to the following lottery. There are six tickets, five of which have a prize of a six-cent bottle of Coke, and one of which has no prize. The fair price is then five cents.

Up in philosophers' paradise, the debate is still going on.

GHOSTS OF VENN, VON MISES, POPPER, AND OTHER FREQUENCY DOGMATISTS: And that, of course, was the fair price, because on average, sailors on the base paid six cents for each bottle of Coke.

GHOST OF *Unhappy Sailor*: I didn't care about the long run. I was only on the island for a day, and I had to pay a dime for my six-cent bottle of Coke. It may have been fair for the people stationed permanently at the base, but it was not fair for me.

GHOSTS OF KEYNES AND OTHER BELIEF DOGMATISTS: Exactly so. Talk of averages in the long run is completely irrelevant. The machine was fair. Putting a nickel in the machine was equivalent to having a ticket in a symmetric zero-sum lottery with six tickets. Five tickets give a prize worth six cents, one ticket gives nothing. So the total prizes added up to 30 cents. There are six players, and each should put in a nickel. The unfairness is not in the lottery. The unfairness is in forcing *Unhappy Sailor* to play this lottery. There are many kinds of unfairness, and being forced to gamble for a soft drink is one of them.

WHY DO WE HAVE DIFFERENT KINDS OF PROBABILITY?

Here is a simple answer. Numerical probabilities began to be used in earnest a long time ago, around 1650. Naturally, people needed simple examples. Gambling was very common, and so were lotteries. A lot of gambling relied on artificial randomizers such as dice, coins, and packs of cards. Lotteries used an artificial randomizer. Moreover, many of the randomizers of choice were supposed to be symmetric. Hence it really did not make much difference what you meant by probability. Let's take a lottery with 1,000 numbered balls placed in an urn, and see why it makes little difference.

Relative frequency talk: On repeated draws with replacement from this lottery box, each ball is drawn as often as every other. So the probability of drawing ball #434 is the relative frequency of drawing that ball, namely $\frac{1}{1000}$.

Propensity talk: The urn, balls, and drawing procedure are arranged so that the propensity for one ball to be drawn is the same as for any other. Hence the probability of drawing ball #434 is $\frac{1}{1000}$.

Personal talk: So far as I'm concerned, every ball is equally likely, so for me, the probability of drawing ball #434 is $\frac{1}{1000}$.

Interpersonal talk: No reasonable person would give greater probability to one ball over another, so the probability of drawing ball #434 is $\frac{1}{1000}$.

Logical talk: The logical relation between any h_j (the hypothesis that ball #j is drawn) and the available evidence, and that between any other h_k and the available evidence, is just the same. So the probabilities are equal, and the probability of drawing ball #434 is $\frac{1}{1000}$.

Principle of insufficient reason talk: There is no evidence favoring one of the 1000 mutually exclusive and jointly exhaustive hypotheses over any other. Hence one should assign them each probability $\frac{1}{1000}$.

MODELING

The next step in the development of probabilities was to model more complex situations on core examples such as urns, lotteries, dice, cards. It still did not matter much how one understood the core examples. Only when we get quite sophisticated modeling does it matter very much how we think of probabilities. Yes, our shock absorber example is naturally understood in terms of frequencies, and our strep throat example is naturally understood in terms of degrees of belief. But until one starts thinking very carefully about statistical inference, only pedantic philosophers care much about the meaning of probability.

MEANINGS

"Define your terms!" How often have you heard that. But definition is not always what we want. Many words are best explained, in the beginning, by examples. Suppose you wanted to explain the meaning of the word "bird" to an alien. You would probably point to small or middle-sized birds that are common where you live. Famous experiments in California showed that most students thought a robin was the prototypical bird. In England you can get the same result, except that the English robin (redbreast) is a completely different kind of bird from the North American robin! Myself, I would not pick a robin but some of those little brown birds that congregate in the tree outside my window. But except for smart alecks who know about this experiment, no one in North America chooses an ostrich as the prototypical bird, let alone a cassowary. Few choose ducks, fewer still swans. Few choose eagles or owls.

Who can define a bird? Maybe some ornithologists can, but most of us get on just fine talking about birds without defining "bird." We think of birds as being more or less like our prototype of a bird. Ostriches are in some ways like my little brown birds. So are eagles, but ostriches and eagles are not much alike. We could think of birds as radiating out from a center, where in the center we have our prototype for birds, and the birds on the periphery have some resemblance to the birds in the center. According to the experiments, those students in northern California have a picture of birds rather like this:

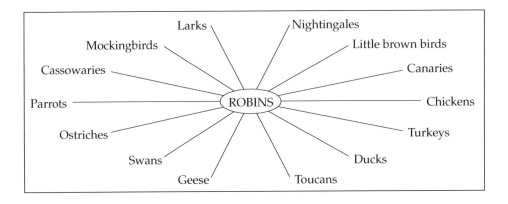

Much the same is true of probability. Our prototypical examples are artificial randomizers. But as we start to think hard about more real-life examples, we get further and further away from the core examples. Then our examples tend to cluster into belief-type examples, and frequency-type examples, and in the end we develop ideas of two different kinds of probability:

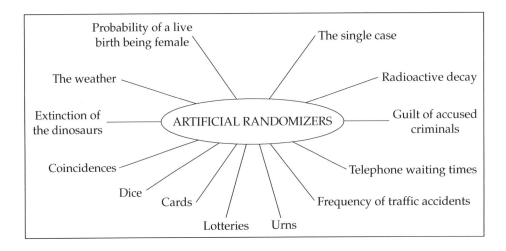

THE LAST WORD

From now on we will be careful about kinds of probability. In previous chapters we tended to speak, wherever possible, in a frequency-type way. It is only fair that we end the first part of the book by letting a belief dogmatist have the last word.

John Maynard Keynes, advocate of the logical theory of belief-type probability, had no use for frequency-type probabilities. He jeered at the idea of relative frequency in the long run. He asked what could be meant by "the long run."

"The long run" is just a metaphor. Infinite long runs may be a nice idealization, but have nothing to do with real life. In another context Keynes remarked:

"In the long run we are all dead."

EXERCISES

1 *Indifference.* Look back at Mario Baguette's problem about meeting Sonia (page 143). If Mario suspects that Sonia will take the budget airline, Eatemup, he may not be indifferent among the five choices. Now he has a problem in personal probabilities; does he think it more likely she would come on Alpha *or* Beta, or on the cheap Eatemup? What would you do?

The remaining exercises are based on an imaginary symposium. Once upon a time four dogmatists were put on a stage and asked to explain their views about probability. We'll call these men

> *Venn*, the frequency theorist.
> *Popper*, the propensity theorist.
> *De Finetti*, the personal probability theorist.
> *Keynes*, the theorist of logical probability.

The master of ceremonies read out several statements and asked each dogmatist to say what it meant, if anything. What did each of the four men say about the italicized statements below?

2 *Happy Harry's Preparation Kit for the Graduate Record Examination (GRE).* "*Students who use Happy Harry's Kit have a 90% probability of success in the GRE!*"

3 *The informed source.* An informed source who did not wish to be identified was asked about the recent spate of bombings and retaliations. She said that *there is little probability of a lasting Middle East peace settlement in the next two years.*

4 *Conditional Happy Harry.* "If your probability of success on the GRE is only 50–50 before you use Happy Harry's kit, it will be 75% after you use it." The emcee told the dogmatists to take this as a compound statement involving two probability statements: "If *your probability of success is 0.5, on condition that you do not use Harry's kit*, then *your probability of success is 0.75, on condition that you do use Harry's kit.*"

5 *The Great One.* Wayne Gretzky, who scored more goals than anyone in the history of ice hockey, developed arthritis at age thirty-eight and started doing paid TV

ads for Tylenol. How could a healthy man have arthritis in his thirties? Dr. Clarfield, a hockey physician, said, "He played enough hockey for three careers, so *the trauma in his joints was probably more than it was for most players.*"

6   *Landing on Mars.* A NASA spokeswoman said that *the first person to set foot on Mars would in all probability be an engineer.*

7   *Lunatic coin tossers.* A fair coin is being tossed. We say that after N tosses, heads is in the lead if heads has come up more times than tails. Conversely, tails is in the lead if tails has come up more often. (With an even number N, they could be tied.) We say that the lead changes at toss N if heads was in the lead at $N-1$, but tails is in the lead at $N+1$. *The probability that in 10,000 tossings of a fair coin, the lead never changes, is about .0085.*

8   *An amazing answer.* Here you are asked about the meaning of probability in a question. The answer to this question is given in the answer section, but you are not expected to know the answer here. But make a guess. *What is the probability that in 10,000 tosses, one side is in the lead for more than 9,930 tosses, while the other side is in the lead for fewer than 70 tosses?*

KEY WORDS FOR REVIEW

Frequency theory   Personal theory
Propensity theory   Logical theory

13 Personal Probabilities

How personal degrees of belief can be represented numerically by using imaginary gambles.

Chapters 1–10 were often *deliberately ambiguous* about different kinds of probability. That was because the basic ideas usually applied, across the board, to most kinds of probability.

Now we develop ideas that matter a lot for belief-type probabilities. They do not matter so much from the frequency point of view.

THE PROGRAM

There are three distinct steps in the argument, and each deserves a separate chapter.

- *This chapter* shows how you might use numbers to represent your degrees of belief.
- *Chapter 14* shows why these numbers should satisfy the basic rules of probability. (And hence they should obey Bayes' Rule.)
- *Chapter 15* shows how to use Bayes' Rule to *revise* or *update* personal probabilities in the light of new evidence. This is the fundamental motivation for the group of chapters, 13–15.

In these chapters we are concerned with a person's degrees of belief. We are talking about personal probabilities. But this approach can be used for other versions of belief-type probability, such as the logical perspective of Keynes and Carnap.

Because Bayes' Rule is so fundamental, this approach is often called *Bayesian*. "Belief dogmatists" are often simply called Bayesians because the use of Bayes' rule as a model of learning from experience plays such a large part in their philosophy. But notice that there are many varieties of Bayesian thinking. This perspective ranges from the personal to the logical.

THOUGHT EXPERIMENTS

We are concerned with degrees of belief. There is a close relation between belief and action. For example:

> You are walking in unfamiliar countryside. On the way home you come to an unmarked fork in a path. You do not know whether to go left or right. You favor going left but are uncertain. You decide, you take a calculated risk. You translate your belief into action. You vote with your feet. You go left rather than right.

How confident are you that this is a good decision? To what degree do you believe that the left fork goes home? A thought experiment provides a clue on how to represent degrees of belief using numbers.

For example:

> If you toss a fair coin to decide which way to go, you must think that it is as probable that home is to the left, as that it is to the right. Your personal probability, for each fork, is $1/2$.
>
> But if you would roll a die, and go right if and only if you rolled a 6, then your personal probability, that home is to the right, must be about 1/6.

This chapter is about thought experiments. Not experiments for your instructor or your neighbor, but experiments for *you*.

FIRST THOUGHT EXPERIMENT: GIFTS

The first thought experiments that you will conduct involve choosing between "gambles." The gambles don't cost you anything. You take no risks.

> Think of being offered a small but desirable prize, a free gift.
>
> It does not matter whether the gift is $10, or a good grade in the course, or being sent roses next Valentine's Day by someone you care about.
>
> Pick your own gift.
>
> Be real. Write down here a small gift that you would like:

_____

RISK-FREE GAMBLES

Now think of two possible events. Here we use a trite example—the weather on the first day of spring.

> Event 1: Heavy snow falls in Toronto next March 21.
> Event 2: Next March 21 in Toronto is a balmy and springlike day.

A **gamble** is a choice to be made between two possibilities. Say you have chosen $10 as your gift. Take your choice:

- $10 if event 1 occurs, and nothing otherwise, or
- $10 if event 2 occurs, and nothing otherwise.

Would you rather "gamble" on event 1 occurring? Or on event 2 occurring?

Be real. Write down your answer:

_____

If you are indifferent between these two options, then you must think that events 1 and 2 are equally likely.

But if you would rather get your gift if event 1 occurs, you seem to think it is more likely that event 1 will occur, than event 2. You attach a higher personal probability to event 1, than to event 2.

Conversely, if you would rather get your gift if event 2 occurs, you seem to think it is more likely that event 2 will occur, than event 1. You attach a higher personal probability to event 2, than to event 1.

EVENTS AND PROPOSITIONS

We have just been using the event language. As usual, we can also use the proposition language. Consider:

Proposition 3: The right claw of a healthy lobster is almost always larger than the left claw.

Proposition 4: The left claw of a healthy lobster is almost always larger than the right claw.

Would you rather have your $10 if proposition 3 is true, or if proposition 4 is true? If you prefer (3) to (4), then you have a higher personal probability for (3) than for (4).

REALITY CHECK: SETTLE SOON

Gambles are worthwhile only if they are settled soon. I have no interest in a gamble on the weather, with the prospect of a gift of $10, a million years from now. Think of this:

5: Heavy snow falls in Toronto on January 1, 2075.
6: Next January 1 is balmy and springlike in Toronto.

I myself think that (5) is much more likely than (6), greenhouse effect or no.

All the same, I would rather have my gift if (6) occurs, than if (5) occurs. I will be dead by the time (5) is settled, so whatever happens, I myself win nothing, and by 2075 ten dollars may be worth nothing anyway. But if I choose (6), there is some small chance that I will get my $10 gift.

From now on, imagine that all gambles and bets are to be settled quite soon.

That may require *a lot* of imagination. Think of the lobsters. Propositions (3) and (4) say "almost always." How do we settle this bet? Or recall Pascal's wager. Think of this gamble:

7: God created exactly this Universe.
8: This universe evolved by chance from an uncaused Big Bang.

Some people—"creationists"—might prefer to gamble on getting their gift if (7) is true. Other people—atheists—might gamble on getting their gift if (8) is true. But few of us believe that the question will be settled in our lifetimes.

REALITY CHECK: UNRELATED PRIZES

The value of the prize used for comparing two events should not be affected by the occurrence of events.

For example, if your chosen gift were a new parka, you would value your prize more if it snowed on March 21 than if spring arrived. So that is not a suitable gift for thinking about events 1 and 2.

Likewise, "eternal bliss" is not a suitable gift for comparing the imaginary gamble involving (7) and (8). For if you think that (7) is very improbable, eternal life will not, for you, be a real possibility at all.

SECOND THOUGHT EXPERIMENT: USE FAIR COINS

So far we have been qualitative. We can use the same procedure to be quantitative.

Choose what you believe to be a fair coin. Think of the following gamble, assuming that the coin is tossed next March 21:

$10 if (1): Heavy snow falls in Toronto next March 21, or
$10 if (9): This fair coin falls heads when first tossed next March 21.

If you prefer option (1), then you must think it more likely that it will snow, than that the coin will fall heads. You assess the probability of snow on March 21 as greater than $\frac{1}{2}$.

Suppose you prefer (1). Then try the following imaginary gamble:

$10 if (1): Heavy snow falls in Toronto next March 21, or
$10 if (10): This fair coin falls heads at least once in the first two tosses made
    next March 21.

The probability of (10) is $\frac{3}{4}$. If you prefer (10) over (1), then your personal probability for (1) is between $\frac{1}{2}$ and $\frac{3}{4}$.

If you prefer (1) to (10), your personal probability for snow on March 21 is more than ¾.

If you are indifferent between (1) and (10), then your personal probability for snow in Toronto next March 21 is about ¾.

You can narrow down your range by choosing to compare to three coins thrown in a row. Or you can think of an urn with k green balls and $n - k$ red balls, to *calibrate* your beliefs as finely as you please.

Thus you can think of these experiments as using an artificial randomizer to calibrate your personal degrees of belief.

You can even explain when, in your personal opinion, a coin is fair. You are indifferent between betting on heads or tails, so long as the stakes and payoffs are the same.

REPRESENTING, NOT MEASURING

After the second thought experiment, we said that when people are indifferent between (1) and (10), then their personal probability is *"about 3/4"*? Can't we be exact?

No. Belief is not the sort of thing that can be measured exactly. This method can never determine your personal degrees of belief to very many places of decimals, but it can be as fine as makes any sense, for you. For example, suppose some people prefer

$10 if (11): This fair coin falls seven heads in a row on the first seven tosses made next March 21,

to

$10 if (12): Heavy snow falls in Columbia, South Carolina, next March 21.

But they prefer $10 if (12) to

$10 if (13): This fair coin falls eight heads in a row during the first eight tosses made next March 21.

Then we could calibrate their personal probability, p, of snow in Columbia next March 21:

$1/256 \leq p \leq 1/128$. Or $0.0039 \leq p \leq 0.0078$.

By this time we have lost any feel for the numbers. If we wanted to *represent* the personal probability by a number, we could say, perhaps, that the personal probability "is," say, 0.006. This is not because we have measured the person's degree of belief. It is because we might find it convenient to represent the person's degree of belief by a number.

BETTING

Our thought experiments never involve taking a risk. You will never lose, in any of these experiments. But now think of more risky situations. Imagine making bets, which you can win or lose.

You can imagine betting on almost anything, so long as you also imagine that the bet will be settled reasonably soon.

Imagine that you and I bet on an event or proposition A—any of the possibilities in (1) to (10) above will do.

Suppose we are betting for money (but any other utility will do).

Say you bet $X *on* A, and I bet $Y *against* A.

This means that if A occurs, or turns out to be true, you collect my $Y.

But if A does not occur, or turns out to be false, I collect your $X.

In such a bet, the sum of the two bets, $(X+Y), is called the **stake**.

BETTING RATES

Suppose that you and I are betting. You bet that it is going to snow on March 21. I bet with you that it is not going to snow. You bet $1 *on* snow. I bet $3 *against* snow.

If it snows, you win the whole $4, for a profit of $3. I lose $3.

If it does not snow, I get the $4, a gain of $1 for me, and a loss of $1 for you.

Under these conditions, your **betting rate** on snow is 1/4. My betting rate against snow is 3/4.

Your betting rate = (Your bet) ÷ (Stake)

PAYOFF

The easiest way to display a bet is in a table called a payoff matrix. This table shows payoffs when the stake is $S, and your betting rate is p.

You bet pS on A.
A person who bets against you bets $S(1-p) = (S-pS)$.

The left column lists the possible outcomes of the bet: A occurs, ~A occurs.

	Payoff for bet on A, given B	Payoff for bet against A, given B
A	$(1-p)S$	$-(1-p)S$
~A	$-pS$	pS

In the future, we will usually omit the dollar signs.

THIRD THOUGHT EXPERIMENT

Suppose that neither you nor your friend knows whether event E will occur. I offer the following deal, for nothing. You can have either.

Option (E): A chance of winning $(1-p)(\$10)$ if E occurs,

or

Option (~E): A chance of winning $p(\$10)$ if E does not occur.

Now you have to divide the cake—choose p. Your friend then chooses either option (E) or option (~E). If in your opinion p is a fair betting rate, then neither option has an advantage.

If, after choosing p, you think that option (E) is preferable to option (~E), then you should increase p.

This argument is just a generalization of our technique for calibrating personal probabilities.

FAIR BETTING RATES

In choosing between those two options, you did not take a risk. But the same argument will apply to anyone who bets. Suppose that the stake is $10. If p is, in your opinion, the fair rate for betting on E, then you should be indifferent between:

- A bet *on* E at rate p: you win $(1-p)(\$10)$ if E occurs, just as in option (E) above.
- A bet *against* E at rate $(1-p)$: you win $p(\$10)$ if E does not occur, just as in option (~E) above.

If you think that a betting rate of p is fair, you see no advantage in betting one way—on E at rate p—rather than the other—against E at rate $(1-p)$.

A quick way to say this:

> The fair rate for betting against E is the *reverse* of the fair rate for betting on E.

NOT REAL-LIFE BETTING

Bettors want to profit from their bets. They don't offer $1 to win $3 if E occurs, and also offer $3 to win $1 if E does not occur. They want an *edge*.

So if they think that ~E is three times as likely as E, they offer $1 to win *more* than $3 if E occurs. They want to win $(3+x)$, so their rate for betting *on* E is

$1/(1+3+x)$. This is because they think this gives them an advantage. They want the bet to be "unfair"—in their favor.

On the other hand, if they are betting against E, and they put up $3, they want to win *more* than $1. So they offer $3 to win $$(1+x)$ if E does not occur. So their rate for betting *against* E is $3/(1+3+x)$.

If you go to a bookmaker, and ask to bet on the next America's Cup challenge race for large yachts, you can get rates on:

   The Australian yacht will win the next America's Cup.
   The Australian yacht will not win the next America's Cup.

You can be sure that the two rates you are offered will not add up to 1!

FAIR MEANS NO EDGE

We are not going to the races. We are doing thought experiments, to find out how to represent our *own* degrees of belief. There is no "edge." A fair personal betting rate p is one where the person thinks there is no advantage in betting either way, at rate p on E, or rate $(1-p)$ against E.

ODDS

Gamblers don't talk about betting rates. They talk about the **odds** (against something happening).

You stake $1, hoping to make a profit of $3. Gamblers say the odds are 3 to 1 against your winning.

A betting rate is the ratio of your stake to the total amount staked, namely $1/4 = 1/(3+1)$. Thus if the odds against E are $y{:}x$, the betting rate on E is $x/(x+y)$.

Betting rates and odds are two ways to express the same basic idea. We use betting rates here because they look more like probabilities.

Moreover, gamblers just love to create a fantasy world of fancy talk. For example, betting on (American) football can use either point spreads (which use even odds) or money-line bets. In money-line bets you either "give" the odds or "take" the odds. If you are familiar with this talk, it is all very simple, but the rest of us just get confused. So we use exactly one idea, betting rates.

CONDITIONAL BETS

Betting rates correspond to personal probabilities. What about conditional probability? We need the idea of a *conditional bet*.

A conditional bet is a bet made on a condition, with all bets cancelled if the condition does not hold.

Examples:

A bet that the Toronto Maple Leafs will win the Stanley Cup, on the condition that they get into the final round.

A bet that it will snow in Toronto next March 21, on the condition that the temperature at the Toronto airport drops below 0°C that night.

A bet that you will go to Heaven, conditional on your following the practices of a certain religion.

A bet that within ten years there will be radical breakthroughs in the treatment of inheritable diseases, thanks to successes in the human genome project.

To stick to the weather, you bet $1, say, that it will snow conditional on a subzero temperature, and I bet $2 that it will not. The stake is $3.

If the temperature stays above zero, *the bet is off*. There is no winning or losing.

If the temperature drops below zero, *the bet is on*, and either you make a net gain of $2 (it snows) or I make a net gain of $1 (it doesn't).

CONDITIONAL BETTING RATES

Conditional betting rates are like ordinary betting rates.

Your betting rate on A, conditional on B, is:

(Your conditional bet) ÷ Stake.

In the above example:

Your conditional bet was $1.
My conditional bet was $2.

The stake was $3.

Your conditional betting rate was 1/3.
My conditional betting rate was 2/3.

To generalize:

If the stake is $S, and you bet **on** A conditional on B, at rate p, then you bet pS, and:

If B does not occur, the bet is off.
If B and A occur, you win $(1-p)S$.
If B occurs, but A does not occur, you lose pS.

Likewise, if you bet *against* A, conditional on B, when the betting rate on A given B is p, then you bet $(1-p)S$, and:

If B does not occur, the bet is off.
If B and A occur, you lose $(1-p)S$.
If B occurs but A does not occur, you gain pS.

THE CONDITIONAL PAYOFF MATRIX

Leaving out the dollar signs, here is a payoff matrix for conditional bets, when the betting rate on A given B is p, and when the total sum staked is S:

	Payoff for bet on A, given B	Payoff for bet against A, given B
A&B	$(1-p)S$	$-(1-p)S$
(~A)&B	$-pS$	pS
~B	0	0

THE ARGUMENT

The Bayesian program has three stages. This chapter has gone through the first stage. Chapters 14 and 15 will explain the second and third stages.

The first stage—this chapter—gets you to represent your personal degrees of belief by betting rates. It seems very simple.

The second stage—Chapter 14—has a rigorous argument.

At the third stage—Chapter 15—we seem to have a simple logical consequence of the first two stages.

In one sense, Chapter 15 is the hardest chapter, because it has a quite precise argument. But in another sense, the present chapter is the hardest one. This is because all the steps are merely plausible steps, quite slippery. You may have the feeling that the whole thing is a confidence trick! So we should say that what really makes the argument interesting is that there are many different versions of it, many more subtle than anything in this book, and all leading to the same conclusions.

EXERCISES

1 *Nuclear power.* You are offered the following gamble that costs you nothing: $100 if
   (a) Energy from commercial nuclear fusion becomes available towards the end of the twenty-first century.
   Or
      $100 if a coin of probability p of heads falls heads on the next toss.
   Could you realistically use this gamble to calibrate personal probabilities for (a)? Could you use a similar gamble to calibrate for (b)? $100 if
   (b) Nuclear energy is abandoned in North America within two years.

2 *Chocoholic.* Alice loves chocolate, and for her, a box of fine chocolates is a great gift. She is sitting in her doctor's waiting room. Could she realistically use this prize to calibrate her beliefs in these possibilities?
   (a) She will be told by her physician to enter a weight-loss program immediately.

(b) She will be told by her physician that she can eat anything she wants, her metabolism can handle it.

3 *Intelligent aliens.* In the summer of 1996, after the announced discovery of evidence for "life" on a Martian meteorite, a large betting company named Ladbroke's "cut the odds on finding intelligent alien life within the next year from 250-to-1 to 50-to-1. For bettors to collect, the United Nations must confirm the existence of alien life forms capable of communication with Earth."

(a) Would a bet with these conditions satisfy the "settle-soon" requirement?

(b) Odds of 50-to-1 on intelligent alien life being confirmed within a year is the same as a betting rate of $\frac{1}{51}$: you give Ladbroke's \$1 and they will pay you back \$51 (net profit of \$50) if you win. Suppose that Ladbroke's allows you to bet the other way at the same odds: you can bet \$50 that intelligent alien life will not be confirmed, for a net profit of \$1 if you win. No one except a true alien-freak believes that it is at all likely that the UN will certify intelligent alien life within twelve months. Many would agree with skeptical Skuli and say that their personal betting rate could be as much as $\frac{999}{1,000}$ that the UN will not confirm intelligent alien life. Skuli says he would be willing to bet \$999 to win \$1 right now, if the payoff were immediate. Explain why Skuli, being a rational man, does not bet a mere \$50 to win \$1.

4 *Bets.* I bet \$9 that you will get an A in this course. You bet the opposite way. The stake is \$12. How much did you bet? What is your betting rate *against* getting an A?

5 *Raising the ante.* Now suppose the total stake, with the same betting rates, is \$100. You bet against your getting an A. What is your "payoff," if you do get an A?

6 *Fair bet.* If you consider 1/4 as the fair rate for betting that you get an A, what would you consider the fair rate for betting against your getting an A?

7 *Make-up tests.* In a large class with frequent tests, you are allowed to do a "make-up" if you missed a test because of illness.

You hear through the grapevine that make-up tests are harder than the original tests.

What might be your own personal betting rate that you will get at least a B on the next test?

What might be your betting rate conditional on your being sick and taking a make-up examination?

Draw a payoff matrix for the conditional bet, if the stake is \$10.

8 *"Not" reverses preferences.* We argued that if your fair personal betting rate for betting on E is p, then your rate for betting on ~E should be $1-p$. In general, you "reverse" your bet when you turn from E to ~E. Here are a few exercises to fix this idea. Let (1) and (2) be any events (or propositions). Suppose that you prefer

$10 if (1) occurs, over
$10 if (2) occurs.

Would you prefer

$10 if (1) does not occur, over
$10 if (2) does not occur?

KEY WORDS FOR REVIEW

Thought experiments
Degrees of belief
Stake
Representing by numbers

Betting rate
Conditional bets
Conditional betting rate
"Fair" betting rate

14 Coherence

> Consistent personal betting rates satisfy the basic rules of probability.
> Consistency in this sense is called coherence.

Personal probabilities and betting rates are all very well. But thus far they have no structure, no rules—in fact, not much meaning. Now we give one argument that betting rates ought to satisfy the basic rules for probability. We have already had three thought experiments in Chapter 13. Here are two more.

FOURTH THOUGHT EXPERIMENT: SETS OF BETTING RATES

A group of beliefs can be represented by a set of betting rates.

> Imagine yourself *advertising* a set of betting rates. For each of the propositions A, B, . . . K in the set, you offer betting rates $p_a, p_b, p_c, . . . , p_k$.

In this imaginary game, you are prepared to bet, say,

on A at rate p_a, or
against A at rate $(1-p_a)$.

FIFTH THOUGHT EXPERIMENT: SIMPLE INCONSISTENCY

These are *personal* betting rates. Couldn't you choose any fractions you like?

Of course. But you might be inconsistent.

For example, suppose you are concerned with just two possibilities, B (for "below zero") and ~B:

B: On the night of next March 21, the temperature will fall below 0°C at the Toronto International Airport meteorological station.

~B: On the night of next March 21, the temperature will not fall below 0°C at the Toronto International Airport meteorological station.

You go through a thought experiment. You feel gloomy. B makes you think of winter. Will winter never end? You think it is more likely than not to be cold. You advertise a betting rate:

(1) Your betting rate on B: 5/8.

You go through another thought experiment. Thinking about ~B cheers you up. Can spring be far behind? You advertise a betting rate:

(2) Your betting rate on ~B: 3/4. Hence your betting rate **against** ~B is (1 − 3/ 4) = 1/4. But that is the same as a betting rate on B of 1/4.

These two assessments are not consistent.
    Now we generalize this idea of inconsistent betting rates.

SURE-LOSS CONTRACTS

A *betting contract* is a contract to settle a bet or a group of bets at certain agreed betting rates.
    A *bookmaker* is someone who makes betting contracts. He pays you your prize if you win the bet. He takes your money if you lose the bet.

> A clever bookmaker named *Sly* sees your advertised betting rates (1) and (2) about the weather. He offers you a contract at your rates. That's fair! But **he** chooses which way to bet. That's fair too! But your rates are bad news for you.
>   "You bet $5 **on** B, at your advertised odds (1)," says *Sly*.
>   So you stake $5. *Sly* stakes $3. You win $3 if it is below zero on March 21. Otherwise you lose $5.
>   "And you bet $6 **on** ~B, at your advertised odds (2)," says *Sly*. So you stake $6. He stakes $2. You win $2 if it is not below zero on March 21. Otherwise you lose $6.

You are in trouble. Look at the table. Your gains and losses are marked plus and minus:

	Bet on B	Bet against B	Payoff
Below zero	+$3	−$6	−$3
Not below zero	−$5	+$2	−$3

You will lose $3 no matter what happens next March 21!
    This is a *sure-loss contract*.

A **sure-loss contract**, for a person X, is a contract with X, at X's betting rates, so that X will lose no matter what happens.

It would be foolish to advertise betting rates open to a sure-loss contract. It is a logical mistake. Your betting rates are not internally consistent. Because the word "inconsistency" has a standard sense in deductive logic, this kind of error in inductive logic is called **incoherence**.

A set of betting rates is **coherent** if and only if it is not open to a sure-loss contract.

We will soon establish a remarkable fact:

A set of betting rates is coherent
if and only if
it satisfies the basic rules of probability.

A THREE-STEP ARGUMENT

1   Personal degrees of belief can be represented by betting rates. (See Chapter 13.)
2   Personal betting rates should be coherent.
3   A set of betting rates is coherent if and only if it satisfies the basic rules of probability.

Therefore:

Personal degrees of belief should satisfy the basic rules of probability.

Now we check this out for each basic rule.

NORMALITY

We require that $0 \leq$ (betting rate on A) ≤ 1.

   This holds because betting rates are defined as fractions between 0 and 1.

CERTAINTY

We require that $\Pr(\Omega) = 1$. That means that the probability of something certain should be 1.

Imagine that A is certainly true, or bound to occur, but that your betting rate on A is $p < 1$. Then *Sly* will ask you to bet against A at rate $1-p$. If the stake is $1, you lose $(1-p)$.

ADDITIVITY

Remember that the additivity rule applies to mutually exclusive events. Let A and B be mutually exclusive. Additivity requires that:

Betting rate on AvB = betting rate on A + betting rate on B.

Suppose that a certain person, *Hilary*, offers betting rates that do not satisfy the rule. Let *Hilary* advertise these betting rates.

> On A: p.
> On B: q.
> On AvB: r.

Suppose that, for example, $r < p+q$, so that the additivity rule is violated.

Sly asks *Hilary* to make three bets at the advertised rates. His trick is to arrange the contracts so that they actually involve *Hilary*'s betting rates. The stake in each of these bets will be $1.

> *Bet (i)*. Bet p on A to win $(1-p)$ if A is true. *Hilary* loses p if A is not true.
> *Bet (ii)*. Bet q on B to win $(1-q)$ if B is true. *Hilary* loses q if B is not true.
> *Bet (iii)*. Bet $(1-r)$ **against** AvB, to win r if (AvB) is false—if neither A nor B is true. But if one or the other is true, then *Hilary* loses $(1-r)$.

These are "unit" bets. To make them more realistic, make the stake, say, $100, so that if, for example, $p = 0.3$, *Hilary* puts up $30 to win $70.

Note that since A and B are mutually exclusive, one or the other might be true, but both cannot be true together. Here is *Hilary*'s payoff table, omitting dollar signs:

	Payoff on (i)	Payoff on (ii)	Payoff on (iii)	Payoff
A&(~B)	$1-p$	$-q$	$-(1-r)$	$r-p-q$
(~A)&B	$-p$	$1-q$	$-(1-r)$	$r-p-q$
(~A)&(~B)	$-p$	$-q$	r	$r-p-q$

If $r < p+q$, $r-(p+q)$ is negative. So *Hilary* loses $[r-(p+q)]$ no matter what happens.

If $r > p+q$, *Sly* asks *Hilary* to bet at the same advertised rates, but the opposite way. *Hilary* is asked to bet $1-p$ against A, $1-q$ against B, and r on AvB at these rates. His profit—*Hilary's* loss—will be $\$[r-(p+q)]$ no matter what happens.

Therefore, coherent betting rates must be additive. We can also use the above table to point out that if they are additive—if $r = p+q$—then there is no way to make sure-loss contracts involving A, B, and AvB.

We have now checked the rules for normality, certainty, and additivity.

> A necessary and sufficient condition that a set of betting rates is coherent is that it satisfies the basic rules of probability.

CONDITIONAL SURE-LOSS CONTRACTS

What about *conditional* bets?

A bet on A, conditional on B, is cancelled when B does not occur. Hence one cannot have a guaranteed sure-loss contract for conditional bets. If B does not occur, no one will win or lose anything.

Instead we can have a *conditional sure-loss contract*. A contract is sure-loss, on condition B, if and only if you are bound to lose whenever B occurs.

We extend the idea of coherence. A set of betting rates is *coherent conditional on B* if and only if it is not open to a conditional sure-loss contract.

CONDITIONAL COHERENCE

We now need to show that conditional bets avoid conditional sure-loss contracts if and only if they satisfy the basic rules, and the definition of conditional probability. That is, we require that when a betting rate on B is not zero:

> Rate for betting A, conditional on B = [betting rate on A&B] ÷ [betting rate on B].

This is not quite so easy as for the first three basic rules. Suppose that Hilary advertises the following betting rates:

On A&B: q.
On B: $r > 0$.
On A conditional on B: p.

Here bookmaker *Sly* does not choose the total sum staked to be $1, but instead uses a function of the betting rates themselves.

Sly asks *Hilary* to make three bets, using her advertised betting rates:

(i) Bet $\$qr$ on A&B [to win $\$(1-q)r$]. The stake is $\$r$.
(ii) Bet $\$(1-r)q$ against B [to win $\$rq$]. The stake is $\$q$.
(iii) Bet $\$(1-p)r$ against A, conditional on B [to win $\$pr$]. The stake is $\$r$, as in (i).

Hilary's payoff table is:

	Payoff on (i)	Payoff on (ii)	Payoff on (iii)	Payoff
A&B	$(1-q)r$	$-(1-r)q$	$-(1-p)r$	$pr-q$
$(\sim\!A)\&B$	$-qr$	$-(1-r)q$	pr	$pr-q$
$\sim\!B$	$-qr$	rq	0	0

Hence, if $p < q/r$, *Hilary* is guaranteed a loss.

For example, suppose that Hilary's betting rates are:

On A&B: 0.6.
On B: 0.8.
On A conditional on B: 0.5.

Sly asks Hilary to:

(i) Bet $48 *on* A&B to win $32 if A&B occurs.
(ii) Bet $12 *against* B, to win $48 if B does not occur.
(iii) Bet $40 *against* A, conditional on B, to win $40 if B occurs, but A does not occur.

If both A and B occur, *Hilary* loses $20
If B occurs but A does not, *Hilary* loses $20.
If B does not occur, the conditional bet is cancelled, and *Hilary* wins and loses $48 on the other two bets, for a net payoff of 0.

On the other hand, if $p > q/r$, bookmaker *Sly* asks *Hilary* to take the other side of all these bets (so that the table above is the table for *his* payoffs), and he makes a profit whatever happens.

When betting rates follow the definition of conditional probability ($p = q/r$), it is impossible to make a conditional sure-loss contract.

A necessary and sufficient condition that a set of betting rates, including conditional betting rates, should be coherent is that they should satisfy the basic rules of probability.

FRANK RAMSEY AND BRUNO DE FINETTI

The first systematic theory of personal probability was presented in 1926 by F. P. Ramsey (page 144), in a talk he gave to a philosophy club in Cambridge, England. He mentioned that if your betting rates don't satisfy the basic rules of probability, then you are open to a sure-loss contract. But he had a much more profound—and difficult—argument that personal degrees of belief should satisfy the probability rules. Where we have throughout this book taken the idea of utility for granted, Ramsey's approach developed the ideas of probability and utility in an interdependent way. Moreover, he allowed for the declining marginal utility of money in his definition.

In 1930, another young man, the Italian mathematician Bruno de Finetti (see page 144), independently pioneered the theory of personal probability. He invented the word "coherence," and did make considerable use of the sure-loss argument.

When Ramsey referred to the argument in passing, he called a sure-loss contract a *Dutch Book*. A "book" is a betting contract made by a bookmaker. But why "Dutch"? I think this was some English undergraduate betting slang of the day, but I don't know. Two Dutch students of mine once tried to find out the source of this ethnic slur, but failed. Nevertheless, the name "Dutch Book" is now standard in inductive logic. We prefer to speak of a *sure-loss contract*.

EXERCISES

1   *Diogenes* is a cynic. He thinks the Maple Leafs will come in last in their league next year. His betting rate that they will come in last (proposition B) is 0.9. His betting rate that they will not come in last (proposition ~B) is 0.2. Make a sure-loss contract against Diogenes.

2   *Epicurus* is an optimist. He thinks the Leafs will come in first in their league next year (T). His betting rate on T is 0.7. His betting rate on ~T is 0.2. Make a sure-loss contract against Epicurus.

3   *Optimistic Cinderella* is at a dance. She has been told that her Cadillac will turn into a pumpkin if she stays at the dance after midnight, but she doubts if that is true. She decides that she will stay at the dance if and only if, when she rolls a fair die at 11.59 P.M., it falls 3 or 4 uppermost.

    She is, then, concerned with these possibilities:

        S: She stays at the dance.
        P: Her Cadillac turns into a pumpkin.

    Her personal beliefs, represented as betting rates, are as follows:

        On P&S: 0.2
        On S: 1/3
        On P, conditional on S: 1/2

    likeMake a conditional sure-loss contract against Cinderella, with a guaranteed profit for you of $1.

4   *Pessimistic Cinderella.*   Same as (3), but where her personal betting rate on P&S is 0.1.

5   *A mysterious gift.* A distant relative tells you she is going to give you a gift. You hope it is cash—in fact, you hope it is at least $100. The possibilities that interest you are:

        C: She gives you a cash gift.   H: The gift is cash of at least $100.

Your personal degrees of belief, represented by betting rates, are:

> Betting rate on C&H: .3.
> Betting rate on C: .8.
> Betting rate on H, given C: .5.

Show how a sly bookmaker could arrange a sure-loss contract, where you lose $100 for sure (you'll need that gift from your relative!).

KEY WORDS FOR REVIEW

Sure-loss contract　　Conditional sure-loss
Coherence　　Conditional coherence

15 Learning from Experience

Bayes' Rule is central for applications of personal probability. It offers a way to represent rational change in belief, in the light of new evidence.

BAYES' RULE

Bayes' Rule is of very little interest when you are thinking about frequency-type probabilities. It is just a rule. On page 70 we derived it in a few lines from the definition of conditional probability.

For many problems—shock absorbers, tarantulas, children with toxic metals poisoning, taxicabs—it shortens some calculations. That's all.

But Bayes' Rule really does matter to personal probability, or to any other belief-type probability.

Today, belief-type probability approaches are often called "Bayesian." If you hear a statistician talking about a Bayesian analysis of a problem, it means some version of ideas that we discuss in this chapter. But there are many versions, ranging from personal to logical. An independent-minded Bayesian named I. J. Good (see page 184) figured out that, in theory, there are 46,656 ways to be a Bayesian!

HYPOTHESES

"Hypothesis" is a fancy word, but daily life is full of hypotheses. Most decisions depend upon comparing the evidence for different hypotheses.

Should Albert quit this course? The drop date is tomorrow. He is a marginal student and has done poorly so far. Will the course get harder, as courses often do? (Hypothesis 1) Or will it stay at its present level, where he can pass the course? (Hypothesis 2)

Should I park illegally? Refer to page 103. What were the hypotheses there? What were the probabilities?

Should we invest in nuclear power or in better scrubbers for coal fired power plants? What are the hypotheses? This is more complicated, for you now have to think about what hypotheses are in question. Can you produce hypotheses and probabilities for them?

Should Louise study for a pharmacy degree? On the one hand, she likes that sort of work, is good at biochemistry, and her uncle is a successful pharmacist with his own store. On the other hand, there have been a lot of recent graduates, and the field may be glutted. What are the hypotheses? Can you formulate hypotheses and corresponding probabilities?

Often you can't state the hypotheses, but the more clearly you can state them, the more clearly you can reason about them. One way to think about hypotheses is to ask how probable you think that each of them is. Sometimes you can even use numbers to represent your personal probabilities.

NEW EVIDENCE

When you think about your personal probability for a hypothesis, you do so relative to your background knowledge, beliefs, prejudices, and so on.

But you don't stop there. We learn new things all the time. Unless you are truly prejudiced, new evidence should have some effect on what you believe— and on your personal probabilities.

We can see this in all the examples just given. Albert may be told that whenever the present instructor teaches the course, it gets harder toward the end.

You learn that the parking inspector patrolled the street last night, and almost never comes two nights in a row.

Researchers who work in environmental studies and energy, and are concerned with nuclear power versus coal, get new information every day. They have to process that into their probabilities.

Louise was thinking of taking a pharmacy degree. She learns that with budget cuts there will be less public money for medication, and that doctors will be penalized for prescribing too many expensive drugs. So sales may go down, and the business may contract.

Judgments of probability may have to be revised or updated any minute of the day. Are there any rules about how to do that? Bayesians say *yes*.

THE BAYESIAN IDEA

Recall Bayes' Rule. It applies to a set of mutually exclusive and exhaustive hypotheses (H_i). Such a set of mutually exclusive and exhaustive hypotheses is called a **partition**.

For any H_j in a partition ($H_1, H_2, \ldots, H_n$), Bayes' Rule states that:

$$\Pr(H_j/E) = \frac{\Pr(H_j)\Pr(E/H_j)}{\Sigma[\Pr(H_i)\Pr(E/H_i)]}.$$

The *Bayesian* idea is that we think of E as new evidence, and the H_i as competing hypotheses. Then it appears that for any H_j,

> $Pr(H_j)$ is our initial probability, before we get new evidence,
> E is new evidence, and
> $Pr(H_j/E)$ should be our personal probability in the light of this new evidence.

This is an idea about *learning from experience*. Now we see why coherence is so important. Our argument is:

(1) Personal probabilities should be coherent.
(2) Coherent personal probabilities satisfy the basic rules of probability.
(3) Hence they satisfy Bayes' Rule.
(4) So they enable us to represent learning from experience.

PRIOR PROBABILITY

In each of our examples, from lazy Albert thinking of dropping the course to energetic Louise thinking about pharmacy, there are some competing hypotheses. Suppose you think about them clearly, and arrange them so that they are mutually exclusive and exhaustive, relative to your present background knowledge and beliefs. Call them:

$H_1, H_2, \ldots, H_n$.

Now suppose you represent your present degrees of belief about these hypotheses by personal probabilities. These are called your *prior* probabilities—probabilities based on an initial consideration of the hypotheses and the information at hand. Any probabilities you offered in answer to the earlier questions would be examples of prior probabilities.

So suppose you have prior personal probabilities:

$Pr(H_1), Pr(H_2), \ldots, Pr(H_n)$.

EXAMPLE: SHOCK ABSORBERS (1)

Here is a repeat of an example from page 52. An automobile plant contracted to buy shock absorbers from two local suppliers, Bolt & Co. and Acme Inc. Bolt supplies 40% and Acme 60%. All shocks are subject to quality control. The ones that pass are called reliable.

Of Acme's shocks, 96% test reliable. But Bolt has been having some problems on the line, and recently only 72% of Bolt's shock absorbers have tested reliable.

A delivery of shocks arrives on a truck. We want to know which company it comes from. The hypotheses are:

$H_1 = A = $ The delivery comes from Acme.
$H_2 = B = $ The delivery comes from Bolt.

The prior probabilities are:

$$Pr(H_1) = Pr(A) = 0.6. \qquad Pr(H_2) = Pr(B) = 0.4.$$

LIKELIHOOD

You have some prior probabilities. Then you learn something new, a new item of evidence E. You want to revise your degrees of belief to take account of E. How should you do it?

Suppose you can consider how likely E would have been, *if* the various competing hypotheses were in fact correct.

That is, you can assess your personal conditional probabilities:

$$Pr(E/H_1), Pr(E/H_2), \ldots, Pr(E/H_n).$$

These quantities are very important. It is handy to have a name for them. R. A. Fisher (page 225), perhaps the most innovative statistician of the twentieth century, chose a name for them. Unfortunately his name is **very confusing**.

He called these quantities the **likelihoods** of the hypotheses $H_1, H_2, \ldots, H_n$, in the light of the evidence E.

The function that gives the likelihoods, for some given set of hypotheses, is called the **likelihood function**.

This is very confusing because in ordinary English, "probability" and "likelihood" in many contexts are synonyms. They mean almost the same thing, in a great many conversations. And now Fisher chooses to use "likelihood" in a technical way where it does not mean exactly the same thing as "probability."

Any individual likelihood such as $Pr(E/H_1)$ is, of course, just a probability. But notice that a set of probabilities for a partition into hypotheses does *not* obey the additivity rule. The likelihoods across a partition do *not* add up to form a new likelihood. But the probabilities of elements of a proposition do add up. So a set of likelihoods, for a partition, is not a set of the probabilities of the members of the partition. Let's take an example of this confusing use of the word "likelihood."

SHOCK ABSORBERS (2)

Evidence: A shock absorber is selected at random from the delivery, and it is found to be reliable on test. On page 52 we called this new evidence R, for reliable.

$$Pr(E/H_1) = Pr(R/A) = 0.96$$
$$Pr(E/H_2) = Pr(R/B) = 0.72$$

These are the likelihoods of the two hypotheses in the light of the evidence E. These likelihoods add up to 1.68. They do *not* add up to 1. (1.68 does not signify anything at all.)

Given some evidence, a set of likelihoods for a partition is well defined. But it is *not* a set of probabilities for the hypotheses in the partition, relative to the evidence.

Why use this confusing terminology? Because it has become absolutely fixed for all statisticians, ever since Fisher introduced it three-quarters of a century ago.

POSTERIOR PROBABILITY

You want to revise your prior probabilities in the light of the new evidence. The revised probabilities are called **posterior probabilities**. *Prior* means before—before the new evidence. *Posterior* means after—after the new evidence. The posterior probabilities for a partition are:

$$\Pr(H_1/E), \Pr(H_2/E), \dots, \Pr(H_n/E).$$

Bayes' Rule now connects posterior probabilities, prior probabilities, and likelihoods:

$$\Pr(H_j/E) = \frac{\Pr(H_j)\Pr(E/H_j)}{\Sigma[\Pr(H_i)\Pr(E/H_i)]}.$$

SHOCK ABSORBERS (3)

The posterior probabilities are:

$$\Pr(H_1/E) = \Pr(A/R). \qquad \Pr(H_2/E) = \Pr(B/R).$$

Applying Bayes' Rule, we calculate the posterior probabilities that the delivery came from Acme, or Bolt:

$$\Pr(H_1/E) = \Pr(A/R) = 2/3. \qquad \Pr(H_2/E) = \Pr(B/R) = 1/3.$$

SUMMARY FORM OF BAYES' RULE

Look back at Bayes' Rule. The denominator is:

$$\Sigma[\Pr(H_i)\Pr(E/H_i)].$$

This is a constant, determined by the partition. In fact, it is just $\Pr(E)$. Hence, for every H_j,

$$\Pr(H_j/E) \text{ is proportional to } \Pr(H_j) \times \Pr(E/H_j).$$

Or, using "$\propto$" as short for "is proportional to":

Posterior probability $\propto$ prior probability $\times$ likelihood.

REPEATED APPLICATION OF BAYES' RULE

We start with prior probabilities defined over a partition of hypotheses.

Then we get some new evidence E. We use Bayes' Rule, and derive posterior probabilities. We take these as our new personal probabilities for the partition.

Next we get some more evidence F. We can use our new personal probabilities as priors in Bayes' Rule, and compute a second set of posterior probabilities.

In summary form, this amounts to:

First posterior of H ∝ [(prior of H) × (likelihood of H in the light of E)].

Second posterior of H ∝ [(first posterior of H) × (likelihood of H&E in light of F)].

Thus let there be a partition into *n* hypotheses, $(H_1, H_2, \ldots, H_n)$.

We start with the prior probabilities $\Pr(H_j)$.

When we learn of new evidence E, we become interested in the first posterior probabilities $\Pr(H_j/E)$. These can be computed by Bayes' Rule.

When we get further evidence F, we become interested in the second posterior probabilities $\Pr(H_j/E\&F)$. We can use Bayes' Rule to compute these, in effect taking the first posterior probabilities as prior probabilities relative to the new evidence F. We obtain a conditional form of Bayes' Rule.

$$\Pr(H_j/E\&F) = \frac{\Pr(H_j/E)\Pr(F/H_j\&E)}{\sum[\Pr(H_i/E)\Pr(F/H_i\&E)]}$$

SHOCK ABSORBERS (4)

We tested one shock absorber taken from the delivery. It tested reliable. That was evidence E. Now we take a second shock absorber at random, and test it. It is *not* reliable. This is new evidence F.

Since our samples are taken at random, and the outcomes are independent,

$$\Pr(F/A\&E) = \Pr(-R/A) = 0.04. \qquad \Pr(F/B\&E) = \Pr(-R/B) = 0.28.$$

Our personal probabilities, given E, were found to be:

$$\Pr(A/E) = 2/3. \qquad \Pr(B/E) = 1/3.$$

Applying Bayes' Rule:

$$\Pr(A/E\&F) = \frac{\Pr(A/E)\Pr(F/A\&E)}{\Pr(A/E)\Pr(F/A\&E) + \Pr(B/E)\Pr(F/B\&E)}.$$

So that $\Pr(A/E\&F) = 2/9$.

SHOCK ABSORBERS (5)

Does it matter what order the evidence comes in? Would it matter if our first shock absorber was not reliable, while our second one was? Not according to Bayes' Rule.

If we first found F, a randomly selected shock absorber was not reliable, we would calculate:

$Pr(A/F) = 3/17.$ $Pr(B/F) = 14/17.$

And then, using Bayes' Rule again,

$Pr(A/E\&F) = 2/9.$

REVERSING THE ORDER

This illustrates a general, and very tidy, fact about Bayes' Rule. The order in which you obtain a series of pieces of evidence makes no difference to the final posterior probability.

EXAMPLE: APPENDICITIS

In the shock absorber example, the prior probabilities and likelihoods were given by objective frequency-style facts about the two companies that deliver shock absorbers. Anyone told exactly the information given in the text would draw the same conclusions. Now we move to more personal probabilities.

We're going to ask about the probability that a person has appendicitis.

Stage 1: A Primitive Prior

From a large urban population I picked an identifying name at random from a telephone directory. I first picked a phone book and then a last name, it was "Waukey." That name is completely strange to me; I did not even know there was such a name. I telephoned the number; a person whose voice sounded young and male answered and said his name is Richard Waukey. So now I know virtually nothing about this person, except that he is probably young, male, lives in a certain region, and answers the telephone (possibly lying about his name).

What is the probability that Richard has appendicitis right now? If I had to pick a probability right now, I'd pick something really small, say 8 parts in a million. Let A be the event that Richard has appendicitis. I might offer some fairly arbitrary—but not entirely arbitrary—small number to represent my opinion:

$Pr(A) = 0.000008.$

Stage 2: More Useful Prior

I put down that very small number because appendicitis is not at all common now among adults, that is, the majority of people listed in phone books. But now I learn a piece of evidence E: Richard is fourteen years old. I am told that in this region, only about six boys per hundred thousand have appendicitis at any one time. Now I can make a significant judgment:

$Pr(A/E) = 0.00006.$

Stage 3: A Likelihood

I learn that Richard has spells of shivering, feels out of sorts and irritable, has a bit of a headache, and vomited after his last meal. Call these symptoms V for vomiting. A large proportion of those who have appendicitis exhibit these symptoms, and I judge the likelihood of vomiting, given appendicitis and the background information, to be:

$Pr(V/A\&E) = 0.8.$

Stage 4: A Partition

But could the boy have something else wrong with him? I think of two other hypotheses.
H: Richard is basically healthy. It is just one of those things, something he ate.
F: He has food poisoning.
Assume, for simplicity, that these are the only three hypotheses in the cards.

I judge that: $Pr(F/E) = 0.00009.$
So $Pr(H/E) = 1 - 0.00009 - 0.00006 = 0.99985.$

Stage 5: More Likelihoods

I judge that Richard's symptoms are slightly more characteristic of food poisoning than of appendicitis. On the other hand, reasonably healthy boys are unlikely to be vomiting today. So I personally judge that:

$Pr(V/F\&E) = 0.9.$
$Pr(V/H\&E) = 0.00001.$

Stage 6: The Illness Develops

The discomfort progresses rapidly. The boy complains of severe pain in his abdomen just above the right of his groin. To keep pressure off this tender area he lies with his right thigh slightly bent. There is a feeling of resistance when the sore area is touched with a finger. Now these symptoms do not always occur in appendicitis when there is vomiting, but they are much less common when there is food poisoning and vomiting, and almost unknown in reasonably healthy boys with serious indigestion. Letting P stand for these detailed symptoms of pain, I assess the likelihoods as follows:

$Pr(P/A\&V\&E) = 0.6.$
$Pr(P/F\&V\&E) = 0.02.$
$Pr(P/H\&V\&E) = 0.00001.$

SUMMING UP THE AVAILABLE INFORMATION

Intuitively at stage 1 you'd say that there is no probability that Richard has appendicitis.

Maybe at stage 2 there is a minute probability, but this is still pretty negligible.

By stage 4 there is a real probability, but you can't tell that this is not food poisoning. Performing an appendectomy on someone with food poisoning, and not appendicitis, is *very* bad: malpractice! But serious appendicitis with no operation is also bad.

Thus by stage 5 you have a serious dilemma. Finally, at stage 6, you would be pretty confident that Richard has appendicitis.

How confident? Bayes' Rule allows for a calculation.

USING BAYES' RULE TO STAGE 4

We require $Pr(A/V\&E)$.

$Pr(A/V\&E) = [Pr(A/E) \times Pr(V/A\&E)] \div K$
where K, the constant of proportionality, is
$[Pr(A/E) \times Pr(V/A\&E)] + [Pr(F/E) \times Pr(V/F\&E)] + [Pr(H/E) \times Pr(V/H\&E)]$

We have the numbers to insert in this formula. We obtain that:

$Pr(A/V\&E) \approx 48/139 \approx 0.35.$
$Pr(F/V\&E) \approx 81/139 \approx 0.58.$
$Pr(H/V\&E) \approx 10/139 \approx 0.07.$

What have we learned from our new piece of evidence, that the boy is vomiting? First, we've learned that he is sick. The prior probability of his being "healthy"— at least having neither food poisoning nor appendicitis—was essentially 1. Now it has dropped to 7%.

This may seem a little high. Surely if he is vomiting then there *must* be something seriously wrong with him?

No. This high figure comes from the *base rates*: neither food poisoning nor appendicitis are common in our region. Stomach upsets are common. Good health is so common, in this population of teenage boys, that the symptom might well have arisen from eating too much cherry pie, for example.

The 7% is an example of how Bayes' Rule keeps you honest. Many of us would jump to the unqualified conclusion: Richard Waukey is sick! Not according to our prior assessment of probabilities and likelihoods.

What about food poisoning versus appendicitis? The posterior probability of food poisoning has increased, relative to appendicitis. But not by very much. The physician cannot make a confident diagnosis yet.

USING BAYES' RULE TO STAGE 5

Learning is (ideally) a cumulative process. You learn something and build on that. Now you can always replace Bayes' Rule by direct calculation from first principles, from the basic rules of probability. But once I have worked out the posterior probability at stage 5, and start to analyze a new piece of information—the pain—I can use the posterior probability at stage 5 as my prior probability at stage 6:

$$\Pr(A/P\&V\&E) = \Pr(A/V\&E) \times \Pr(P/A\&V\&E) \div K^*.$$

The constant of proportionality K^* is:

$$[\Pr(A/V\&E) \times \Pr(P/A\&V\&E)] + [\Pr(F/V\&E) \times \Pr(P/F\&V\&E)]$$
$$+ [\Pr(H/V\&E) \times \Pr(P/H\&V\&E)].$$

Inserting the numbers, we obtain roughly:

$$\Pr(A/P\&V\&E) \approx 160/169 \approx 0.947.$$
$$\Pr(F/P\&V\&E) \approx 9/169 \approx 0.053.$$
$$\Pr(H/P\&V\&E) \text{ is negligible.}$$

The new information about specific abdominal pain has swamped the rates. I am virtually certain that he has something worse than indigestion. And in my considered opinion, it is extremely probable—although not completely certain—that Richard Waukey has appendicitis.

DO NOT STOP THINKING!

There are now diagnostic computer programs that in effect employ Bayes' Rule. It has been found that when a program and a physician disagree, then given the same or similar data about a patient, other doctors, reviewing the case, more often agree with the program than with the first physician. *But do not use mechanical calculations as an excuse not to think!*

Coherence is a type of inductive consistency. After reaching stage 6, a physician can review her judgments of personal probability and likelihood. All that Bayes' Rule can do is ensure that the whole system of degrees of belief is consistent. After reaching stage 6, a prudent physician may think, "You know, perhaps I underestimated the probability of Richard having this kind of pain as a result of food poisoning. I'd better think this out again." She may revise some of the earlier probabilities and likelihoods, and come to a different posterior probability at stage 6.

LIKELIHOOD RATIOS

What does evidence really tell you? Bayes' Rule suggests an answer to people who can represent their degrees of belief by coherent personal probabilities. Different people have different prior probabilities. But given new evidence E, they all update their probabilities in the same way—multiplying by the likelihoods. An hypothesis with a larger relative likelihood, in the light of E, moves up, in everyone's scale of beliefs, while a hypothesis with a lower relative likelihood moves down. The *ratios* among the likelihoods determine how a piece of new evidence affects beliefs.

This is one reason that Fisher thought the likelihoods of hypotheses, relative to some evidence, are so important. What a pity he chose such a confusing name for such an important idea!

Another reason they are important is that people tend to agree on the relative likelihoods of hypotheses, in the light of some evidence, far more readily than they agree on the probabilities.

The example of appendicitis diagnosis illustrates the value of likelihood ratios. We wrote down the likelihoods at each stage in our examination of Richard Waukey. Once the relative likelihoods were given, the subsequent stages of the calculation were mechanical.

In general, here is what happens when we use Bayes' Rule:

■ We start with prior probabilities.
■ We obtain new evidence and become interested in some posterior probabilities.
■ We obtain these by (as the summary form of Bayes' Rule shows us) *multiplying by the likelihoods*.

The likelihood ratios convey all the information (relevant to the hypotheses under consideration) which is given by the new evidence.

> From the Bayesian point of view the likelihood ratios between competing hypotheses sum up the evidential meaning of new information.

A mathematician would express this idea in terms of the *likelihood function*. The likelihood function for a given piece of evidence E is the function that computes the likelihoods of the hypotheses in the light of E.

A MODEL OF LEARNING?

Some philosophers say: your personal probability that Richard has appendicitis, after you have found out that he is fourteen years old, has been vomiting, and has pain as described, ought now to be 94.5%. Thus we have shown exactly how you ought to process new information. Moreover, the relative likelihoods of competing hypotheses are a good indicator of the significance of new evidence.

Some philosophers say that this lesson is entirely general. We have found the key to reasonable learning from experience. To repeat, the idea comes from combining three different ideas:

Idea 1: It is plausible to connect personal degrees of belief and personal betting rates.

Idea 2: There is a plausible argument that betting rates should satisfy the basic rules of probability (and hence Bayes' Rule).

Idea 3: Bayes' Rule can be used to modify initial judgments of probability in the light of new experience.

Some philosophers take Bayes' Rule as the key to learning from experience. It seems to help even with David Hume's problem of induction. We discuss that application at the end of the book, in Chapter 21. That is a philosophical chapter. There we will also *question* the use of Bayes' Rule as a strict model of learning by experience.

JEFFREY'S RULE

There is a problem. Even a liberal use of Bayes' Rule may not be enough to analyze learning from experience. Why not?

Because Bayes' Rule assumes that learning proceeds by tidy steps:

We learn a definite new truth, E.
We apply Bayes' Rule.
We then learn another definite new truth, F.
We apply Bayes' Rule.
And so on, constantly updating our posterior probabilities.

Some learning is like that, especially in a laboratory or survey sample where we collect definite observations. But in real life we often change our opinions on the basis of less precise observation or experience.

For an example, recall Louise, who was considering studying for a pharmacy degree.

Louise hears a rumor that with budget cuts there will be less public money for medication, and doctors will be penalized for excessive prescribing of expensive drugs. So sales may go down, the business may contract.

That is a useful rumor, but there is no absolutely definite evidence, no established truth, no settled fact upon which she can rely. She has only rumors.

The inductive logician Richard Jeffrey has extended Bayes' Rule to cover such situations.

Here is a sketch of the idea. Let Louise's partition of hypotheses be G and ~G, where:

G = Good job opportunities for pharmacists in four years time.
Let C (for cuts) = there will be less public money for medication, and doctors will be penalized for excessive prescribing of expensive drugs.

Louise figures that if C is true, it is bad news for young pharmacists.

$Pr(G/C) = 0.1$

Otherwise, the chance of a good job is pretty good, although there could be a lack of jobs for other reasons than budget cuts:

$Pr(G/\sim C) = 0.8$.

Louise hears the rumor. But she does not learn that C is true. She only learns that it is probably true.

Let us represent probabilities in the light of the rumor by Pr*, so that

Pr*(G) stands for the probability of G, in the light of the rumor.

We want to know Pr*(G).

Hearing the rumor, Louise figures that the probability of C is 3/4.

$Pr^*(C) = 0.75$. $Pr^*(\sim C) = 0.25$.

We cannot apply Bayes' Rule, because the rumor gave us no certain information E to plug into Bayes' Rule.

Jeffrey's revision of Bayes' Rule is reminiscent of the rule for total probability. For a partition into two hypotheses, G and ~G, his rule states that:

$Pr^*(G) = Pr(G/C)Pr^*(C) + Pr(G/\sim C)Pr^*(\sim C)$.

Thus Jeffrey advises Louise to conclude that $Pr^*(G) = 0.275$.

Before she heard the rumor, Louise thought it was quite probable that a pharmacy degree would lead to a good job. If she reasons according to Jeffrey's rule, the job situation looks quite bleak.

LOGIC-BAYESIANS

Throughout this chapter we have been thinking of purely personal judgments of probability. There is a whole spectrum of belief-type probabilities. At one end are purely personal probabilities. At the other end is the idea of logical probability.

A logical probability is thought of as a logical relation between a hypothesis and the evidence for it. We mentioned that the economist J. M. Keynes and, much later, the philosopher Rudolf Carnap both favored a logical theory of probability. Both presented axioms for this idea. Their logical probabilities obey the basic rules of probability. Hence they obey Bayes' Rule. Hence logical probabilities can also represent learning from experience by Bayes' Rule.

The most important contributor to what we could call Logic-Bayesianism was a working scientist, the English geophysicist Harold Jeffreys. His *Theory of Probability* (1939) contains an enormous number of applications to practical problems in science, and is still a rich source of real-science Bayesian thinking.

THE REQUIREMENT OF TOTAL EVIDENCE

A personal probability is just that: the representation of a person's degree of belief. Our notation for categorical probability, Pr(A), suits personal probabilities very well. But logical probability is thought of as a relation between a proposition and evidence for it, and so the notation of conditional probability, Pr(H/E), is what is needed.

Personal probabilities represent degrees of belief, and we have a good idea of how to combine these with utilities to calculate expected utilities and use decision theory. Personal probabilities have a directly practical interpretation.

What is the practical interpretation of logical probability? The basic idea is that rational people should maximize conditional expectation using logical probabilities conditioned on all the *available evidence*. Carnap called this the *requirement of total evidence*.

LOGIC VERSUS OPINION

Personal probability theory says that a person's probability judgments are a private matter. They are up to the individual. But not anything goes. There are some rational constraints. Personal probabilities should be inductively consistent. They should, that is, be coherent. If they are coherent, they satisfy the basic rules of probability.

Otherwise, there are no constraints on personal probability. One candidate might be what on page 137 was called the *frequency principle*: if the only information about a hypothesis is a frequency-type probability, then you should make your personal probabilities, in that situation, equal to the frequencies.

Logical probability theory maintains that there are far stronger constraints than mere coherence. It maintains that there are uniquely correct, uniquely rational judgements of the probability of hypotheses in the light of evidence. Rudolf Carnap weakened this idea, holding that there was a continuum of what he called *inductive methods*, each corresponding to a set of prior logical probabilities. However, the system that he published in *Logical Foundations of Probability* (1950) and *The Continuum of Inductive Methods* (1952) is too simple. It does not appear to have practical applications in either the sciences or everyday life.

L. J. SAVAGE

The theory of personal probability was independently invented by Frank Ramsey and Bruno De Finetti. But the success of the idea—and the very name "personal probability"—owes everything to the American statistician L. J. Savage (1917–1971). He made clear the importance of this idea, combined with Bayes' Rule. His most famous contribution is *The Foundations of Statistical Inference* (1954).

Here is an odd fact, a coincidental (?) connection between the early days of the Bayesian philosophy and the early days of computer science.

During the Second World War, Savage was the chief "statistical" assistant to John von Neumann, the great mathematician who built the first electronic computers, and introduced the modern age of computers and information.

There was one other great advocate of Bayesian ideas directly after World War II, the English probability theorist I. J. Good. I. J. Good was an assistant to A. M. Turing. Turing defined the idea of the ideal computer and proved the fundamental theorem about ideal computation. That is why today we speak of Turing machines.

It is as if the modern Bayesian idea is a byproduct of the age of computers.

EXERCISES

1 *Likelihoods.* State the prior probability, posterior probability, and likelihood in:
   (a) Spider problem, page 71. Do the likelihoods of G and H (relative to T) add to 1?
   (b) Taxicabs, page 72. Do the likelihoods of G and B (relative to W_b) add to 1?

2 *Lost notes.* Imagine that you have lost your notes for your inductive logic course. You have two hypotheses, and are unsure which is true:

   > L: You left your notes in the library.
   > C: You left them in the classroom where inductive logic is taught.

   (a) Assign to L and C what are, for you, sensible prior probabilities. Use easy numbers, but be sure the assignments throughout this question are fairly realistic.
   You obtain some evidence:

   > E: A friend says she saw someone's notes lying in the library, but has no reason to think they are yours.

   (b) Assign your personal likelihoods to L and C in the light of E.
   (c) Compute the posterior probability of L and C in the light of E.
   You later obtain some more evidence:

   > F: Another friend says he saw something or other with your name on it in the library.

   (d) Assign likelihoods to L&E and C&E in the light of F.
   (e) Compute new posterior probabilities of L and C from the previous posteriors, and the likelihoods.

3 *Mushrooms.* Jack Waukey is brought in from a campsite to your hospital, late at night. He is vomiting, has the shivers, and abdominal pain.
   In your judgment, the probability that he has appendicitis, Pr(A), is 0.8.
   Then his brother Richard tells you that Jack had picked some wild mushrooms at dusk, and cooked them for his supper in the near-dark. You ask him about these mushrooms. He can describe the shape well enough. Amanite, almost certainly. What color? The light orange *Caesar's Amanite* is a tasty morsel, but the white *Amanita Phalloides* is deadly poison. Its popular name is *Death Cap*.
   The mushrooms were picked at dusk. Neither Richard nor Jack is sure of the color. Young *Death Cap* mushrooms are white inside, while young *Caesar's Amanite*, otherwise very similar, are yellowish inside. There is no definite evidence about that. "Well, probably yellowish," says Richard. On being pushed, you'll take Pr(Y) = 0.7.
   Use Jeffrey's rule to work out the new probability Pr*(A) that Jack has appendicitis.
   Notice how critical the decision is. The stomach pump is essential on the diagnosis of poisoning, while an operation for appendicitis would be fatal. But on

the other diagnosis, the stomach pump would be terribly dangerous for a rup-tured appendix, and an operation is essential.

4   *Rumors, rumors.* Just before the final examination, Joy, who is a student in this class, heard a rumor that the instructor told someone there would be no questions on the final about gambler's fallacies. Let:

> G = There will be a question about a gambler's fallacy.
> I = The instructor told a student there would be no such question.

Before she heard the rumor, assuming the instructor gave no hints, Joy thought there was a decent chance of a question on a gambler's fallacy: 0.3.

She thinks the instructor is fairly reliable: $Pr(\sim G/I) = 0.9$.

She thinks this rumor is pretty likely to be right, so after having heard the rumor, her $Pr(I) = 0.8$.

(a) Determine the probability she assigns to G after having heard the rumor. State and name any rule for updating probabilities that you use.

(b) For Joy, the utility of reviewing a topic, if it is asked on the exam, is 20. The utility of studying a topic that is not on the exam is −5. Compute Joy's expected utility for a decision to review gambler's fallacies, before she hears the rumor. And after hearing the rumor. She studies for a question only if the expected utility of doing so is positive. Does she review gambler's fallacies after hearing the rumor?

5   *Buses.* You are visiting Gotterdam, a large city in a foreign country that is new to you. The only other large city in this country is Shamsterdam. Both cities have excellent bus services, but that is about all you know about them.

At the airport, you find two city bus schedules. But part of each schedule is torn off—the part with the name of the city. All that is left is the last six letters, "...terdam." You see that one of these "dam" cities has 20 bus routes, while the other has 200. Since Gotterdam is larger than Shamsterdam, you suspect that Gotterdam has 200 bus routes, while Shamsterdam has 20. Let:

> [200] = The proposition that Gotterdam has 200 bus routes
> [20] = The proposition that Gotterdam has only 20 bus routes.

(a) Make your own personal judgment of probabilities Pr([200]) and Pr([20]).

(b) You arrived late at night, and were taken to the home of a friend. You are about to go for an early morning walk. So far as you know, you are in a "typical" part of town. State Pr(*n*), your personal prior probability that the first bus you see will be numbered *n*.

(c) What is your personal prior $Pr(1 \leqslant n \leqslant 20)$? $Pr(21 \leqslant n \leqslant 200)$?

(d) You go for an early morning walk. The first bus you see is No. 19. You think: "It is far more likely that I'd see a low number bus, if there are only low numbered buses, than that I would see a low numbered bus, if there are 200 routes."

What is the likelihood—your personal likelihood—of [200] in the light of this new piece of evidence?

What is the likelihood of [20]?

What is the ratio of the likelihood of [20] to that of [200]?

(e) What is your personal conditional probability Pr([200]/19)? Pr([20]/19)?

(f) You go on a very long, wandering walk through all parts of Gotterdam. You encounter 100 buses, all of which are from routes 1 through 20. What is your personal conditional probability that Gotterdam has 200 bus routes?

(g) How does this story illustrate the idea of "learning from experience"?

6 *Doom.* Professor John Leslie has used seemingly similar reasoning to reach startling conclusions. He uses Bayes' Rule to prove that the human race will probably come to an end very soon! He first considers an urn problem where

> there is a 2% probability that an urn with my name in it contains ten names only, and a 98% probability that it contains a thousand. These "prior" probabilities are my personal estimates, before any names are drawn. If my name is among the first three drawn, then Bayes' Rule tells me the "posterior" probability of there having been only ten names is _____.

(a) Complete the blank. What is the posterior probability in this case?

You will agree with Leslie, who continues,

> An estimated probability of only two out of a hundred has been revised to about two out of three.

He now proposes

> a rather similar calculation, applied to one's temporal position. Simplifying greatly, let us say that the sole alternatives are (i) that the human race will end before A.D. 2150, and (ii) that it will survive for many hundred thousand more years. Simplifying again, let us say that the chance that a human will be in the first decade of the 21st century is 1/10 in the case of a short-lasting race, while in the long-lasting race it is only 1/1000.

Where does the figure 1/10 come from? Leslie reckons that about 10% of all the people alive up to the year 2150 were alive in the 1990s, the decade in which he was writing. By contrast, if human beings continue to exist and multiply, at most 1/1000 of the "long-lasting" race were alive in the 1990s. He continues,

> Well suppose you start by thinking that the chance that the race will end by 2150 is only 1%.

So far, let us accept all of Professor Leslie's assumptions. Next he argues that you know *you* are alive in the twenty-first century. Take that as the evidence (compare to a bus numbered 19, or having your name drawn in a lottery). Using Bayes' rule, he claims, the revised estimate of the probability of Doom Soon is _____

(b) Complete Leslie's calculation, as if you could sensibly use Bayes' Rule, just as in the bus problem or the lottery example.

The argument is robust. It does not seriously depend on assignments of personal probability—change the 1/10, the 1/1000, and the 1% somewhat. Leslie's extraordinary conclusion still follows. It is as probable as not that the human race will come to an end quite soon. In fact, this argument works even better for the hypothesis that the world will come to an end in the next few minutes!

(c) Explain why.

Leslie argues that the conclusion is not so surprising with a vast store of nuclear weapons, new killer viruses on the way, global pollution, greenhouse warming, nuclear winter, asteroids on the loose, and so on. These gloomy reflections do help to show that the *conclusion* (doomsday by 2150) is more probable than we at first thought.

(d) But do they strengthen Leslie's *argument* using Bayes' Rule?

Now go back to the buses of Gotterdam. When all the buses encountered are from routes numbered 20 or less, we became virtually certain that there are only 20 bus routes in Gotterdam. Professor Leslie has encountered or heard about millions upon millions of human beings, all of them born within the next year!

(e) Using Leslie's doomsday argument, what is the posterior probability, on all this evidence, that the human race will come to an end within a year?

7   *Fallacy.* Your answer to (e) is a *reductio ad absurdum* of this form of argument— we have used it to derive an absurd conclusion. It is not virtually certain that the human race is about to become extinct. Still, what is wrong with the argument?

   The bus argument is a good one. Leslie's argument strikes most of us as crazy. Find at least one fallacy in Leslie's argument.

8   *Total evidence.* Briefly discuss Leslie's argument from the perspective of logical probability and the requirement of total evidence.

KEY WORDS FOR REVIEW

Prior probability	Learning from experience
Posterior probability	Likelihood ratio
Likelihood	Jeffrey's rule
Bayesian	Logic-Bayesians

16 Stability

Some core connections between the basic rules of probability, frequency-type probability, and statistical stability. These facts provide the foundations for frequency reasoning. The chapter ends by stating Bernoulli's Theorem, one of the most fundamental facts about probability.

Now we move from three chapters using the belief perspective to four chapters using the frequency perspective. Chapters 13 and 14 gave one reason why belief-type probabilities should satisfy the basic rules of probability. Chapter 15 showed how to apply that result to "learning from experience." Chapters 16–19 do something similar from the frequency perspective.

THE PROGRAM

- *This chapter* describes some deductive connections between probability rules and our intuitions about stable frequencies.
- *Chapter 17* extends these connections.
- *Chapter 18* presents one core idea of frequency-type inductive inference—the significance idea.
- *Chapter 19* presents a second core idea of frequency-type inductive inference—the confidence idea. This idea explains the way opinion polls are now reported. It also explains how we can think of the use of statistics as *inductive behavior*.

All the results described in this chapter are *deductions* from the basic rules of probability. The results are only stated, and not proved, because the proofs are more difficult than other material in this book.

BELIEF AND FREQUENCY COMPARED

The basic rules are for any type of probability. Belief-type and frequency-type probabilities emphasize two fundamentally different types of consequences of the basic rules.

The most important idea for belief-type probability is Bayes' Rule. This is deducible from the basic rules of probability, which hold for all types of probability. But Bayes' Rule is not very interesting for frequency-type probabilities.

The most important single idea for frequency-type probability is the way in which frequencies become stable as the number of trials increases. A basic result that helps us to understand this idea is known as Bernoulli's Theorem. Like Bayes' Rule, it is deducible from the basic rules of probability, although the proof is much harder than for Bayes' Rule. So it holds for all types of probability. But Bernoulli's Theorem is not so interesting for belief-type probabilities.

Bernoulli's Theorem is only the first of a great many important *laws of large numbers* and *central limit theorems* developed by generations of mathematicians, but we think that Bernoulli's original theorem contains the core idea that has been so fruitful in so many ways.

Think of it this way: the belief perspective fixes on one fundamental logical property of the probability rules—Bayes' Rule. The frequency perspective fixes on another fundamental logical property of the probability rules—laws of large numbers. Both of these logical properties have been truly rich in suggestions and consequences, both philosophical and mathematical.

NEW WINE IN OLD BOTTLES

Bernoulli's Theorem is 300 years old. Bayes' Rule is almost 250 years old. They are not out of date. Each is at the heart of one or the other of the two fundamental approaches to inductive inference that are flourishing today. Many dogmatists say that only one of those two approaches is correct. Our approach says that both are useful, not only in practice, but also, as we shall see in Chapters 21 and 22, for bringing fresh perspectives to the philosophical problem of induction. That problem was definitively stated by David Hume about thirty years after Bernoulli proved his theorem, and about thirty years before Bayes' contribution was published. Hume's problem is not out of date either. Analytic philosophers still drive themselves up the wall (to put it mildly) when they think about it seriously.

STATISTICAL STABILITY

And now to work. One of our fundamental ideas about probability is stable relative frequency in the long run. The basic rules do not seem to say anything about frequencies being stable, let alone about long runs. We have already emphasized that frequency in the long run is a pretty obscure idea. "In the long run we are all dead." Yet most of us have the idea that the more trials are made on some types of setup, the more stable the relative frequency will become. We now have to show that this idea really can be explained in terms of the basic rules.

AN EXPERIMENT

But first let's see whether we do get stability. Toss a fair coin 20 times, and note the number of heads. You expect it to be around 10, but of course on occasion there will be very few heads, and on occasion there will be many more than 10. Each member of a large class studying elementary probability was given a penny and asked to toss it twenty times. The 250 results were then plotted. Nobody got 0, 1, 19, or 20 heads. In fact, only 25 students got exactly 10 heads, while 32 got 11 heads, and 29 got 9 or 12 heads.

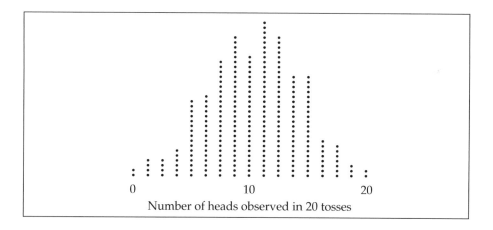

Number of heads observed in 20 tosses

Despite the irregularity, if we draw a smooth curve around these columns, it will look roughly like a "bell." This is an experimental "bell-shaped curve."

We expected that if every student in the university had tossed the coin 20 times, the plot would have looked much smoother: the approximation to a "bell" would fool the naked eye. And, if we had used fair coins throughout, and tossed fairly (a tall order!), the curve would have peaked at 10.

SAMPLE MEAN

Our experiment consisted of 250 mini-experiments, each with a result k, the number of times the coin fell heads. We can ask, what is the "average" value of k, in the 250 trials? This is a lot of adding. If you want you can check that the average value is 9.76, very close to 10.

Each student performed a mini-experiment, tossing a coin 20 times. We can think of our big experiment of 250 such minis as a *sample* from a much larger, or indefinitely large, set of such experiments. The average value of k is called the *experimental* or *sample mean* of the number of heads.

If the students had recorded k/n, the relative frequency (or proportion of times) that the coin fell heads, then the sample mean would have been 9.76/20 = 0.49. That's very close to ½.

SAMPLE STANDARD DEVIATION

The sample mean is just an average. Averages do not tell the whole story. If every student in the class had tossed the coin 50 times, we expect that the clustering around the average would be much more noticeable. Hence the bell-shaped curve would have looked much "thinner." There would have been less spread or dispersion in the results.

We would like a measure of dispersion around the mean X. This would be a number d such that we could say, very roughly, that most of the results are between X$-d$ and X$+d$.

A natural way to measure the dispersion is to note the differences between the mean X and each observed result X_i. In our case, there are 250 observed proportions k/n, and the mean X = 0.49.

Now if we simply took the differences (X_i-X) and added them up, some would be positive and some negative, and they would cancel out. Instead, the usual way to measure dispersion is to add up the squares of these differences—all of which are positive—and then take the square root of this sum. This is called the *sample standard deviation*, abbreviated SD.

$$SD = \sqrt{[\Sigma(X_i - X)^2/n]}$$

In our example, the sample standard deviation is about 2.9.

Now look back at our graph. You will see that 162 of the results, or 65%, lie between (10$-$3) and (10$+$3).

In an absurd experiment using 10,000 university students, we would expect to find a smaller standard deviation. We will soon see that it should be less than 2.3.

ODD QUESTION 1

Our idea is that many frequencies tend to stabilize in a long sequence. The longer the sequence, the more the stability. The larger the number of trials, the less likely are large deviations from the average. That was the idea behind Odd Question 1 (page xv), which ran as follows:

> About as many boys as girls are born in hospitals. Many babies are born every week at City General. In Cornwall, a country town, there is a small hospital where only a few babies are born every week.
>
>   A **normal** week is one where between 45% and 55% of the babies are female.
>
>   An **unusual** week is one where more than 55% are girls, or more than 55% are boys.
>
>   Which of the following is true:

_____(a) Unusual weeks occur equally often at City General and at Cornwall.
_____(b) Unusual weeks are more common at City General than at Cornwall.
_____(c) Unusual weeks are more common at Cornwall than at City General.

Large deviations, in this case unusual weeks, are more common in a small population like Cornwall, than in a large population in the city. That is why (c) is the right answer. This answer implicitly assumes—what seems to be true— that sex at birth is a matter of chance. In almost all populations until very recently, the probability of a live male birth is around 0.51, and the probability of a live female birth is 0.49. Assuming that births follow a theoretical model like a slightly loaded coin, then (c) is certainly the right answer.

Of course, the model might be wrong. It is now quite easy to determine the sex of a child during early pregnancy. In some populations, male children are much more desirable than females, and so female fetuses are aborted during the first trimester. Hence the ratio of live male births, to female live births, is increased.

BERNOULLI TRIALS

In this chapter we are concerned with repeated independent trials with constant probability p for some event E. These are often called *Bernoulli trials*. We have been thinking of tosses of a coin, spins of a roulette wheel, and draws from an urn (with replacement) as Bernoulli trials.

Now we will summarize, without formulas, the fundamental theorems described later in this chapter.

We can ask:

If the probability of event E is p, what is the relative frequency with which E occurs in a long sequence of Bernoulli trials?

All the theorems described in this chapter are, in one way or another, answers to this type of question.

LIMITS

The basic rules of probability entail that the relative frequency will almost always be around p.

In most long sequences of Bernoulli trials
the relative frequency of Es will be close to p.

Moreover:

> The longer the sequence of trials the greater the probability that the relative frequency of E will be close to p.

We can make stronger statements than that. For any small *margin of error ε* as the number of trials increases without bound, it becomes increasingly probable that the relative frequency of E is within ε of p.

Let us use the name *accuracy-probability* for the probability that the relative frequency of E is within a margin of error ε of p.

> For any given margin of error ε as the number of trials increases the accuracy-probability approaches 1.

This is the effect of *Bernoulli's Theorem*. It clearly implies that the probability of large deviations of the relative frequency from p decreases as the number of trials increases.

These are qualitative statements, but we shall use a quantitative approximation for some accuracy-probabilities.

We have now stated all the results to be discussed in this chapter. We now need to state them more carefully, and to give a few examples of what they mean in practice.

AN URN MODEL

Imagine an ideal urn together with a device for sampling with replacement. Independent trials, no bias: on any draw from the urn, the probability of any ball is the same as that of any other. Draws from the urn are Bernoulli trials.

The urn contains green and red balls in a definite proportion p. The probability of drawing a green ball is p.

REPEATED DRAWS

Now consider a new type of trial, a compound trial:

We make n repeated independent draws with replacement—Bernoulli trials. We note the number k of green balls drawn. The possible outcomes of trials of this type are $0, 1, 2, \ldots, n$.

Now we present some simple results about repeated and compound trials.

MOST PROBABLE NUMBER

What number of green balls are we "most likely to get" in drawing n balls with replacement?

Obviously, if p is small, we don't expect to get many green balls, while if p is large, we expect to get a lot. But we can answer the question exactly.

We can compute the probability of getting 0 green balls, 1 green ball, 2 green balls, ... , n green balls.

Which numbers from 0 to n have the highest probability? Here we speak of the most probable number of green balls.

The most probable number of green balls is roughly pn.

In addition to the most probable *number* of green balls in n trials, we can consider the most probable *proportion* or *relative frequency* of green balls.

The most probable relative frequency of green balls is roughly p.

Why "roughly"? For two reasons. First, pn is usually not an integer. When $p = \frac{1}{2}$ and $n = 5$, $np = 2\frac{1}{2}$ which is not a whole number. In drawing from an urn 5 times, you never draw exactly $2\frac{1}{2}$ green balls. Second, there are sometimes two equally most probable numbers. When $p = \frac{1}{2}$ and $n = 5$, the two most probable numbers of green balls to be drawn are 2 and 3.

In exercises 7 and 8 we illustrate the fact that the most probable number is in effect the integer or pair of integers "closest" to pn. It is the integer that lies between $pn - (1 - p)$ and $pn + p$, unless both those quantities are integers.

MOST PROBABLE RELATIVE FREQUENCY

Let k_o stand for the most probable number in n trials. Then the most probable relative frequency of green balls is k_o/n. This fraction is close to p. In fact, as is confirmed in the exercises:

$$(p - (1-p)/n) \leq k_o/n \leq (p + p/n).$$

As the number of trials n increases, both p/n and $(1 - p)/n$ approach zero. Hence the numbers on the left and right in that formula very quickly become very close to p. Hence for large n, the most probable relative frequency is essentially p.

> *Theorem: For a large number of trials the most probable relative frequency of green balls, k_o/n, is essentially just p.*

This is the first connection between probability and frequency in a long run.
Comparison to our experiment. In our experiment of 250 students tossing a coin

20 times, the most common observed relative frequency was not 1/2. 32 students got 11 heads in 20 tosses, so the most common relative frequency was not 10/20 = 0.5, but 11/20, or 0.55.

EXPECTED NUMBER OF GREEN BALLS TO BE DRAWN IN n DRAWS

We can also ask about the *average* number of green balls drawn in n draws with replacement. Here we are thinking of drawing n balls over and over again, occasionally getting no green balls, sometimes getting one green ball, most often getting k_o green balls, and so forth We can average all these outcomes, to get the average or expected number of green balls in n draws. It is quite easily proved from the basic rules of probability that *the expected number* is pn.

EXPECTED RELATIVE FREQUENCY OF GREEN BALLS IN n DRAWS

The expected relative frequency is just the expected number divided by n. Hence:

Theorem: The expected relative frequency of green balls is p.

This is the second connection between probability and relative frequency in a long run.

Comparison to our experiment. In our experiment of 250 students tossing a coin 20 times, the actual relative frequency of heads was very close to ½, namely 0.49.

CONVERGENCE AND STABILITY

Given that $\Pr(\text{green}) = p$, we expect that in a sample we will obtain about pn green balls.

But how large a sample is needed, in order that the observed proportion k/n will, very probably, be close to p?

More precisely: For some small "margin of error" ε, what is the probability that the relative frequency of greens in n trials will be within ε of p?

Jacques Bernoulli proved that as n increases, this probability approaches 1.

MARGIN OF ERROR AND ACCURACY PROBABILITY

Using formulas, for some margin of error ε we are interested in the probability that in n trials, we get a number k of green balls such that:

$$p - \varepsilon \leqslant k/n \leqslant p + \varepsilon.$$

This is an unusually complicated "event"! The numbers p and n are fixed by the question. The number k is the outcome of an observation of n trials.

For example, suppose $p = 0.3$. If we made $n = 100$ draws, and took $\varepsilon = .01$ as our margin of error, the event

$$p - \varepsilon \leqslant k/n \leqslant p + \varepsilon$$

is the event of getting k such that:

$$(0.3 - 0.01) \leqslant k/100 \leqslant (0.3 + 0.01).$$

So, this event happens when we draw $k = 29, 30,$ or 31 green balls.

We are interested in the probability of events like that. For a given margin of error, we will call that the *accuracy-probability*.

For a given margin of error ε,

the accuracy-probability is the probability that k is within εn of np.

Or, in symbols, the accuracy-probability is:

$$\Pr\left[(np - \varepsilon n) \leqslant k \leqslant (np + \varepsilon n)\right].$$

The accuracy-probability is also the probability that k/n is within e of p, or, in symbols:

$$\Pr\left[(p - \varepsilon) \leqslant k/n \leqslant (p + \varepsilon)\right].$$

THEOREM:
As the number of trials increases, the accuracy probability approaches 1. Relative frequencies tend to converge on probabilities.

This is the third connection between probability and frequency in a long run.

BERNOULLI'S THEOREM

Bernoulli's Theorem is usually stated in a slightly different way: In the limit, k/n converges on p with a probability that is increasingly close to 1.

To state this result precisely, we want the difference between p and the relative frequency to be as small as we please. That is, we want k/n to be within some small *margin of error* ε of p, as just discussed.

Second, we want the *accuracy-probability*, that k/n is within ε of p, to be as close as we want to 1. That is, we want the difference x between this probability and 1 to be as small as we choose, so long as we make enough trials. These ideas are put together to form Bernoulli's Theorem.

> For any small error ε, and
> for any small difference x,
> there is a number of trials N,
> such that
> for any $n > N$,
> the probability is greater than $1 - x$, that
> the proportion of green balls k/n is within ε of p.

That's worth framing.

BERNOULLI'S THEOREM
For any small error ε,
and any small difference x,
there is a number of trials N,
such that for any $n > N$,
$Pr[(p-\varepsilon) \leq k/n \leq (p + \varepsilon)] > (1 - x).$

This is the fourth and most fundamental connection between probability and frequency in a long run. There is one more fundamental connection to come in the next chapter.

JACQUES BERNOULLI

Bernoulli's theorem is named after the Swiss mathematician Jacques Bernoulli (1654–1705), uncle of Daniel (page 94). His chief work on probability, *The Art of Conjecturing*, was written in the early 1690s but not published until after his death in 1713. This book is important for the mathematics of probability. But it is also important for the philosophy. In the fourth and final part, Bernoulli gives the core of the "confidence" approach to learning from experience, to be presented in Chapter 19.

EXERCISES

1 *Hungry Clara.* Bottle-fed baby Clara is fed 7 times during a 24-hour period. Her "intake" at each feeding was measured in fluid ounces:

6 oz., 4 oz., 7 oz., 4 oz., 2 oz., 7 oz., 5 oz.

(a) What was the average, or mean, amount of food that Clara had at each feeding? (b) What is the standard deviation?

2   *Sick Sam.* Sam is ill and eating irregularly. His parents try to feed him 7 times, but he has only one big meal and his intake throughout the 24 hours is only:

3 oz., 1 oz., 2 oz., 2 oz., 8 oz., 1 oz., 4 oz.

(a) What was the average, or mean amount of food that Sam had at each feeding?
(b) What is the standard deviation?
(c) Why is the mean for Sam smaller than Clara's, while the standard deviation is larger?

3   *Median income.* The arithmetical mean, or average, income of a group is the sum of all incomes divided by the size of the group. That is one kind of "middle." We could also look at the income that divides the population in two, with as many people above that point as there are people who fall below that point. This is called the *median*. The median will be halfway between the lowest income in the upper-half group, and the highest in the lower half group.

   A small start-up company has six employees, A, B, C, D, E, F, including the person who cleans and tidies, part-time at night. Their incomes are as follows.

   A: $31,000   B: $16,000   C: $85,000
   D: $38,000   E: $122,000   F: $74,000

What is the (a) mean income, (b) median income?

4   *Incomes.* In exercise (3) the mean and median differ. Is this because we have such a small population? No. Here are the average and median incomes for Canada, using the most recent figures available.

Household type	Average income	Median income
Family	$57,146	$50,316
Unattached person	25,005	18,856
All households	46,556	37,979

Does the difference between the median and the mean suggest anything about the distribution of incomes?

5   *Poverty line.* There are many definitions of "the poverty line." In the United States, when people talk about the poverty line they usually mean the *poverty thresholds*. In Canada they mean the *low-income cutoffs*. In Canada, the poverty line for a family of four in a big city is 34,000 Canadian dollars, or about 23,000 U.S. dollars, about 6,000 U.S. dollars higher than the American poverty threshold for a family of four namely $17,029.

   The usual "poverty lines" for international comparisons are (i) 50% of the median income of the population, or (ii) 50% of the average income. Compute the Canadian poverty lines for a family, using each of these two measures.

6   *Quick fixes.* The British prime minister announced that before the next election his government would lift 30% of the people, now living in poverty, above the poverty line. (a) What would be a cheap way to do this, assuming the poverty line is defined in terms of average income? Don't simply force the same number of people now above the poverty line below the poverty line! (b) Would your method work if the poverty line were defined in terms of the median income?

7   *Most probable numbers.* The most probable number is seldom exactly pn because the most probable number is a whole number, an integer, such as 5 or 1097. But

pn may be a fraction or decimal number. For example, if $p = 0.3$ and $n = 13$, $pn = 3.9$, which is not a whole number. Moreover, there might be two equally most probable numbers.

Consider 5 draws with replacement from an urn with an equal number of green and red balls, so that $p = \frac{1}{2}$. Pr(0) means the probability that no green balls are drawn, Pr(1) means that 1 green ball is drawn, and so on.

(a) In how many equally probable distinguishable ways can we draw five balls from the urn?

(b) What is Pr(0)? Pr(5)?

(c) What is Pr(1)? Pr(4)?

(d) What is Pr(2)? Pr(3)?

(e) What are the most probable numbers?

(f) Let k_o denote the most probable number of green balls in n Bernoulli trials with probability p. Define k_o as that integer or pair of integers such that:

$$np - (1 - p) \leq k_o \leq np + p.$$

Confirm that in our example of $p = \frac{1}{2}$, $n = 5$, that the numbers 2 and 3 are the most probable numbers.

8 *Most probable number.* What is the most probable number when $p = 0.3$, $n = 13$?

9 *Success.*

(a) Find the most probable number of successes (S) in 11 Bernoulli trials where Pr(S) = 0.3.

(b) What is the expected number of successes?

10 *Coastal rain.* As the result of observations taken every year since 1843, it has been found that the probability of rain in Victoria, British Columbia, on July 1 is 4/17. Find the most probable number of rainy July the Firsts for the next fifty years.

11 *Particle accelerators.* Particles of a certain type are being studied in a physics experiment. Under experimental conditions A, on average 60 particles appear per second, and each has, with probability 0.7, a velocity greater than v. When the conditions are changed to B, there appear on average only 50 particles, but they tend to be faster: the probability that the velocity exceeds v is 0.8.

(a) Under conditions A and B respectively, what is the most probable number of particles per second going faster than v?

(b) Do the average numbers of fast (velocity $> v$) particles per second differ from the most probable numbers? Is this usual or unusual?

(c) If you wanted to study fast particles, would you rather work under conditions A or conditions B?

KEY WORDS FOR REVIEW

Sample mean	Most probable number
Sample standard deviation	Bernoulli's Theorem
Bernoulli trials	Expected number

17 Normal Approximations

We have seen that relative frequencies converge on theoretical probabilities. But how fast? When can we begin to use an observed relative frequency as a reliable estimate of a probability? This chapter gives some answers. They are a little more technical than most of this book. For practical purposes, all you need to know is how to use is the three boxed **Normal Facts** below.

EXPERIMENTAL BELL-SHAPED CURVES

On page 191 we had the result of a coin-tossing experiment. The graph was roughly in the shape of a bell. Many observed distributions have this property.

Example: Incomes. In modern industrialized countries we have come to expect income distributions to look something like Curve 1 on the next page, with a few incredibly rich people at the right end of the graph. But in feudal times there was no middle class, so we would expect the income distribution in Curve 2. It is "bimodal"—it has two peaks.

Example: Errors. We can never measure with complete accuracy. Any sequence of "exact" measurements of the same quantity will show some variation. We often average the results. We can think of this as a sample mean. A good measuring device will produce results that cluster about the mean, with a small sample standard deviation. A bad measuring device gives results that vary wildly from one another, giving a large standard deviation.

AN IDEAL BELL-SHAPED CURVE

There is a mathematical formula for a family of perfectly symmetrical bell-shaped curves. We will not do the mathematics. We just state some useful properties of these curves, which are called are called *normal* (because people thought they occurred empirically, in the normal course of events) or *Gaussian* (because the

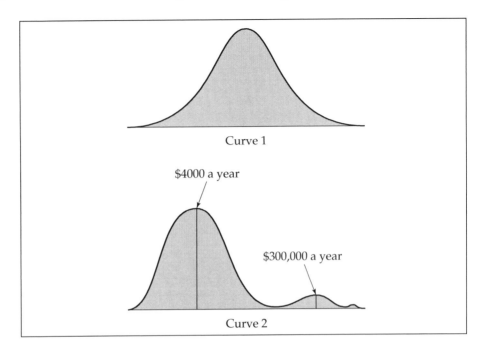

German mathematician C. F. Gauss (1777–1855) made deep studies of these curves).

Each curve in this family is defined by two numbers. One is called the (theoretical) mean, represented by μ (a Greek letter, pronounced *mu*). This is the value of the curve at its peak.

The second parameter is a measure of the width of the curve, the theoretical standard deviation σ, the lowercase Greek letter *sigma*.

In sampling from a population with a normal distribution, the sample mean X tends to the theoretical mean μ, and the sample standard deviation SD tends to be close to the theoretical standard deviation σ.

MEANING OF THE CURVE

In our graph of the coin-tossing experiment, we had 20 columns. Column *n* represented the number of students who threw *n* heads in 20 tosses. The normal distribution is continuous, so the mathematics is harder. But the meaning is quite simple. Instead of one or more columns, think of the *area* under a segment of a curve.

Example: We are measuring the boiling point of sulfur, which is 112.8°C. If we're doing the job well, our measurements will be normally distributed around this number, the mean of the distribution. How many of our measurements will be within 0.4°C of the true melting point? The proportion of measurements between 112.4° and 113.2° will be represented by the proportion of the shaded area of the curve, to the total area:

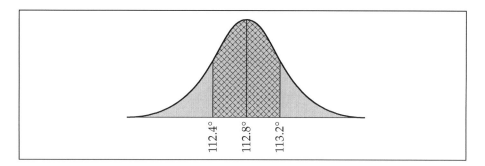

APPLICATION: NORMAL FACT I

Suppose that some variable is normally distributed with mean μ and standard deviation σ. It might be the error of a measurement, or income, or height. We observe a value E of this variable. Then:

The probability that E is within σ of *pn* is about 0.68.
The probability that E is within 2σ of *pn* is about 0.95.
The probability that E is within 3σ of *pn* is about 0.99.

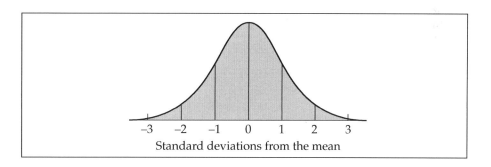

Standard deviations from the mean

APPLICATION: NORMAL FACT II

Bernoulli proved his theorem in the 1690s. A few years later—and before Bernoulli had published his results—Abraham De Moivre made an even more powerful discovery: the normal distribution is a very good approximation for Bernoulli trials. Think of the probability of getting k occurrences of event E on n Bernoulli trials where the probability of E, Pr(E), is fixed at p.

Let $b(k;n,p)$ = the probability of getting k occurrences of event E in n trials when $\Pr(E) = p$.

This is called the *binomial distribution* because it is about two (*bi*) terms (*nom*) such as heads and tails. Working out the function b is horribly complex when n is large, but there is a simple approximation: $b(k;n,p)$ is approximated by a normal distribution (unless p is very close to the end points 0 or 1—there we need another approximation).

A binomial distribution $b(k;n,p)$ is approximated by a normal distribution in which $\mu = pn$, and $\sigma = \sqrt{[(1-p)pn]}$.

HOW GOOD AN APPROXIMATION?

This graph shows how good the normal approximation is, even for as few as 10 coin tosses, and even when Pr(heads) is quite small, say 0.2. Note that if the probability of heads is only 1/5, we are unlikely to get more than 5 or 6 heads.

On the Y axis the heights of the bars show the probability of getting exactly k occurrences of heads.

The curve is the normal curve, with

$\mu = np = 10 \times 0.2 = 2.$
$\sigma = \sqrt{[(1-p)pn]} = \sqrt{[(1 - 0.2)(0.2 \times 10)]} = 1.6.$

Note how tidily the curve matches the columns.

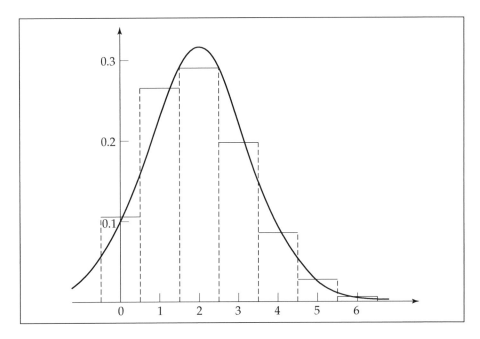

HOW FAST DOES RELATIVE FREQUENCY CONVERGE ON PROBABILITY?

We answer by putting together Normal Facts I and II. Normal Fact II tells us that the binomial distribution is approximated by a normal one.

NORMAL FACT III

We are considering a sequence of Bernoulli trials with a probability p of heads. The number of heads in n tosses is k. We want to know the probability that k is close to pn. We give the answer for three special cases, which follow directly from Normal Facts I and II.

The probability that k is within σ of pn is about 0.68.
The probability that k is within 2σ of pn is about 0.95.
The probability that k is within 3σ of pn is about 0.99.

For example, there is a 99% probability that k lies between $pn - 3\sigma$ and $pn + 3\sigma$.
   This is the fifth and most practical connection between probability and frequency in a long run.

LAWS OF LARGE NUMBERS

Our sequence of five connections between probability and relative frequency in a long run, has been explained for the most simple case. It is also the most familiar case, for the usual examples are tossing coins or drawing balls from an urn. However, many practical situations involving a yes/no answer are modeled on Bernoulli trials. The simplest polls can be modeled like that. The pollster asks, "Are you in favor of this new abortion law?" and divides respondents into "Yes" and the rest. We classify the shock absorbers from a production line as "OK" or "Below standard." Urn models are not so very far away from real life.

   Many deeper, subtler, and more sophisticated limiting results were proved after the work of Bernoulli and De Moivre. Such results are often called *laws of large numbers*. Bernoulli's Theorem itself is often called *the weak law of large numbers*. More general and all-encompassing results are often called *Central Limit Theorems*. But Bernoulli's Theorem plus the Normal Facts just stated are enough to get a decent sense of what is going on.

LIGHT BULBS

VisioPerfect, a light bulb manufacturer, has a long production line of bulbs. Of these, 96% percent have a "long life"—they burn for more than 8,000 hours—

and 4% are more short-lived. Since bulbs are marketed in six-packs, the shortest production run is 400 six-packs, or 2400 bulbs.

The distribution of long-life and short-life bulbs from this process appears to be random, so we model it by Bernoulli trials.

In a run of 2400 bulbs, the expected number of long-life bulbs is 0.96 × 2400 = 2304.

We do not often get exactly 2304 long-life light bulbs, even though that is both the most probable number and the expected number of long-life bulbs. How likely is it that we get close to this number? The quantity d is:

$$\sigma = \sqrt{[p(1{-}p)n]} = \sqrt{[0.96 \times 0.04 \times 2400]} = 9.6.$$

Hence the probability that in a production of 2400 bulbs the number of long-life bulbs:

Lies between 2294 and 2314 is better than 2/3.
Lies between 2284 and 2324 is much better than 0.95.
Lies between 2275 and 2333 is better than 0.99.

We have said "better than" in the first line because the bounds of 10 around the expected number are wider than $\sigma = 9.6$. We have said "much better than" in the second line because the bounds of 20 around the expected number are much wider than $2\sigma = 19.2$.

A BORED PRISONER

James, a stockbroker, was caught defrauding his company and had to spend several years behind bars with nothing much to do.

He decided to toss an apparently fair coin 10,000 times. On the hypothesis that the coin and tossing arrangements are fair,

The expected number of heads is 5000.
$\sigma = \sqrt{[p(1{-}p)n]} = \sqrt{[½ \times ½ \times 10,000]} = 50.$

Hence the probability that the number of heads he observes in 10,000 tosses:

Lies between 4950 and 5050 is about 2/3.
Lies between 4900 and 5100 is about 0.95.
Lies between 4850 and 5150 is about 0.99.

ONE-HALF IS THE WORST-CASE SCENARIO

The stockbroker tossed his coin 10,000 times. That long run of tosses is more than four times as long as VisioPerfect's run of 2400 bulbs. Yet the margins of error for the same accuracy-probabilities are much larger.

This means that there is far more potential variability in the stockbroker's tosses than in the manufacturer's production line. To see this even more clearly, suppose that James tossed his coin exactly 2400 times. Then the expected number of heads is 1200, and:

$$\sigma = \sqrt{[p(1-p)n]} = \sqrt{[½ \times ½ \times 2400]} = 24.5.$$

Compared to 9.6 for VisioPerfect. That means that, for example, with a 95% accuracy probability, the margin of error for the coin-tosser is about 50, while for VisioPerfect it is about 20.

Conversely, in a run of 10,000 light bulbs, the expected number of long-life bulbs is 9600, and:

$$\sigma = \sqrt{[p(1-p)n]} = \sqrt{[0.96 \times 0.04 \times 10,000]} = 19.6.$$

For James it is 50. That means that, for example, with a 99% accuracy probability the margin of error for James is 150, while for VisioPerfect it is about 60.

So the margin of error, for the same accuracy-probability, is about 2½ times larger for James tossing coins in prison than for the manufacturer of light bulbs.

The only numerical difference between the light bulbs and the stockbroker was the probability.

Light bulbs: $p = 0.96$ (the probability of a long-life bulb).
Coin tosses: $p = 0.5$ (the probability of heads).

The margin of error is greatest when $p = ½$.
That is to be expected. The margins of error depend on $\sigma = \sqrt{[p(1-p)n]}$.
For fixed n, the largest value of $p(1-p)$ is $½ \times ½ = ¼$.
You can check this out with examples. If $p = 0.3$, then $p(1-p) = 0.21 < 0.25$.
Exercise 6 asks you to prove that a probability of ½ is a "worst-case scenario" in the sense that, for accuracy-probabilities like 0.95 or 0.99, the margin of error is greatest for $p = ½$.

ABRAHAM DE MOIVRE

Abraham de Moivre (1667–1754), who established the normal approximation for Bernoulli trials, was from a family of French religious refugees who fled to England. For many years he earned his living as a tutor for pupils sent to him by Isaac Newton. His book *The Doctrine of Chances* was, for over fifty years, the most important English-language textbook on probability theory. Later he wrote the first fundamental book about the theory of annuities.

EXERCISES

1 *Bimodal.* Give some more examples of bimodal distributions.

2   *Normal.* Which of these would you expect to be roughly normal, roughly bi-modal, or neither?
    (a) The distribution of heights in an ethnically homogeneous group of males.
    (b) The distribution of heights in a similarly homogeneous group of people.
    (c) The distribution of rainfall in your town, per weeks of the year.
    (d) The volume of milk produced per cow, in a herd of Jersey cows.

3   *Inferior products.* Suppose that only ¾ of the bulbs from VisioPerfect's production line are long-life. Suppose the process can be modeled by Bernoulli trials, as in the text.
    (a) What is the expected number of long-life bulbs in a production batch of 4800?
    (b) What is the probability that the number of long-life bulbs in this batch lies between 3540 and 3660?

4   *Showers after sports.* Do male high school students use the school showers after participating in school sports? Once upon a time they almost all showered. But now it turns out that only about half of them do so. The rest, well, smell.
    Suppose we randomly sample 3136 male high school students in the city, who participate in school sports. We would expect that about 1568 of these will take showers after sports. Find a number x such that there is only a 1% probability that we find more than $1568+x$ or fewer than $1568-x$ boys who do not shower after sports.

5   *Other regions.* The showering customs may differ in different regions. Suppose samples of 3136 students are made in several widely separated school districts, urban and rural, northern and southern, western, central, eastern, and so forth.
    Find x of question 4 in districts where the proportion of boys who shower after school sports is:
        (a) 0.3. (b) 0.7. (c) 0.1. (d) 0.9.
    In each case, x will be a whole number such that there is no more than a 1% probability that the sample deviates from the expected number by more than x.

6   *Worst-case scenario.* Prove that for an accuracy-probability of 0.95, the largest margin of error in Bernoulli trials occurs when $p = \frac{1}{2}$.

KEY WORDS FOR REVIEW

Normal distribution   Theoretical mean
Binomial distribution   Theoretical standard deviation
Normal approximation

18 Significance and Power

Statistical hypotheses are compared with data, often collected in carefully designed experiments. Evidence may lead us tentatively to accept or reject hypotheses. Evidence can be good or bad; it can be more, or less, convincing. When is it significant? What are the underlying ideas about accepting and rejecting hypotheses? This chapter introduces two fundamentally different ways of thinking about these issues, both of which are deeply entrenched in statistical practice. One idea is that of **significance tests**. Another is the **power** of a test to discriminate false hypotheses.

ASTROLOGY

Four members of this class went for coffee after the first meeting. Two of them had the same astrological sign (of the zodiac). There are 12 signs of the zodiac. Is this significant? Were they fated to meet?

We need to consider plausible models and ask, how likely is it, that this phenomenon would occur by chance alone?

Theoretical probability model: each person is assigned a sign by a chance setup with equal probability for each sign—just as if you drew your sign from a pack of twelve different cards, say a pack of all the clubs except the ace.

Think of a deck of cards with the aces removed, leaving 4 suits of 12 different cards each (analogous to the 12 signs and the 4 people). If we select at random a card from each suit, what is the probability that we get at least two cards that match in value?

"At least" problems are usually most easily solved by turning them upside down. The probability that no two cards match is:

1 − (the probability that at least 2 cards match).

Start with 2 suits, say spades and diamonds. The probability of no match is 11/12, since there is only a 1/12 chance that a spade and a diamond have the same value. The probability that a club will differ from the other two cards is 10/12, and the probability that a heart will differ from the other 3 is 9/12. So the probability that none of the four cards match is

$$\frac{11 \times 10 \times 9}{12 \times 12 \times 12} = \frac{55}{96}.$$

Hence the probability of at least one match—that at least two people have the same sign—is 41/96, or somewhat better than 4/10.

Hence almost as often as not we expect at least two people among four drawn at random to have the same sign of the zodiac. Intuitively we conclude that the meeting of two people with the same sign of the zodiac, at a coffee table for four, is not significant.

ALERT LEARNER

On page 31, *Alert Learner* saw that a roulette wheel stopped at black 12 times in a row.

She thought that this information about twelve spins was significant. She thought that it might suggest—indicate, but not prove—that the wheel was biased toward black.

Why did she think that 12 blacks in a row are significant? They are significant in terms of the assumption that the wheel is fair.

It is quite unlikely that a fair wheel would stop at 12 blacks in a row. Even if there were no zeroes on the roulette, so that the probability of black is ½, only one sequence of 12 spins in 4096 would, on average, be 12 blacks in a row. The probability is about 0.00024.

Alert Learner could see that:

Either the wheel is biased toward black, *or* the wheel is fair and an unusual run of blacks has just been observed.

This simple "either-or" is the basis of **tests of significance.**

STATISTICAL HYPOTHESES: ROULETTE

In our chapter on the gambler's fallacy, *Fallacious Gambler, Stodgy Logic,* and *Alert Learner* started with an assumption about the roulette wheel. "The wheel is fair."

We analyzed this assumption: the wheel is a chance setup in which the outcomes black and red are equally probable, and outcomes are independent.

This assumption can be thought of as a *hypothesis* about the wheel. We call it a *statistical hypothesis.*

STATISTICAL HYPOTHESES: VISIOPERFECT

In our example on page 205, VisioPerfect has a run of 2400 light bulbs. According to the company's publicity, 96% of the bulbs manufactured by its production process are long-life.

We modeled this as a claim about Bernoulli trials, on which the probability of a long-life bulb is 0.96.

That is a *statistical hypothesis* about the process by which VisioPerfect manufactures light bulbs. Call this hypothesis H.

We computed that if H is true, then:

◆ The probability of getting between 2275 and 2333 long-life bulbs in a run of 2400 is more than 99%.

◆ Conversely, the probability of getting more than 125, or fewer than 67, short-life bulbs is less than 1%.

IS THE HYPOTHESIS TRUE?

Statistical hypotheses involve frequency-type probabilities. They are definite claims about how the world is. The gambler's hypothesis was that the roulette wheel is fair. That is either true or false. There is no "frequency" about that.

Likewise, the light bulb hypothesis H involves a frequency-type probability. It is either true, or it is false.

Is H true? There are many ways H could be false:

■ VisioPerfect may be mistaken about its production process—and not know that.

■ The publicity people who work for VisioPerfect may be misleading us. They could even be lying.

■ Or maybe it is we logicians who jumped to conclusions—perhaps the production process does not behave like simple Bernoulli trials (there might be glitches, when the process produces a whole string of short-life bulbs).

We can ask if H is true. But from the frequency perspective we cannot talk about the probability of H, or the probability that H is true.

This is because H is a definite claim about a single state of affairs—the process by which VisioPerfect makes light bulbs. H is true—or H is false. There is no "frequency" about it.

TWO FREQUENCY-TYPE IDEAS

If frequency-type statisticians cannot tell us about the probability of H, in the light of some evidence, how can they help us with inductive inference? In many ways. We will emphasize two:

◆ The significance idea.
◆ The confidence idea.

The significance idea is easy to understand, although people often abuse it. The confidence idea is harder to understand. People often abuse it, too. In this chapter, we illustrate the significance idea. In the next chapter we will illustrate the confidence idea.

BAD LIGHTS

The monthly magazine *Consumers' Advocate* asserts that it tested a run of 2400 light bulbs—400 six-packs—from VisioPerfect. It found 133 short-life bulbs.

H is the statistical hypothesis of Bernoulli trials with a 96% probability of long-life bulbs. From the frequency perspective, you can infer that:

- *If* hypothesis H is true, *then* an event of probability less than 1% (more than 125, or fewer than 67, short-life bulbs) has occurred.

This is because we deduced from H that:

- The probability of getting more than 125, or fewer than 67, short-life bulbs, is at most 1%.

But we cannot infer that:

"The probability is less than 1% that H is true."

From the frequency perspective, such a statement does not make sense!

FUNNY COINS

James the jailed stockbroker (page 206) was tossing a coin that he thought was fair. He tossed it 2400 times, and observed 1279 heads.

His result deviated from 1200 by a surplus of 79 heads. He worked out that one would get a surplus or deficit of more than 75 heads, in 2400 tosses, less than 1% of the time.

He was entitled to say,

- *If* the hypothesis of a fair coin is true, *then* an event of probability less than 1% (more than 1275 heads, or fewer than 1125 heads) has occurred.

But he cannot infer that:

"The probability is less than 1% that the coin is fair."

From the frequency perspective, such a statement does not make sense. He was either tossing a fair coin, or he wasn't.

SIGNIFICANCE

From the frequency perspective, we cannot talk about the probability of H. All the same, *Consumers' Advocate* has drawn attention to a significant fact. There were too many short-life bulbs.

Of course, the 133 short-life bulbs might have been a fluke. That could happen by chance. But most of us would guess that H is false.

Statisticians have evolved a vocabulary here. They say that the *Consumers'
Advocate* data is **significant at the 1% level.**

EXPERIMENTAL FARMS

Some statistical methods were first developed in agriculture. Experimental farms
tested new seeds, new fertilizers, new pesticides.

To begin with, they cared about yields—the new product had to produce
more food, either because it was more bountiful, or because there was more pest
resistance, drought resistance, storm resistance, or whatever.

The method was simple enough. The new seed or fertilizer was tried out in
some well-organized experiment. Nowadays we would have a lot of plots of
land, and randomly assign the new treatment to some, and leave others as
controls.

We call the plots with new fertilizer, or the new seed, or the new pesticide,
the *treated* plots. If the difference between the yields of *treated* and *untreated* plots
is small, then the treatment seems pointless. If the difference is sizable, then the
treatment may be desirable. That is obvious. The question is:

◆ How to sort significant from insignificant differences in yield?

EXPERIMENTAL DESIGN

The question was thought of in terms of *testing* the hypothesis that the treatment
made no material difference to the crop yield. The hypothesis of "no worthwhile
effect" was called the **null hypothesis.**

The procedure for answering the question seems straightforward:

- Make a statistical model of the experiment. This will include the method by
  which some plots are treated, and some are not—for example, the assignment
  may be random.
- Clearly define, in terms of this model, the null hypothesis, that the treatment
  makes no difference.
- Decide how the yields from treated and untreated plots will be measured.
- Divide possible differences between yields from the two kinds of plot into
  two exclusive and exhaustive classes, *Little* and *Big*. If the experimental results
  fall into the *Big* class, there is a big difference in yield.
- Choose *Big* and *Little* so that there is a low probability, *according to the model
  and the null hypothesis*, of getting a *Big* difference—say, 1%.
- Intuitively, we think that a result in the *Big* class is significant.

Once there is an experimental design, the yields from treated and untreated plots
are measured and compared. If the difference between the two yields is *Big*, then
this result is called *significant at the 1% level*. Other phrases are used, such as *1%
significant*.

EXAMPLE: PESTICIDE

A particularly nasty bug is attacking barley crops. It is proposed that coating the seed with a certain chemical will decrease the damage. So a controlled experiment is designed. Very roughly, we grow barley in a number of patches, some treated, some untreated, and compare the yield at harvest. Then we have:

- The null hypothesis. The treatment does not help.
- The conjecture that the pesticide increases yield.
- Data: the relative yields of treated and untreated plots.
- The probability of obtaining the data, or even less probable data, on the supposition that the null hypothesis is true.
- This probability is found to be p.

The probability p is called the **significance level** of the result.

REGIONS OF SIGNIFICANCE

Something is missing from the account so far. Suppose the null hypothesis is that a certain coin is fair. It is tossed 12 times. We obtain:

H, H, T, H, T, T, T, H, T, T, H, H.

6 heads and 6 tails: no evidence against the null hypothesis, that the coin is fair.
    But the probability of getting exactly that sequence of heads and tails is 1/4096, or about 0.00024. Does that mean that the outcome *is* significant?
    No. Most significance tests are designed in the following way.
    We divide possible data into two groups, which we will call S (for significant) and N (for not significant). The groups have two features.

1. If the null hypothesis is true, then the probability of getting any individual test result in S is smaller than the probability of getting any individual test result in N.
2. If the null hypothesis is true, then the probability of getting some result or other in S is p, where p is the significance level of the test.

The first feature implicitly involves likelihood, as defined on page 174. The likelihood of H, in the light of E, is the probability of getting E, if H is true. Feature (1) says that the likelihood of the null hypothesis, in the light of any result in S, is less than the likelihood of the null hypothesis, in the light of any result not in S.

TEST DESIGN

Features (1) and (2) leave a lot of freedom. There are many ways in which to design significance tests. People who design tests typically choose a particular statistical summary of the data, a *statistic*.

The test consists of running the experiment, summarizing the data by the statistic. If the experimental statistic lies in a "1% region" then the results are declared significant at the 1% level.

The 1% region, as in (1) and (2) above:

1. Includes all the results that have lowest probability according to the null hypothesis.
2. Is such that the probability of getting the statistic in that region is 1%, according to the null hypothesis.

How do you choose a statistic? That is the direct and practical question about significance tests. One important theoretical notion is that of a *sufficient statistic*. In a certain sense, a sufficient statistic is a summary of raw data that conveys all the relevant information in the raw data. That is a technical idea for a statistics course, but it is connected with the Bayesian idea (page 181) that likelihood ratios sum up the evidential meaning of a piece of information. Here we are concerned not with such questions about test design, but with the basic logic of significance tests.

THE INDUCTIVE LOGIC OF SIGNIFICANCE TESTS

The upshot of a significance test is never:

"There is at most a 1% chance that the null hypothesis is true."
"The probability that the null hypothesis is false is 0.99."
"The probability is 99% that the treatment increases yields."

The upshot of a significance test is typically:

If a designated null hypothesis is true, then, using a certain statistic that summarizes data from an experiment like ours, the probability of obtaining the data that we obtained, or less probable data, is 0.01.

We often shorten this statement to:

The probability of the data, according to the null hypothesis, is 0.01.

But as we saw above, the probability of the actual data we observed is usually miniscule. What has low probability is a certain region of possible outcomes, which includes our actual data.

What can we say about the truth of the null hypothesis in the light of our data? Only this:

Either the null hypothesis is true, in which case something unusual happened by chance (probability 1%), *or* the null hypothesis is false.

AT HOME WITH FARMERS

Significance tests were invented for farmers. There is an important lesson there. Farmers know an immense amount about their plants, their animals, the weather, their pests, their land. But very little agricultural knowledge is "theoretical" in the way that physics or molecular biology have deep theories behind them. It takes complex chemistry to make a fertilizer or a pesticide. But we can find out if it works, for certain conditions, only by experiment. In the end, theory does not help. Practice tells. To put the matter in strong words:

> Significance tests are for situations where we do not understand, in any theoretical sense, what is happening.

MEDICINE

Significance tests have become very common. The first obvious extension is to medicine. Medicine and farming are very similar. We usually do not understand very well why various medications or treatments are effective. We have only a little theoretical understanding of what is really happening. Even researchers who think they do understand have to convince skeptics.

We can nevertheless tell, empirically, that some medications are more effective than others. Significance tests help us test new medicines and treatments. They also help us to find out when different health factors are *associated* or *correlated* with one another.

EXPERIMENTAL PSYCHOLOGY

Experimental psychology has become the heartland of significance testing. This fits our paradigm. We understand, in a deep theoretical way, almost nothing about human psychology. So we do lots and lots of purely empirical experiments. We design experiments, obtain results, and quote significance levels.

Many research journals that publish experimental psychology insist on significance levels or other more sophisticated statistical indicators. If you open a research journal today, you will soon find tables of results, with a last column that indicates the extent to which two variables are associated.

For example, in a memory test, the length of time between exposure to a stimulus, and testing for recognition of it, may affect the ability to recognize the stimulus. In the table of results, there may be a column of numbers indicating the extent to which time and recognition are associated. Some of these numbers will be marked with a single asterisk (*). Others are marked with a (**). At the bottom of the table you will see:

* $p < 0.05$.   ** $p < 0.01$.

This means that the associations marked (*) are significant at the 0.05 level, and those marked (**) are significant at the 0.01 level.

SOCIAL SCIENCES

Very much the same practice is common in many social sciences. Here are some examples taken from issues of mainline research journals that appeared just as I was finishing this chapter:

Sociology: A paper comparing (a) the educational achievement and occupational status of children whose parents moved from one part of the country to another during their childhoods, to (b) the same achievements for age-matched children whose parents stayed in the same region or town.

Economic Geography: A paper arguing that despite superficial economic agreements, there has been no real tendency toward the formation of distinct trade blocs on the part of the three major powers (Germany, Japan, and the United States) over the past twenty years.

Political Science: A paper (about the causes of the collapse of the Soviet Union) arguing that in only four countries around the world was there a significant association between educational level, and a preference for individuals taking care of themselves whenever possible, as opposed to government responsibility for the general welfare of all individuals.

History: A paper explaining why, before 1914, capital-importing countries such as the United States, Canada, Australia, Italy, and Argentina did their best, despite enormous difficulties, to keep on the "gold standard"—to ensure that their currencies were exchangeable for gold bullion. (Reason: the capital-exporting countries of Europe, such as France, Germany, and Britain, charged lower interest rates to countries on the gold standard, even though they said this made no difference.)

Psychiatry: A paper arguing that a questionnaire for screening dissociative identity disorder (multiple personality) correlates well with other tests favored by psychiatrists who believe in this diagnosis.

As an exercise, you could go to a college library and see how many different types of journals use the same practice of citing 0.01 and 0.05 significance levels.

STATISTICAL PACKAGES

One of the reasons for the popularity of 0.01 and 0.05 (or their complements, 99% and 95%) was a sort of mathematical accident. Any phenomenon approximated by or modeled by a normal distribution or bell-shaped curve has the property we used for our Normal Fact on page 203: it is unusually easy to compute 99% and 95% accuracy probabilities for some phenomena.

Long before pocket calculators made some calculations trivial, these figures became easy standards for comparison, simply because you could compute them without weeks of back-breaking labor. Today many investigators use a statistical software package without really understanding what it does. You can just enter data, and press a button to select a program.

As a result, some research seems quite mindless. It looks for associations, without having any theoretical model in mind at all. It produces tables with those stars (*) and (**) indicating a significance level. Remember, all that the (**) means is:

Either the null hypothesis is true, in which case something unusual happened by chance (probability 1%), *or* the null hypothesis is false.

The situation is sometimes even worse with more sophisticated statistical techniques contained in easy-to-use software packages. Often people who use them have no idea what the packages are for.

p-VALUE

The value of 1% for significance level is purely arbitrary. An experiment can be designed for any low probability, 0.05 or .001 or whatever. The significance level is often called the *p*-value. Papers will report some work, do some calculations, and conclude, "The *p*-value is such-and-such." That means the level of significance is such-and-such.

The procedure is only slightly different from the first agricultural field trials. There, in advance, we divided treatment differences into *Big* and *Little*, where *Big* was chosen so that the probability of getting a yield difference in the *Big* class was (say) 0.01.

Instead we could have proceeded as follows:

- We observe a difference in yield of x.
- We work out the probability of getting a yield difference of **at least** x, according to the null hypothesis and the statistical model of the experiment.
- We find that this probability is q.
- We take the nearest tidy small number a little larger than q—it might be 0.1 or 0.001 or 0.03 or 0.006, or whatever. We call this number the *p*-value.
- We report the experiment result and conclude with the words, "The *p*-value is 0.00006 (or whatever)."

FAT AND BEANS

Often *p*-values are useful as quick indicators of the relative importance of different findings. They are used not only in experiments but also, for example, in surveys to detect associations. There is no ethical way to conduct an experiment on human beings, to see whether smoking cigarettes is an effective treatment for producing lung cancer. But we can compare the incidence of lung cancer among smokers and nonsmokers. It is significant. That observation was the *beginning* of our present knowledge about the dangers of nicotine addiction. It took much more than surveys to show that there is a causal connection.

You may have heard of studies of the incidence of lung cancer among male smokers. Now for something completely different: the incidence of lung cancer among female nonsmokers. A statistically sophisticated paper in the *Journal of the National Cancer Institute* examined some relationships between diet and lung cancer among nonsmoking women in Missouri. We quote from only one aspect of this paper.

Missouri women with lung cancer were matched for age, income, race, marital history, and so forth with randomly selected Missouri women. All the women (or near relatives, in the case of patients near death) were asked about various factors in their diets, such as the frequency with which they ate peas or beans. After eliminating many of the women for one reason or another (unreliable diet information, other health problems, etc.) 429 nonsmoking women with lung cancer were compared to a control group of 1021 women who did not have lung cancer. It was found that the more fat was eaten, the more the ratios of women who had lung cancer, to women who did not have lung cancer, increased. The ratios decreased the more peas and beans were eaten. Were these and other results significant?

In the following quotation, "univariate" means the authors are in each case comparing just one variable (say, the frequency of eating peas or beans) with the incidence of lung cancer.

> Among the macro-nutrients, daily intake of total fat ($p = .02$), saturated fat ($p = .0004$), oleic acid ($p = .07$), percent of calories from fat ($p = .02$) were univariately associated with an increasing risk of lung cancer, while percent of calories from carbohydrates ($p = .09$) was associated with a decreasing risk. In evaluating the role of food fiber, the intake of fiber from beans and peas ($p = .002$) was significantly related to decreasing risk.

The null hypothesis, in each case, was that a factor such as consuming oleic acid has no association with lung cancer. The test statistic was based on the trend for increasing rates of lung cancer for a given foodstuff. Using a standard measure of trend, results were not divided in advance into two classes, *Big Trend* and *Little Trend*. Instead, the *p*-value indicates the degree of probability of getting, in each case, the observed trend or greater (as measured by a standardly used statistic).

The numbers just quoted help you to see at a glance which trends seem most significant—in fact, the authors even use the word "significantly" in the last sentence quoted.

The last number—$p = 0.002$—does not mean (to repeat!) that the probability is 0.998 that eating peas and beans reduces the risk of lung cancer. It means that the observed trend of decreasing incidence of lung cancer among pea and bean eaters would very seldom be observed, if eating peas and beans was not associated with the low incidence of lung cancer in a regular way.

CAUSES

Does eating peas and beans *cause* a lower incidence of lung cancer, while eating foods high in saturated fats *causes* a greater incidence?

In this book we do not discuss causation. That deserves another textbook. But notice an obvious fact. The report does go along with a lot of other work suggesting that saturated fats are bad for a long life and that fiber is good for a long life. But the facts reported are different from some better-known facts.

For example, we can begin to guess why saturated fat might be associated with *heart* problems; according to our present-day folk medicine, the arteries get clogged. We can begin to guess why fiber might diminish problems like *colon* cancer; according to our present-day folk medicine, more regular bowel movements diminish the chance of colon cancer. But why on earth should fiber or fat have any effect on *lung* cancer?

> Proposing a biological mechanism for the observed association between dietary fat and lung cancer would be speculative at this time in light of the inconsistent pattern of risk observed [in the literature surveyed by the authors].

The significance levels give us a basis for further research. The article tells us to look for causes, but not whether there are causes, or what they might be. There is a shred of evidence that a great deal of a certain type of fat molecule may produce certain types of cancer cells in mice. That is about as far as we have gone, so far.

This study alone would not be enough to set off a big search for connections between fat and lung cancer. Work like this gains momentum when put together with other studies. The authors write that

> A large case-control study conducted in Toronto found a relationship between lung cancer risk and dietary intake of total fat, saturated fat, and cholesterol in both men and women and in both smokers and nonsmokers.

COMMON CAUSE

The cause of variation in lung cancer rates might nevertheless not be diet. For example, look at where the fat is coming from, and remember that we are talking about older women, not kids going to a fast-food chain:

> In this study, the leading contributors of dietary saturated fat were hamburgers, cheeseburgers, and meat loaf.

We may be looking at a relatively poor part of the population (that's meat loaf, not steak). Maybe the people who eat peas and beans have a more active life, contributing to better lungs, than the people who eat cheeseburgers. Maybe the fat and beans have nothing causal to do with lung cancer, although there is a *common cause* of high cheeseburger consumption and a high lung cancer rate (poverty, or an inactive life style). Maybe there is a *common cause* of a low incidence of lung cancer and eating peas and beans (an active, health-conscious life). In fact, that was a first line of defense against the claim that smoking cigarettes causes lung cancer. Maybe some factor, be it genetics or stress, causes people both to like nicotine and to get lung cancer.

Everyday folklore is all that most of us use when we guess that an "active lifestyle" and no cheeseburgers are good for health. Do not be so sure about that. There is an old Woody Allen movie, *Sleeper*, in which people wake up late next century and find everyone gulping down cheeseburgers and milkshakes at health clinics. They laugh at *our* folklore that peas and beans are good for you, and fat is bad.

That is why we need significance tests or more powerful kinds of statistical inference. We need statistics when we don't understand. That is why we use techniques originally developed for agriculture.

Medical research papers often use fancy words. The word *etiological* comes from a Greek word for "cause." Doctors use it to mean "causal." The paper we have been looking at ends by saying:

> In summary our paper finds a strong, increasing trend in lung cancer risk associated with increased saturated fat consumption among nonsmoking women. . . . A smaller protective effect was also observed with bean and pea consumption. While our results support the public health admonition to reduce fat and saturated fat consumption, *additional etiological studies are needed before we can fully understand the nature of this association.*

We have emphasized the conclusion. Perhaps it is a bit of an understatement!

STANDARDS

Significance tests used in experiments and other types of study can be quite sophisticated. But the logic is pretty much the same. Either a certain hypothesis is false, or else something unusual has occurred.

What is the point of those little numbers, the 1% or the *p*-values?

The point is to standardize experimental and survey work. If experiments and surveys use some standard experimental designs, some standard tests of significance, and report significance levels, we have a way to compare different reports.

Unfortunately, a lot of routine work, especially in the social sciences, now tends to report the significance of an experimental result, and leave things at that. But significance should be just the beginning.

Think about the word "significance" itself. A result is significant if it means *something*. But what? A significant result is a beginning, not end. Eating beans and peas "significantly" decreases the probability of getting lung cancer. But why on Earth?

Once we have got a fix on the significance of some evidence, we have only just begun to work or think. If we actually care about a fertilizer, a medicine, a diet, and are told a significance level, we have an intersubjective way of assessing the result, and comparing it to other results in other fields we know more about. But you should not think of a significance test as a purely intellectual event: "The significance level in a test of the null hypothesis H is 1%. So H is false!"

The point of the test was to see, for example, if a treatment is effective, or a type of diet is associated with lung cancer. If we get significant results, we become interested in applying the treatment or looking further into the diet. A *p*-

value or significance level test is just one step in the development of useful knowledge and techniques.

RIVAL HYPOTHESES

Significance tests are tests of a null hypothesis. Back on the farm, the null hypothesis states that a certain experimental treatment has no material effect. Naturally, there is a rival hypothesis: the treatment has noticeable good effects. So far, we have taken that for granted. But as significance tests became generalized beyond medical and agricultural trials to psychology, sociology, political science, and so forth, it became necessary to specify alternative hypotheses more carefully. We can see this even with our two examples, the prisoner tossing coins, and VisioPerfect producing light bulbs.

The prisoner tosses his coin and finds he gets too many heads. But he would have been equally suspicious about possible bias if he found too many tails. The situation is different with *Consumers' Advocate*. The editors are suspicious in one direction only: VisioPerfect's bulbs are not good enough. The veins of suspicion run differently in the two cases:

- *Coin.* Null hypothesis: fair coin.
  - ➤ Experiment: 2400 trials.
  - ➤ Significant result: too many heads, or too many tails.
- *Light bulbs.* Null hypothesis: 96% long-life bulbs.
  - ➤ Experiment: 2400 trials.
  - ➤ Significant result: too many short-life bulbs.

It seems clear that although so far we have described significance tests on the two null hypotheses as strictly parallel, they ought not to be.

In the case of the coin, the region of significance should be what is called "two-sided." The region of significance should include both what are, according to the null hypothesis, too many heads, and too many tails.

In the case of the light bulbs, the region of significance should be what is called "one-sided." It should include only what are, according to the null hypothesis, too many short-life bulbs.

In both cases, we will take an experimental result to be significant at the 1% level when we get a result that is in a class of results that happens only 1% of the time. But we will choose the classes differently, depending on the *rival hypotheses* that interest us.

Some investigators think this should be done in an ad hoc way, from case to case. In real life, situations differ a good deal, and the design of a significance test requires a subtle appreciation of the circumstances. Other investigators favor a more systematic approach derived from the work of Jerzy Neyman and E. S. Pearson. Instead of a framework of *significance*, they use a framework of *acceptance and rejection* of statistical hypotheses.

ACCEPTANCE AND REJECTION

Suppose a researcher tests a null hypothesis and gets results significant at the 1% level. That may indicate to her that some treatment or intervention does have some effect. The investigator might be said to "reject" the null hypothesis, but that, in the original framework of significance tests, would be misleading. It would suggest that she first believed in the null hypothesis, and then rejected it. The usual course of events is just the opposite. The investigator hopes that a treatment is effective—hopes that the null hypothesis is false. A significant result is encouraging.

Likewise, an investigator might be said to "accept" a null hypothesis if test results are not significant. But that does not mean that the null hypothesis becomes part of her set of accepted beliefs. More likely, she just forgets about it!

All that makes sense in the significance framework. But now we consider a new framework. Just as there are frequency dogmatists and belief dogmatists, so, within the frequency perspective, there have been significance dogmatists and acceptance dogmatists. As usual, our approach is eclectic. There are important uses for both approaches.

THE NEYMAN–PEARSON FRAMEWORK

Neyman and Pearson produced a new framework. They think of an investigator as having a certain policy for sorting hypotheses in the light of experimental results. Some hypotheses are rejected, and others are accepted. Sometimes this might be literal rejection, not of hypotheses but of, say, manufactured objects. Thus VisioPerfect may use quality control to reject the hypothesis that a certain batch is up to 96% long-life. That means rejecting the batch, not offering it for sale under the famous brand name VisioPerfect.

Neyman and Pearson considered a method of analysis that in the end leads to one of two decisions:

◆ Reject a hypothesis under consideration.
◆ Accept that hypothesis.

They design tests that divide experimental outcomes into two mutually exclusive regions:

◆ R: Reject the hypothesis H if the outcome falls in R.
◆ A: Accept the hypothesis H if the outcome falls in A.

At first this looks very much like significance testing. The rejection region is just what we earlier called the class S of significant results. But S was chosen without any explicit mention of rival hypotheses. In the new framework, we choose rejection and acceptance regions using all the hypotheses that interest us.

TWO TYPES OF ERROR

In the Neyman–Pearson framework, we can make two different types of mistake:

◆ Error of **Type** I: Reject H when it is true.
◆ Error of **Type** II: Accept H when it is false.

Neyman and Pearson say we should design tests that keep both types of error as small as possible.

That involves a balancing act. It is easy to keep Type I errors small. Never reject H. (Or make the probability of rejecting H vanishingly small.) It is easy to keep Type II errors small. Never accept H. (Or make the probability of accepting H vanishingly small.)

To make the balancing act simple, we can think first of keeping the probability of Type I error conveniently small, say 0.01.

So we could design a test such that

$$\Pr(R/H) = 0.01.$$

Thus far, this rationale is no different from significance tests. (Neyman and Pearson renamed the significance level the "size" of the test, but we will keep the older language.)

POWER

It is the next step that counts.

Given a chosen small probability of Type I error, we want to minimize the probability of Type II error. That is, we want to *minimize*:

$$\Pr(A/H \text{ is false}).$$

Or, to say the same thing differently, we want to *maximize* the probability of rejecting a hypothesis when it is false:

$$\Pr(R/H \text{ is false}).$$

Neyman and Pearson called this the **power** of the test. They said that we want to maximize power.

Power is not so easy to work out as significance. This is because even when H is a statistical hypothesis, the assertion that "H is false" is not usually a straightforward statistical hypothesis at all.

For example, James tossing his coin had a simple statistical hypothesis H: the coin is fair. The alternative is any number of hypotheses involving bias, nonindependence, or both. We can compute the probability of any sequence of outcomes or set of outcomes from a coin, on the hypothesis that the coin is fair, or $\Pr(\text{heads}) = 0.33$, or any other specific hypothesis. But we cannot compute the probability of heads with a coin, on the supposition that "the coin is not fair."

We have to specify the class of hypotheses that are *rivals* to the hypothesis under test. In some questions it may be impossible to do this, at a certain stage of scientific knowledge, in a meaningful way.

Here we will not show how Neyman and Pearson design tests. They usually require quite specific assumptions about the rival hypotheses, although there are a few generally applicable techniques. The problems of designing exact Neyman–Pearson tests are formidable. The important logical point is this.

> Neyman–Pearson tests try to maximize the probability of rejecting a false hypothesis, and minimize the probability of rejecting a true hypothesis.

A common way to do this is to choose a small probability of rejecting a true hypothesis, as in a significance test, while trying to maximize the power, the probability of rejecting false hypotheses.

UTILITIES

There is no reason to go through life with a fixed significance level and a fixed power which one tries to obtain in every test design.

Sometimes one is concerned about power. Sometimes one wants to make very sure that one rejects a hypothesis if it is false. For example, let H be the hypothesis that a certain medication for schizophrenia has no harmful side effects not found with other medications for that disorder.

Sometimes one is concerned with significance. Sometimes one wants to make very sure that one does not reject a hypothesis that is true. For example, let H be the hypothesis that a certain cheap and palatable diet improves the quality of life of the large numbers of East Africans suffering from an immune deficiency disease.

R. A. FISHER

The significance test framework is the work of the English statistician R. A. Fisher (1890–1962). He contributed more fundamental ideas to applied statistics than anyone else. He was also the most original contributor of his generation to statistical genetics, and to the great synthesis in evolutionary biology involving biometrics, Mendel, and Darwin.

Significance tests are only a small aspect of his work. Numerous statistical tests are named after him. Central concepts such as significance, likelihood ratios, and maximum likelihood originate with him. He invented the analysis of variance, which has become standard practice in medical and biological research. He created the general theory of the design of experiments, and developed key concepts of statistical information, such as the idea of a sufficient statistic. We now take for granted that experiments to see whether a treatment is effective should use randomized procedures. That was an innovation for which Fisher had to fight surprisingly hard.

Fisher was always strongly opposed to a *universal* theory of statistical inference. Although many "cookbook" statistical ideas are due to Fisher, he fought long and hard against cookbooks. We have, he thought, a large number of inductive techniques, and we should consider practical situations carefully to see which is appropriate. He thought Bayesian reasoning was fine in its place, when one had good scientific ground for a prior probability. He thought that the Neyman–Pearson framework was fine for quality control, but not for determining single, important scientific quantities. Above all, he thought that statistics and frequency-type probabilities were an essential tool for the communication of information among scientists working in fields where there may not be very good theories about nature, but where there is a great deal of data which needs to be understood.

EXERCISES

1 *Birthdays.* In the astrological example at the start of this chapter, we considered four people, two of whom had the same sign of the zodiac. Was this surprising? No, we found that almost as often as not we expect at least two people among four drawn at random to have the same sign of the zodiac.

You could discuss the astrology example by asking this question: how large a group do you need, so that there is about a 50:50 chance that two people have the same sign of the zodiac? The answer is, four. So it is not surprising that among the four friends, two had the same sign of the zodiac.

Here is a famous example. How large a group do you need, so that there is a 50:50 chance that two people have the same birthday? If you do not know the answer, think about it. Would you be surprised, for example, if in a group of 4, two people had the same birthday? In a group of 8? In a group of 128?

Describe how you might use the method of the astrology example, to answer the birthday question. You do not have to compute the answer.

2 *Statistics in law.*   From a 1980 court case:

> If a 5% level of significance is used [in testing the hypothesis that a coefficient is zero] then the chances are less than one in 20 that the true coefficient is actually zero.

What is wrong with that statement?

3 *Vitamin E and heart failure.*   From a 1996 newspaper story:

> Ten cents worth of vitamin E seems to reduce heart attacks by 75% when taken daily by people with bad hearts, report British researchers led by Dr. Nigel Brown in London. The British team enrolled 2002 people with serious heart disease and randomly assigned them to take either placebos or pills containing 400 or 800 international units of vitamin E a day. After 17 months, 50 people had died of heart disease and 55 had suffered nonfatal

heart attacks. Fourteen of the nonfatal heart attacks occurred among vitamin takers, 41 in the placebo group. The deaths from heart disease were evenly split between the two groups.

(a) Perhaps two distinct null hypotheses were being tested here. What would they be?

(b) The data were significant for one null hypothesis, but not for the other. Explain.

(c) After reading the entire paragraph, the opening sentence seems misleading. Why?

4 *Vitamins: two tests.* In this example, it seems that two null hypotheses were tested. Suppose significance tests were used, and the comparison of 14 to 41 nonfatal heart attacks was significant at the 1% level. The comparison of actual deaths was not significant at the 1% level.

(a) What is the probability that when *one* 1% test is conducted, by chance you will get a significant result even if the null hypothesis is true?

(b) What is the probability that when *two* 1% tests are conducted, by chance you will get at least one significant result even if both null hypotheses are true?

5 *Fat and beans.* In the example on page 218, five different p-values were given for trends associated with consuming fat. A further p-value was given for a trend associated with eating peas and beans. Since so many factors were examined, were the investigators bound to find some associations with p-values lower than 0.05?

6 *Psychology: one hundred tests.* Jerry is a psychology graduate student. He does a couple hundred experiments. Each has a distinct null hypothesis. In two cases, he finds results that are significant at the 1% level. The results of the other experiments are not significant, even at the 5% level. He publishes just these two experiments. *Comment!*

7 *The department at work.* Jerry is a student in a large psychology department, with 100 graduate students, each of whom is exactly as successful as Jerry. Each student publishes two experiments, and each gets a Ph.D. "What a great department" says Jerry's friend Bobby. "What a lot of discoveries those students are making!" *Comment.*

8 *Power.* As a matter of fact, experimental psychologists usually publish p-values, using the significance test framework. But they are usually not testing a null hypothesis about the noneffect of a treatment. Critics of this practice suggest that experimental psychology should use the Neyman–Pearson framework. In particular, psychology journals should insist that authors publish not only p-values but also the power of the test they are using. Do you agree?

9 *Vitamins again.* In question 3, let H_E be the hypothesis that taking fairly large doses of vitamin E cuts down on nonfatal heart attacks. Rival hypothesis K_E states that taking vitamin E has no effect on the incidence of nonfatal heart attacks, or anything much else.

Let H_A be the hypothesis that taking large doses of vitamin A (in the form of beta-carotene), thought to discourage lung cancer, has no side effects for heart disease among heavy smokers. A rival hypothesis K_A states that taking vitamin A increases the incidence of heart failure among heavy smokers.

If you were constructing Neyman–Pearson tests for these H against their rivals K, would you use tests of the same power?

10 *More statistics in law.* This quotation is from a textbook about probability and jurisprudence.

> In large samples a value of the statistic t of approximately 2 means that the chances are less than one in twenty that the true coefficient is actually zero and that we are observing a larger coefficient just by chance. . . . A t-statistic of approximately 2½ means the chances are only one in a hundred that the true coefficient is zero.

What is wrong with that?

11 *Bayesian lawyers?*   OK: so the authors in questions 2 and 10 are not good at inductive logic. But can't we be generous? Don't they really mean something Bayesian? Take, for example, question 10. Is there any difficulty with this Bayesian version of the statement?

> In large samples a value of the statistic t of approximately 2 means that the personal probability, that the true coefficient is actually zero, is less than one in twenty that the true coefficient is actually zero. . . . A t-statistic of approximately 2½ means the personal probability that the true coefficient is zero should be only 0.01.

12 *Overconfident physics.* Don't think we are down on lawyers. The following statement is taken from a recent advanced physics textbook with the title *Techniques for Nuclear and Particle Physics Experiments, A How to Approach*. It is explaining the practical use of confidence intervals. It asserts that in experimental physics we should not state the result of a measurement as an exact number x, but as a number with a margin of error indicated by the standard deviation σ. The author states that:

> The presentation of a result as x plus or minus σ signifies, in fact, that the true value [of what we are measuring] has (about) 68% probability of lying between the limits $x - \sigma$ and $x + \sigma$ or a 95% probability of lying between $x - 2\sigma$ and $x + 2\sigma$.

What is wrong with this assertion?

KEY WORDS FOR REVIEW

Statistical hypothesis	Acceptance and rejection
Significance level	Type I and Type II errors
Significance test	Power
p-value	

19 Confidence and Inductive Behavior

Our final example of inductive logic denies that we make inferences at all. Instead, we behave inductively, in such a way that our system for making decisions has good overall consequences for us. This is the theory of confidence intervals.

SAMPLES AND POPULATIONS

In Chapter 2 there was a box of 60 oranges—a population of oranges. We drew 4 oranges at random—a sample. In Chapter 2 we distinguished two forms of argument:

Statement about a population.
So,
Statement about a sample.

Statement about a sample.
So,
Statement about a population.

Bernoulli's Theorem, applied to sampling with replacement from an urn, makes a statement about a sample on the basis of knowledge about the population of the urn and the sampling method. It is an example of the first type of argument.

Now we want to go in the other direction. We take a sample. We want to draw a conclusion about a population. A significance test involves one type of reasoning but does not go very far. We often want to use a sample to *estimate* something about a population. The most familiar type of estimate based on a sample is the opinion poll.

OPINION POLLS

Before we do some inductive logic, we should pause to think realistically about survey sampling. Consider a controversial survey topic.

Population: A population of university students asked about a proposed new abortion law. The students' answers are classified as:

favorable / unfavorable / indifferent / don't know.

Sample: An actual sample of 1000 students from this population, taken without replacement (no student is asked the same question twice). The result is a large number of survey forms, with responses, but also coded by the pollsters who asked questions, where the students study, the date the questions were asked, and so forth.

Statistical summary: The proportions of the four responses to the question.

Theoretical probability model: The sample was so conducted that there was an equal probability of sampling any student as of sampling any other.

There are two distinct kinds of worry about this survey.

WORRY 1: THE MODEL

Even with urns it is hard to make a fair drawing device, in which draws are completely unbiased and independent. But think about the real world!

The theoretical model for the survey sample cannot be literally correct. Suppose we try to be very random. We write down every ordered pair {university, student number} and use a computer randomizer to sample from this list.

Practical problems: Some students have dropped out. Some students are enrolled at two universities. Some students have impersonators taking their courses. A couple of dogs, four cats, one horse, and a parakeet were enrolled last year, not to mention some dead people.

Worse problems: It is hard to contact students. No matter how hard we try to make a random sample, stay-at-home students, or go-to-class students, or students-who-have-a-phone-and-answer-it, will show up more often than students who are in the hospital, or out of town, during the survey.

In fact, the theoretical probability model is *false*. It is not a literally true description of the population and sampling method.

We use it because it is not far from the truth. It is a *model*, no more, no less.

Models are not exact, but they are useful.

WORRY 2: THE DATA

In a survey about their favorite TV shows, students might answer honestly, or truly say they never watch television. But: one student is a couch potato who feels guilty, and says he never watches. Another watches only pornography—but denies that. A third lies, thinking it is better to watch a popular program, such as Oprah, though really he watches only opera. Another says he watches only opera, but in fact watches only Oprah.

That's bad enough, but in a poll about a really controversial topic, like abortion, we might expect a great many students to conceal their real attitudes.

WHAT INDUCTIVE LOGIC IS NOT ABOUT

Both problems, the *model* and the *data*, are important. But inductive logic is like deductive logic. Deductive logic is concerned with the validity of arguments. As we said on page 7, logicians study the relations between premises and conclusions. As logicians, they do not comment on whether the premises are true. This is the case for both deductive and inductive logic.

- Inductive logic is about arguments. It is not about the truth or falsehood of premises.
- It is about whether premises provide good reasons for conclusions.

Inductive logic, using frequency-type probabilities, has two kinds of premises: the sample data, and the theoretical model. We then consider what inferences to draw from the premises, or what decisions to make.

There are a lot of deep ideas about how to check the data, and how to check the model. For example, a theoretical probability model is itself a statistical hypothesis. We can use statistical methods to check the model. But in this course, we stick to the simplest questions, about what conclusions to draw from a theoretical model and some data.

ESTIMATION

The most familiar type of estimate is based on proportions. The inference goes:

Population: Balls in an urn.
Sample: A series of 60 draws from an urn, in order, classified by color, as green, red.
Statistical summary: The proportion of green balls drawn in the sample is (say) 18/60, or 3/10.
Theoretical probability model: Sampling was with replacement, draws were independent, and the probability of drawing any ball equals the chance of drawing any other.
Inference: **So**, the proportion of green balls in the population is around 0.3.

That is an estimate of the proportion of green balls in the population. How reliable is it?

RELIABILITY

We all make estimates on the basis of averages. Is that a fact of human psychology? Cultural conditioning? Is there a good theoretical reason for estimating this way?

There is another, more practical question. Three centuries ago, Jacques Bernoulli said something like: "Every peasant knows how to reason this way." The interesting question is, how reliable is an estimate?

Perhaps everyone knows that the larger the sample, the more reliable the estimate. But how much more reliable? When is an estimate reliable?

POINT ESTIMATES

A point **estimate** is an estimate of a quantity or parameter which states a single number.

I am fixing part of a wooden shed. How much lumber will I need to finish the job? I'll need 96 feet. If I tell the lumber yard that I want "between 92 and 98 feet of 6-inch pine," I'll be asked, "But how much do you actually want?"

I usually have to act on point estimates.

But point estimates are usually not exactly right. As a matter of fact, when I am doing carpentry I leave a *margin of error*. I get a few feet to spare. If there are any leftovers, they go into the next job, or are used as firewood. Isn't that wasteful? Not necessarily; it might be more wasteful to make an extra trip to the lumber yard for the few extra feet I would need, if I were short.

Statisticians make point estimates, but they also make *interval estimates*.

INTERVAL ESTIMATES

If q is some quantity of interest—the number of leaves on a mango tree, the proportion of good oranges in the box—I may state that the quantity lies in an interval.

> The number of leaves on the tree is between 236,000 and 237,000.
> The proportion of good oranges in the box is between 0.9 and 0.96.
> The probability of drawing green from this urn is between 0.37 and 0.43.

How reliable are such estimates? Belief-type, or Bayesian, analysis can in principle give a quick answer. We find the posterior probability, given the sample data, that the true value of the quantity q does lie in the interval.

Frequency-type probability cannot do that. Either q is in the interval, or it is not. There is no frequency about it.

> The number of leaves on the tree is between 236,000 and 237,000. Or it is not. But there is not a frequency with which *this* tree has that many leaves.
> The proportion of good oranges in the box is between 0.9 and 0.96—or it is not. There is no frequency about it.

Frequency-type probability needs a way to make interval estimates and to indicate how reliable they are. Can we do that? Of course we can. We are familiar with public opinion surveys.

SMOKE

The city council has been debating whether to ban smoking in restaurants, bars, and cafés. There are several possibilities: a complete ban, smoking allowed only in separate rooms with their own ventilation systems, or segregated smoking and nonsmoking areas.

A poll released last week said that a survey of city residents over 18 years of age determined that 78% favored at least segregated areas, and 57% favored limiting smoking to separate rooms with their own ventilation. Only 38% favored a complete ban. These results are based on a poll of 1026 residents conducted between July 5 and July 9, and are considered accurate to within three percentage points, 19 times out of 20.

WHAT THE REPORT DOES NOT SAY

19 times out of 20 is 95%.

A margin of error of three percentage points around 57% is $57 \pm 3\%$. To say that a proportion is within 3% of 57% is to say it lies between 54% and 60%.

There is no problem with those two explanations, but we are not done yet. The report does *not* say:

"There is a 95% probability, that the proportion of adult residents who favor limiting smoking to separate rooms with their own ventilation is between 54% and 60%."

From the frequency perspective, such a statement does not make sense.

Either the proportion of residents who favor separate smoking rooms is between 54% and 60%—or it is not. There is no frequency about it.

What then does the report mean?

BERNOULLI TRIALS

Polls are easy to model as Bernoulli trials on an urn. We think of sampling with replacement with a constant probability of p of getting a green ball—of selecting a person at random who answers "Yes" to a question.

Opinion polls sample without replacement. But we have seen that in large populations—the 655,000 adult residents of a city, say, and not the 60 oranges in the single box—the probabilities of sampling with and without replacement are pretty much the same. There are many other complications about real-life sampling, but here we care only about the basic idea.

DEDUCTION

Bernoulli's Theorem tells us a lot. Take any population divided into two groups, the Gs and the not-Gs. The population could be adult residents of the city, the Gs could be the adults who favor a total ban on smoking, and the not-Gs could be the rest of the adults. The population could be married couples living together, and the Gs could be couples in which both spouses are faithful. Or the population could be balls in an urn, and the Gs could be the green balls.

Knowing the proportion p of Gs in the population, we can deduce that:

For any small margin of error,
there is a high probability (the accuracy-probability)
that a large sample from the population
will have a proportion of Gs close to p.

In Chapter 17, Normal Fact III (page 205), we stated formulas for some special cases, where the accuracy-probability is about 2/3, 0.95, and 0.99. The formulas depend on standard deviation in the normal approximation, $\sigma = \sqrt{[p(1-p)n]}$, which determines the margin of error.

Knowing p, we can use the table on page 205 to calculate that, for example:

The probability—the accuracy probability—that the proportion of Gs in our sample is within $2\sqrt{[p(1-p)n]}/n$ of p is 0.95

That is a deductive inference. We would like the opposite, an inductive inference. We make a sample of size n. Suppose that the proportion of Gs in the sample is s.

Knowing s, we want to make a statement about p. How can we do that, when the frequency perspective does not allow us to make a probability statement about p? We use one other item from Chapter 17, the "worst-case scenario."

THE WORST-CASE SCENARIO

The accuracy-probability depends on p.

But we also found a worst-case scenario—when $p = \frac{1}{2}$.

In that case the largest possible margin of error is $\frac{1}{2}\sqrt{n}$.

Now we know that for any value of p, there is, for example, a 95% accuracy-probability that the proportion s of Gs in the sample is within $2\sigma/n$ of p.

But for any value of p, the largest possible value of σ—the worst-case scenario—is $\frac{1}{2}\sqrt{n}$.

Hence:

For any possible value of p, the probability is **at least** 2/3 that the proportion s of Gs in the sample is within $1/(2\sqrt{n})$ of p.
For any possible value of p, the probability is **at least** 95% that the proportion s of Gs in the sample is within $1/\sqrt{n}$ of p.
For any possible value of p, the probability is **at least** 99% that the proportion s of Gs in the sample is within $3/(2\sqrt{n})$ of p.

For example, if $n = 10,000$, there is, *regardless of the value of* **p**, at least a 95% probability that the proportion s of Gs in the sample is within $1/\sqrt{(10,000)} = 1/100 = 1\%$ of p.

And there is at least a 99% probability that the proportion s of Gs in the sample is within $3/[2\sqrt{(10,000)}] = 3/200 = 1.5\%$ of p.

THE CONFIDENCE IDEA

Now let us sample a population and see what we can infer about that population.

Let s be the proportion of Gs in a sample of size 10,000.

Then there is *at least* a

95% probability of obtaining a sample such that s is within 1% of p.

Hence—*and here is the logical trick*—there is at least a

95% probability of obtaining a sample such that p is within 1% of s.

That is the basis of confidence intervals.

But be careful! Remember that p is fixed, and that what varies from sample to sample is s.

Suppose that we make a sample of 10,000 individuals, and find that 3000, or 30%, are G. You might look at the above and conclude:

"The probability is 0.95 that the proportion of Gs in the population is within 1% of 30%."

"The probability is 0.95 that the proportion of Gs is between 0.29 and 0.31."

From the frequency perspective, *these statements are absolutely incorrect*.

The proportion of Gs in the population is either between 0.29 and 0.31, or it is not. There is no frequency about it.

So what *should* we say?

CONFIDENCE INTERVALS

The interval 0.29 to 0.31 is called a *confidence interval*. It is used as an *estimate* of the proportion of Gs—an *interval estimate*.

Our *method* for making the estimate, based on a random sample of 10,000 individuals, is:

◆ To select 10,000 individuals at random.
◆ To determine the proportion s of these 10,000 that are G.
◆ To estimate that the proportion p of Gs in the entire population is between $(s-0.01)$ and $(s+0.01)$.

Of course, the proportion s of Gs in the sample will vary from sample to sample. But the probability on any trial of getting a proportion s, such that the unknown proportion p lies between $(s-0.01)$ and $(s+0.01)$, is 95%.

In particular, if our sample of 10,000 gave us $s = 0.30$, we can estimate that p is between 0.29 and 0.31. We can say that our "confidence" in this interval is 95%.

This means that we have made this estimate by a procedure that gives a correct estimate at least 95% of the time.

A confidence statement has the form:
On the basis of our data, we estimate that an unknown quantity lies in an interval. This estimate is made according to a method that is right with probability at least 0.95.

It is completely incorrect to assert anything like this:

"The 95% confidence interval estimate for quantity q is I. So the probability that q lies in the interval I is 0.95."

EXACT INTERVALS

Our purpose is to explain the logic of confidence intervals. Hence we use easy numbers. Our table on page 205 does tell us how to get 99% confidence intervals. For the sample of 10,000, in which the proportion of Gs is 30%, a 99% confidence interval will have a margin of error of no more than $3/(2\sqrt{n})$. Hence we can estimate that p is between 0.285 and 0.315. We can say that our "confidence" in this interval is 99%.

That means that we have made this estimate by a procedure that gives a correct estimate at least 99% of the time.

But our table does not tell us how to compute intervals with any other confidence level than 95% or 99% (or 2/3). Moreover, our use of the "worst-case scenario" means that our intervals may not be very efficient. A mathematician would be very unsatisfied with our intervals. A statistician likes *exact confidence intervals*, partly for elegance, and partly because they are usually more informative. Here is a brief explanation.

Suppose we are estimating some quantity q (like a proportion, or the average height of high school basketball stars, or the mean family income in Kansas). We have some method for collecting data, and making an interval estimate I of quantity q. Now suppose our method for making the estimate has this great property: regardless of the value of q, the probability of getting data that leads to an interval I that includes q is *exactly* 95% (not just greater than or equal to 95%). In that case, I is an *exact confidence interval*. Unlike the confidence intervals we work out in this book, most confidence intervals you find quoted in real life will be exact confidence intervals. It is hard to design exact confidence interval estimators from scratch. But in every case, the logic of a confidence statement is just as explained in the box above.

MORE SMOKE

Recall our poll about smoking in public places:

> A poll released last week said that a survey of city residents over 18 years of age, determined that 78% favored at least segregated areas. . . . These results are based on a poll of 1026 residents conducted between July 5 and July 9, and are considered accurate to within three percentage points, 19 times out of 20.

The "19 times out of 20" is just a standard probability for stating confidence intervals, 0.95.

The "accurate to within three percentage points" is a statement of the margin of error.

The quotation means:

> The 95% confidence interval (based on the poll data) for residents who favor segregated smoking areas is (0.75, 0.81).

This means, in turn:

> On the basis of our data, we estimate that the unknown proportion of residents who favor segregated smoking areas is between 0.75 and 0.81. This estimate is made according to a method that is right with probability of at least 0.95.

THE THREE PERCENT SOLUTION

Where did the "three percentage points" come from in the report of the smoking poll?

According to the theory just explained, the 95% confidence interval is
$$1/\sqrt{n} = 1/\sqrt{1026} = 0.031 \approx 3\%$$
So that is where the 3% came from.

Of course, the pollsters did not make their sample and then work out the margin of error. They designed a poll which had a 95% accuracy probability, and a 3% margin of error.

MORE CONFIDENCE, MORE ERROR

The same poll entitles us to derive 99% confidence intervals. With a 99% probability, the margin of error is within:

$$3/(2\sqrt{n}) \approx 0.047 < 0.05.$$

Hence with the same data and the same logic the pollsters could have said:

> These results, based on a poll of 1026 residents conducted between July 5 and July 9, are considered accurate to within five percentage points, 99 times out of 100.

NOT ALWAYS TIDY: MORE FAT

Polling examples try to get quite narrow intervals, like 3% on either side of 79%. But confidence intervals are used in a very wide variety of applications. Often they are used only to give an indication of the reliability of an estimate.

Recall from page 218 the paper on fat, beans, and lung cancer published in the *Journal of the National Cancer Institute*. We reported only "univariate" associations, for example, a comparison of saturated fat consumption with lung cancer rates. The investigators also wanted an estimate of the effect of saturated fat, and all the other variables that are correlated with saturated fat. This is quite a feat, but there are standard ways to do it. Their conclusion was:

> Comparing the class of women who ate a great deal of saturated fat (and other correlated substances) to the class of Missouri women who ate very little saturated fat:
>
> The incidence of lung cancer in one group was 6.14 times the incidence in the other group.

This was, however, an estimate based on combining a large number of variables, and making allowance for various statistical side effects. The researchers thus stated a confidence interval for this estimate, writing CI for confidence interval:

> 95% CI = (2.63, 14.40).

Notice how valuable this calculation is.
    It is quite scary to read:

> The risk of lung cancer for nonsmoking women, that is associated with high fat consumption, is six times greater than the risk with very low fat consumption.

Optimistic nonsmoking women who love cheeseburgers might find it less scary to read:

> The risk of lung cancer, associated with high fat consumption, may be as low as 2.6 times greater than the risk with very low fat consumption. It could also be as high as 14.4 times greater.

WHAT THESE STATEMENTS MEAN

In their sample of 1026 adult residents, the pollsters in the smoking study found 38% who favored a complete ban on smoking. On the basis of this information, they are entitled to say:

> We estimate that the proportion of residents who favor a complete ban on smoking lies in the ***interval*** 38% ± 3%.
>   Our estimate is made according to a ***method*** which (assuming the theoretical

population model and properties of the sampling method) gives correct interval estimates 19 times out of 20.

Likewise, the researchers studying diet are entitled to say:

> We estimate that the risk of lung cancer for nonsmoking women who consume a great deal of fat, is between 2.63 and 14.4 times greater than the risk for nonsmoking women who eat very little saturated fat.
>
> Our estimate is made according to a **method** which (assuming the theoretical population model and properties of the sampling method) gives correct interval estimates 19 times out of 20.

AN IDEALIZED PICTURE

The second part of these assertions is completely idealized, even for the example of polling.

If we were to sample the adult city residents over and over again, people would start changing their opinions. If we did 10,000 samples, of about 1000 people each, we would sample many individuals several times. They would stop answering, because they would be annoyed. Word would get out that there was a big super-sample going on, and some people would try to fool it. (I would.)

There is a sense in which no one takes the rationale of confidence intervals really seriously as a literal account. You should think of it as a logical picture of the underlying structure of an argument.

STRATIFIED SAMPLING

Pollsters have much more sophisticated methods than simple random sampling of a population. The most familiar polls are political polls. How can one tell something about the entire voter population of a country by asking about 1000 people?

We want a representative sample, but if we sampled only 1000 individuals in a haphazard way, we would likely miss major chunks of the population. We might not sample a single blue-collar union worker. We might not sample a single voting-age university student. We might not sample any rich people. We might miss all the deeply religious people; we might miss all the profoundly atheistic people; we might miss all the divorced parents, or we might miss all the couples who have been married for 35 years and are still going strong.

So pollsters use *stratified* samples. Their polls are built upon a vast background of previous polls. They know that numerous subpopulations are fairly homogeneous in their opinions about many issues, and in their tastes in deodorants or television shows. Each such subpopulation is thought of as one among many strata in the population. The poll is designed so that it first of all randomly selects strata (making due allowance for the different sizes of different strata). It then randomly selects individuals for strata that have themselves been selected randomly.

That sounds pretty complicated. In the United States a lot of commercial polls simply use postal Zip codes, like Beverly Hills 90210. Relative to the immense diversity of Americans, the individuals in any one Zip code tend to be fairly alike in income, race, attitudes, tastes, even if they are not quite as uniform as the folks in 90210. You won't do all that badly in getting a representative sample if you randomly select a couple of people in each and every Zip code in America. But if you are selling only top-of-the-line merchandise, you sample only prosperous Zip codes to find out how rich consumers will take to your product.

Naturally, the mathematics of stratified sampling is more complicated than simple random sampling. But the *meaning* of the resulting confidence statements is always the same:

> We estimate a parameter as lying in such and such an interval. If our theoretical population model is correct, then this procedure of estimation gives a correct interval most of the time.

TECHNICALITIES

Here we are concerned only with the rationale for confidence interval estimates. There are many technical problems for mathematicians to solve. For example, confidence interval estimators, as we have described them, are not unique. That is, we can construct several procedures which give 95% confidence intervals for the same data—yet the intervals are not necessarily the same.

This need not trouble Neyman. If several procedures give 95% confidence intervals, take your pick. You might prefer one over the others because it is more informative, or for other reasons. But so long as you settle on one procedure, you will be right 95% of the time (assuming that your theoretical model is correct). There is, however, a substantial literature on how to find the "best" confidence interval when there are several possibilities. The ideal is an "exact" estimator which gives the narrowest intervals.

CONFIDENCE INTERVALS AND NEYMAN–PEARSON TESTS

There is a close connection between Neyman's theory of confidence intervals and the Neyman–Pearson framework for testing statistical hypotheses. Neyman first coinvented the theory of testing described in Chapter 18, and then developed his idea of confidence intervals. Here is one connection.

Suppose a scientist is testing the null hypothesis that a certain pesticide has no effect on the yield from a tomato crop. Many plots of tomatoes are treated, and the pesticide is applied to half the fields, at random. The null hypothesis implies that the difference between the average yields per plot is 0. But the difference could be positive (more pounds of good tomatoes from treated plots) or negative (fewer pounds of good tomatoes from treated plots).

The tomatoes are harvested. Yields are evaluated. Instead of using a statistical test, the scientist could use a 95% confidence interval, say. If 0 lies in the confidence interval, then we could conclude that we do *not* have any reason to think the pesticide is effective. We do not reject the null hypothesis of no effect.

In many common models of experimental situations, confidence interval reasoning like this is equivalent to testing using the Neyman–Pearson framework. Many researchers prefer to use the confidence interval approach, because they find that people get confused with the idea of power. But recall that confidence interval estimators are not unique. Often the choice of a confidence interval estimator is equivalent to the choice of the most powerful test.

RESEARCHERS AT WAR OVER CHILD DEATHS

You may think that inductive logic is getting too abstract and messy for you! Inductive logic matters. We have just quoted a newspaper headline, "Researchers at War." The story begins:

> Are children dying of leukemia in excessive numbers around our nuclear power stations?

A null hypothesis would be: it makes no difference to a child's chance of contracting leukemia, whether or not the child grows up close to a nuclear power station.

> The answer depends on who is looking at the statistics. A governmental agency and an environmental research group have issued conflicting studies, based on the same data.
>
> The Atomic Energy Control Board, the federal nuclear watchdog, has found a higher-than-expected incidence of childhood leukemia deaths near the plants, but says the result could be due to chance.
>
> Energy Probe, an environmental research group, calls the government's position nonsense.

The story goes on to quote a lot of anger. A man at Atomic Energy said of the man at Energy Probe, "He's full of buffalo bricks." What was at issue?
Energy Probe was using a simple significance test, and citing a p value of 0.0001. By contrast,

> The AECB found leukemia deaths 34% above the provincial average near the Pickering generating station, and 173% higher near Douglas Point. It concluded that the rates are probably due to natural variations that scientists have found in the occurrence of the disease.
>
> In the language of statistics, the results are within a normal range a researcher might expect to find 19 times out of 20 in any large sample, and thus were likely due to chance.

Energy Probe is using significance tests. That "19 out of 20" suggests to us that Atomic Energy is using confidence intervals. The argument was just that of the preceding section. In effect, Atomic Energy found that a quantity that indicated "no effect" lay in a 95% confidence interval. The AECB statistician was quoted as saying,

> "The confidence intervals give useful information that is not contained in the p values quoted by Energy Probe."

We could express the argument in a different way. The Energy Probe significance test ignored power.

This confrontation is just the beginning of the story. This course does not tell how to resolve such issues. We need to do a lot more analysis to understand the ways in which the two groups are using the data. As a rule of thumb, however, someone who uses a most powerful test, or a confidence interval, is *usually* making a deeper analysis of the data and the rival hypotheses than someone who uses only a simple significance test.

Anyone who cares about leukemia deaths of children—or any of literally *thousands* of other immediate and perhaps terrifying questions—should get clear about the conceptual foundations of inductive logic.

AGAINST INFERENCE

Now we move to a more abstract issue.

The method of confidence intervals, as we now know it, is due to Jerzy Neyman. He was a frequency dogmatist. In his opinion, there is only one type of probability: frequency-type.

He went so far as to say: *There is no such thing as inductive inference.* What he meant by this was that we can never make statements of inductive probability about any particular matter of fact or unknown quantity.

All we can do is make (frequency-type) probability statements about the method by which we estimate a parameter. (The reason that Neyman wanted to replace the word "significance" by "size" in the Neyman–Pearson framework (page 224) was that "significance" suggested "inference"!) So what does Neyman want us to say?

INDUCTIVE BEHAVIOR

We *can* say that if we use this procedure repeatedly, we will be right most of the time. The procedure has reliable "operating characteristics." But we can never make a probability statement about a particular application of the procedure.

Neyman said that when we use the method of confidence intervals, we are not making *inductive inferences*. Instead, we are practicing *inductive behavior*. If we use 95% confidence intervals, our behavior will have the desired result 95% of the time. If we use 99% intervals, our behavior will have the desired result 99% of the time.

SIGNIFICANCE TESTS

The idea of inductive behavior transfers at once to tests of statistical hypotheses. Imagine that Bosco, a statistician, has learned the Neyman–Pearson theory of testing presented at the end of Chapter 18. He has the policy of choosing a powerful test and then *rejecting* a hypothesis if and only if he obtains experimental data which is significant at the 1% level.

Bosco would wrongly reject a true hypothesis at most 1% of the time. That is because (if his theoretical model is correct) when a hypothesis under test is true, the probability of getting an experimental result that is significant at the 1% level is just 1%.

Bosco never makes the stupid mistake of saying, about a particular hypothesis H:

There is only a 1% probability that null hypothesis H is true.

Bosco does go further than a person using the significance framework who says only:

Either the null hypothesis H is true, in which case something unusual happened by chance (probability 1%), **or** the null hypothesis H is false.

Bosco says:

I reject the hypothesis H. I am using a rejection method that wrongly rejects a hypothesis at most 1% of the time.

Neyman would call that inductive behavior.

NEYMAN'S FOES

Neyman said that we never make *inductive inferences*. We only engage in *inductive behavior*, he said.

We do not have to agree with Neyman about inference.

We should first remember why he rejected the idea of inductive inference. This is a historical point. He was writing in the 1930s. He was doing battle with people who wanted to attach a probability to an inference. He had several types of enemy, of whom we will mention just two.

(a) People who are simply confused.
(b) Bayesians, who are not confused, but whose philosophy is repugnant to the frequency dogmatist. When Neyman was formulating his philosophy in the 1930s, the Bayesian philosophy was not influential. So his prime target was (a).

(a) *Confusion*. When confused people learn about a significance test or a confidence interval, they want to say:

"There is only a 1% probability that hypothesis H is true."

"The probability that q lies in the confidence interval I is 95%."

Undoubtedly, confused people think that when they say there is only a 1% probability that H is true, or that there is a 95% probability that q lies in some interval, they are making an "inductive inference" from the data. But they are simply confused. Neyman may have thought that if he got us all to talk in terms of *inductive behavior*, then we would be less prone to confusion.

(b) *Bayesian*. Neyman made some important contributions to Bayesian analysis. But he opposed across-the-board belief dogmatists who believe that their theory about learning from experience was the one true theory for inductive inference.

FOR INDUCTIVE INFERENCE

We agree philosophically, in this textbook, with Neyman about (a) and (b). But we do not, many years after he wrote, have to agree with him that there is no such thing as inductive inference. We can be more relaxed. We can perfectly well say that a person who uses a confidence interval is *making an inference*. She is doing so because the practice of using confidence intervals to make inferences is right (say) 95% of the time.

Likewise, we can say that when Bosco rejects a hypothesis, because he has data that are significant at the 1% level, he is *making an inference*. He is inferring from his data that hypothesis H is false.

Part of the theory of inductive inference is about statistical inferences of this sort.

We will return to the philosophical idea of inductive behavior in Chapter 22. It suggests a quite profound way to think about the problem of induction. But let us not forget practical matters, such as the life and death of small children.

JERZY NEYMAN

Jerzy Neyman (1894–1981) was a Polish mathematician who went to London to work in the department established by Francis Galton and Karl Pearson, inventors of correlation, the chi-squared test, and much more. There, collaborating with E. S. Pearson, the son of Karl, he coinvented the Neyman–Pearson theory of testing statistical hypotheses, discussed in Chapter 18. He is also responsible for the theory of confidence intervals and many other fundamental contributions. Neyman moved to the University of California at Berkeley. There he created what was for a long time the most important powerhouse of mathematical statistics.

"Fisher and Neyman were the two greatest statisticians of the twentieth century," writes David Freedman, a statistics professor at Berkeley. The two men did not agree with each other. At the time that Neyman began work in London, Fisher was the most influential working statistician in the world. Both men liked a good argument, and their polemics got pretty fierce. In fact, one reason that Neyman was so hostile to the idea of inductive inference was that Fisher had yet another frequency-based concept for drawing inferences about statistical hypotheses. (He called it "fiducial probability," but the theory did not win general acceptance.) Neyman insisted that the only sound theory was the theory of confidence intervals. He called that inductive *behavior* to separate himself from Fisher's idea of statistical *inference*.

EXERCISES

1 *Missed tests.* In a poll of size 625 based on a random sample of undergraduates, 125 reported that they had missed at least one class quiz or midterm because of illness. (a) Find the margin of error for a 95% confidence interval. (b) For a 99% confidence interval. State the actual confidence intervals in both cases.

2 *Smaller sample.* Same problem, based on a sample of 81 students, 16 of whom reported illness. Here the proportion of students who missed a test because of illness is about the same as in question 1, namely almost 20%. Compare the precision of the estimates made on the basis of the larger sample (625) and the smaller (81).

3 *Parapsychology* is defined as the study of mental phenomena, such as telepathy, which are beyond the scope of normal physical explanation.

> *Telepathy*: communication between people of thoughts, feelings, images, desires, and so on, in ways that cannot be understood in terms of current scientific laws.
> *Poltergeists*: mischievous spirits that make a lot of noise, throw dishes about, and generally make a nuisance of themselves in haunted houses.
> *Medium*: a person who, usually during a trance, makes contact between the dead and the living.
> *Clairvoyance*: the ability to see into the future.

Parapsychology studies these phenomena, as well as ghosts, intimations of deaths in the family, the ability to move objects at a distance just by thinking, and so on.

Do you believe in any parapsychological phenomena? Many people, in many different cultures, do. Here is the result of a recent poll.

> A poll released yesterday said that 63% of all residents of San Francisco believe in parapsychological phenomena.
>
> The poll reported that 58% of the residents of San Francisco believe in telepathy, 31% in the ability of mediums to make contact with the dead, 43% believe in apparitions such as ghosts, 26% believe in poltergeists, and 37% believe that some persons can make objects move without touching or otherwise physically affecting them. In all, 63% believe in at least one of these phenomena.
>
> This result is based on a survey of 1041 people conducted between February 15 and February 18, and is considered accurate to within three percentage points, 19 times out of 20.

(a) State all the confidence intervals implied in this report, and say what they mean.
(b) If you were writing for a newspaper, how would your editor tell you to summarize this interval?

KEY WORDS FOR REVIEW

Point estimate	Confidence interval
Interval estimate	Inductive behavior
Margin of error	Inductive inference

20 The Philosophical Problem of Induction

> For philosophers, this is the most important question about induction. It is not a problem within inductive logic. It questions the very possibility of inductive reasoning itself.

DAVID HUME

In 1739, David Hume (1711–1776), the Scottish philosopher, published *A Treatise of Human Nature*, one of the half-dozen most influential books of Western philosophy. He was twenty-eight years old at the time. In 1748, he published *An Enquiry Concerning Human Understanding*.

These books, especially the second, include the classic statement of what came to be called **the problem of induction**.

Hume's problem about induction is only a small part of a very general theory of knowledge. Here we study just this one aspect of Hume's philosophy.

SKEPTICISM

In ordinary English, a *skeptic* is:

◆ Someone who habitually doubts accepted beliefs.
◆ A person who mistrusts other people or their ideas.
◆ Someone who rejects traditional beliefs, such as religious beliefs.

PHILOSOPHICAL SKEPTICISM

Philosophers attach a far more sweeping sense to the idea of skepticism. A philosophical skeptic is someone who claims to:

◆ Doubt that any real knowledge or sound belief about anything is possible.

There are more specialized types of philosophical skepticism, depending upon what kind of knowledge is in doubt. Think of any field of knowledge or belief X, where X may be religious, or scientific, or moral. X may be knowledge about other people, or about the reality of the world around us, or even knowledge about yourself.

A philosophical skeptic about X is someone who claims to:

◆ Doubt that any real knowledge or sound belief about X, or of type X, is possible.

The doubt is of a peculiar sort. A philosophical skeptic argues that, in principle, nothing can help.

Skeptical doubt is not ordinary skepticism. Someone may doubt that we will ever find out why the dinosaurs became extinct—and yet admit that some new evidence, some new growth in theoretical understanding, would help clear up the mystery. Such a person is not a philosophical skeptic. A philosophical skeptic argues that nothing can remove the skeptical doubt.

David Hume appears to have been a philosophical skeptic about induction.

A SKEPTICAL PROBLEM

Hume's problem is not about some aspect of inductive logic. He is not skeptical about this or that argument. Frequency dogmatists are skeptical of Bayesian approaches to inductive reasoning. Belief dogmatists are skeptical of frequency approaches to inductive reasoning.

Hume seems to be skeptical about every inductive reason whatsoever.

But don't people reason inductively?

Yes, Hume seems to say, but that is just a habit.

PAST AND FUTURE

Inductive reasoning can lead us back into the past: why did the dinosaurs become extinct? Why did you not speak to me yesterday? It can lead us to the present, somewhere else: who is she talking to now? But most often when people think of induction, they think of inferring something about the future, from what we know at present.

People often argue that we can infer something about the future, from what we know at present, because we know that the future is like the past.

So here is one picturesque way to start Hume's problem:

How do you know that the future will be like the past?

CAUSE

One obvious answer to this question is that we know that present states of affairs *cause* some future events.

Hume is a philosophical skeptic about the very idea of cause.

Where do we get this idea? he asks. We will quote his own words (replacing one or two old-fashioned phrases by their modern equivalents). The quotations are from an advertisement Hume wrote for his own book.

Everything indented below was written by Hume. His famous example of cause and effect involves two billiard balls:

> Here is a billiard ball lying on the table, and another moving toward it with rapidity. They strike; and the ball which was formerly at rest now acquires a motion. This is as perfect an instance of the relation of cause and effect as any which we know by sensation or reflection.

Sensation or reflection: it is part of Hume's general theory of knowledge that all our knowledge comes through our senses (sensation), or by reasoning (reflection). He continues:

> It is evident that the two balls touched one another before the motion was communicated, and that there was no interval between the shock and the motion.

What do we have here? The two balls *touched* each other. Moreover,

> the motion which was the cause is prior to the motion which was the effect. *Priority* in time is, therefore, another requisite circumstance in every cause. But that is not all. Let us try any other balls of the same kind in a like situation, and we shall always find that the impulse of one produces motion in the other.

Like causes always produce like effects. He calls this *constant conjunction*. But:

> Beyond these three circumstances of contiguity, priority, and constant conjunction, I can discover nothing in this cause. The first ball is in motion, touches the second, immediately the second is in motion—and when I try the experiment with the same or like balls, in the same or like circumstances, I find that upon the motion and touch of one ball motion always follows in the other.

And that is *all* that Hume can find, in our experience, corresponding to the idea of cause and effect.

EXPERIENCE

Hume then wonders whether we might have an innate sense of causation. He imagines "a man such as Adam created in the full vigor of understanding," who has not yet had any experience. Adam would have had no idea what would happen when one billiard ball hit another. But as soon as he played with billiard balls, and acquired a sufficient number of instances of this kind, whenever he saw one ball moving toward the other, he would always conclude without hesitation that the second would acquire motion. His understanding would anticipate his sight and form a conclusion suitable to his experience.

It follows, then, that all reasonings concerning cause and effect are founded on experience, and that all reasonings from experience are founded on the supposition that the course of nature will continue uniformly the same. We conclude that like causes, in like circumstances, will always produce like effects.

Thus cause and effect cannot justify our belief that the future will be like the past, because the very notions of cause and effect are founded upon an assumption of uniformity. Yet cause and effect were offered as the basis for reasoning about the future! To repeat Hume: *all reasonings concerning cause and effect are founded on experience, and all reasonings from experience are founded on the supposition that the course of nature will continue uniformly the same.*

"The course of nature will continue uniformly the same" means, roughly, the future will be like the past. Where do we get the idea that the future will be like the past?

It may now be worth while to consider what determines us to form a conclusion [that the future will be like the past] of such infinite importance.

NOT PROBABILITY

Hume says that it is obvious that Adam cannot prove, by deduction, "that the course of nature must continue uniformly the same, and the future" must be like the past. (Hume used the old-fashioned phrase *conformable to the past* instead of "like the past.")

Nay, I will go further and assert that Adam could not so much as prove by any *probable* arguments that the future must be conformable to the past. All probable arguments are built on the supposition that there is this conformity between the future and the past . . .

The emphasis on the word *probable* is Hume's own. However, he perhaps did not mean quite what we, more than 250 years later, mean by the word.

A FAMOUS CIRCLE

Could we not justify our expectation, that the future will be like the past, from our previous experience? No, that would be circular reasoning.

This conformity is a *matter of fact*, and if it must be proved it will admit of no proof except from experience. But our experience in the past can be a proof of nothing for the future but upon a supposition that there is a resemblance between them. This, therefore, is a point which can admit of no proof at all, and which we take for granted without any proof.

Anyone who tries to argue that the future will be like the past, on the ground that past futures have been like past pasts, is arguing in a circle.

CUSTOM

So why do we expect the future to be like the past? Because that's how we are. We have some inductive habits. But we cannot justify those habits. Reason cannot provide justification. Reasoning itself is based upon our habits and customs.

> We are determined by *custom* alone to suppose the future conformable to the past. When I see a billiard ball moving toward another, my mind is immediately carried by habit to the usual effect, and anticipates my sight by conceiving the second ball in motion. There is nothing in these objects—abstractly considered—which leads me to form any such conclusion: and even after I have had experience of many repeated effects of this kind, there is no argument which determines me to suppose that the effect will be conformable to past experience.
>
>   It is not, therefore, reason which is the guide of life, but custom. That alone determines the mind in all instances to suppose the future conformable to the past. However easy this step may seem, reason would never, to all eternity, be able to make it.

WAS HUME REALLY A PHILOSOPHICAL SKEPTIC?

Hume, it appears, thought that the past gave no reason or justification for beliefs about the future. Did he then think that "anything goes," or that nothing goes? Was he incapable of any action, having no "reason" for expectations about the future?

   Not exactly. Hume's overall conclusion is that, as a matter of custom or habit (perhaps even as a matter of a sort of psychological necessity or "hard-wiring") we do make inductions. We do expect the future to be like the past. But there is no justification in reason for this. It is just what we do.

PROBABILITY EVASIONS

Hume himself thought that probability would not help with his problem of induction. We cannot, he wrote, "so much as prove by any *probable* arguments that the future must be conformable to the past."

   We will not argue that Hume was wrong. But we can do more with probability than Hume imagined. Probability theory was just beginning in Hume's day. Hume was pretty up to date. I think he had read Abraham de Moivre's book *The*

Doctrine of Chances (first edition 1718, see page 207). But probability theory had hardly begun when Hume proposed the problem of induction.

We will not suggest that probability ideas *solve* Hume's problem. But we will present some ways in which, perhaps, Hume's problem can to some extent be *evaded*.

To **evade** means to get around, or avoid—people evade the law, or imprisonment. We also evade questions. An evasive person does not answer directly. In this sense we will try to evade Hume's problem of induction. We will not answer him directly, but claim it may not be necessary to do so.

An *evasion* of the problem of induction has this form:

Hume, you're right!
There is no justification of inductive inference.
But it doesn't matter much.
We can get along without inductive inferences just fine!

One "evasion," to be described in Chapter 21, uses belief-type probability, and the Bayesian theory of learning from experience. The other, presented in Chapter 22, uses frequency-type probability, and Neyman's notion of inductive behavior. These two probability evasions are:

BAYESIAN EVASION:
Argue that Bayes' Rule shows us the rational way to *learn from experience*.

BEHAVIOR EVASION:
Argue that although there is no justification for any individual *inductive inference* there is still a justification for *inductive behavior*.

AN ANTI-INDUCTIVE EVASION

But first we'll look at a philosopher who says he agrees with Hume, but has a nonprobability evasion of Hume's problem.

The major twentieth-century philosopher of science, Karl Popper, begins one of his essays with the words, "I think that I have solved an important philosophical problem, the problem of induction."

Popper says that Hume is right. There is no justification of inductive inferences.

But there are two questions about induction. One is *psychological*, and one is *logical*.

Psychological: Why, as a matter of human psychology, do we make inductions? Popper says that we do respond to our environment and what has happened to us. But that, as Hume says, is just custom and habit. In this respect we are no different from cats or, for that matter, bacteria. Microorganisms move around, respond to experience, and "learn" about their environment, says Popper. We are much the same, except more complicated.

The psychological questions raise interesting empirical issues. But Popper and Hume, the philosophers, are interested in the logical question.

Logical: But don't we have reasons for our expectations, reasons that cats and bacteria don't have? Hume said **No**. Popper agrees.

But it doesn't matter! Inductive reasoning is invalid, but luckily people don't make inductions, says Popper. Or at any rate, they do not need to.

Popper's thesis: The only good reasoning is deductively valid reasoning. *And that is all we need in order to get around in the world or do science.*

Thus Popper is "evading" the philosophical (logical) problem of induction, because he says that induction is invalid, but luckily we don't (or shouldn't) ever make inductive inferences. What do we do instead? We make guesses and test them. In science, "guess" sounds too haphazard. The fancier word for "guess" is *conjecture*. One of Popper's books is called *Conjectures and Refutations*. Those are two key words in his philosophy of science. Popper's picture of the logic of science is this:

- Make a conjecture C.
- Deduce a *test implication* of C: If C is true and if test T is made, then experimental result R will be obtained.
- Perform the test.
- If R is obtained, then C is **corroborated**. That just means it has passed the test. It is not "verified" or "confirmed," let alone "proven." All our beliefs are **fallible**. No theory or belief about the world is ever proven. We must retain a critical attitude; we must constantly deduce new test implications and then experimentally test our beliefs.

In ordinary English, the verb "to corroborate" just means to confirm or support by providing fresh evidence. Popper does not believe in inductive confirmation or support. He deliberately gave the word "corroborate" a technical meaning having to do with passing a test.

- If R is not obtained, then C is **refuted**. When that happens, we know by experimentation and deduction that C is false. We have learned something *deductively*, not *inductively*.
- When C is refuted, revise it, or try to devise a new conjecture that fits what we now know, including the fact that R does not occur when test T is made.

That is a very simple version of Popper's idea of scientific methodology. He liked to call himself a **deductivist**. Everyone else who tried to solve the problem of induction, especially using probability ideas, was, he said, an **inductivist**.

Popper always emphasized the *fallibility* of human knowledge. "Fallible" means "may be wrong, may mislead, may be erroneous." One of his moral lessons was that all science is fallible.

DAVID HUME

Many would say that David Hume (1711–1776) is the most important philosopher who ever wrote in English. He spent most of his life in Edinburgh, Scotland. The guidebooks to that city, directing you to the apartment building where he lived, used to say, "David Hume, the historian." That is because Hume wrote a six-volume *History of England* which for many years was a best-seller. Hume is said to have been the first person anywhere to get quite rich on royalties alone.

Hume did less well at first with his youthful masterpiece, *A Treatise of Human Nature*, which he wrote while living in France. He once said that this book fell "dead-born" from the press—his child was not born alive, but dead at birth because nobody read it. That was why he wrote the anonymous self-advertisement we have used as a summary of his ideas about induction.

Hume's *Dialogues Concerning Natural Religion* are a lively, powerful, and skeptical examination of some of the arguments for the existence of a Supreme Being, Creator, or God. These dialogues were considered too controversial to be published during his lifetime. In fact, when he was dying of cancer a crowd gathered outside his home jeering and asking when the "atheist" was going to repent.

Hume's fear about not being read as a philosopher was misplaced. He soon became well known to intellectuals all over Europe and colonial America. His *Treatise* ranges over many of the questions of metaphysics and epistemology, and then turns to an equally powerful discussion of morality. Many of the ways in which philosophical questions are discussed in English today were set, rather permanently, by David Hume.

His philosophical problem of induction is only one among many contributions. Yet in one way it is typical of his type of mind. Hume was ever cautious, doubting, querying, skeptical. Although Immanuel Kant (1724–1804) had permanently changed the philosophical scene by the end of the eighteenth century, it was Hume, Kant said, who awakened him from his "dogmatic slumbers."

KARL POPPER

In 1935 the Austrian philosopher Karl Popper (1902–1994) published *The Logic of Scientific Discovery* (in German). This is his fundamental contribution to the philosophy of science. A much-extended English version was published in 1959. During the Nazi regime he emigrated, and taught at the London School of Economics. He wrote many other books about the philosophy of science, covering almost everything from quantum mechanics to the pre-Socratics.

He also wrote influential books of liberal but cautious political philosophy: *The Poverty of Historicism* and *The Open Society and Its Enemies*. He especially disliked Plato and Hegel, because, in his opinion, they were afraid of an open society, the critical discussion of ideas, and the recognition that all our beliefs, including political ones, are fallible. In recent years Popper has had unusual influence in countries with authoritarian regimes, such as China and Iran: because he is a philosopher of science, he is allowed to be widely read, but his liberal views make him a hero for antiestablishment thinkers.

KEY WORDS FOR REVIEW

David Hume	A circular argument
Skepticism	Custom is the guide of life
Philosophical skepticism	Evasions of the problem of induction
Will the future be like the past?	Karl Popper
Cause and effect	Popper's evasion: we never reason inductively
Constant conjunction	Conjecture and refutation
Not probability	Fallibility

21 Learning from Experience as an Evasion of the Problem of Induction

How belief-type probability can be applied to the problem of induction using the idea of learning from experience by Bayes' Rule.

The idea is already present in Chapters 13–15.

- We can represent degrees of belief by numbers between 0 and 1.
- Degrees of belief represented by these numbers should satisfy the basic laws of probability, on pain of being "incoherent" if they don't.
- If they do satisfy these laws, then Bayes' Rule follows.
- Hence we can update earlier degrees of belief by new evidence in a coherent, "rational" way.

This evasion of the problem of induction is called Bayesian.

The Bayesian does not claim to be able to justify any given set of degrees of belief as being uniquely rational. He does claim that he can tell you how it is reasonable to change your beliefs in the light of experience.

The Bayesian says to Hume:

Hume, you're right. Given a set of premises, supposed to be all the reasons bearing on a conclusion, you can form any opinion you like.

But you're not addressing the issue that concerns us!

At any point in our grown-up lives (let's leave babies out of this), we have a lot of opinions and various degrees of belief about our opinions. The question is not whether these opinions are "rational." The question is whether we are reasonable in modifying these opinions in the light of new experience, new evidence.

That is where the theory of personal probability comes in.

On pain of incoherence, we should always have a belief structure that satisfies the probability axioms. That means that there is a uniquely reasonable way to learn from experience—using Bayes' Rule.

The Bayesian *evades* Hume's problem by saying that Hume is right. But, continues the Bayesian, all we need is a model of reasonable change in belief. That is sufficient for us to be rational agents in a changing world.

CONVERGENCE

You should be worried here.

If every person starts with his or her own bundle of opinions and prejudices, and learns in a Bayesian way, each will be internally consistent, but everyone could have completely different opinions forever.

We would never reach consensus. And coming to an agreement is, we think, part of what it is to be reasonable.

The Bayesian has a theorem waiting for us.

I can prove [says the Bayesian, who does indeed have a theorem in mind] that if two people start out with divergent degrees of belief, and agree only on what is possible, then even though their prior probabilities may be very different, with increasing evidence they will tend to converge in their "posterior," after-the-evidence degrees of belief.

By "agreeing on what is possible," the Bayesian means that the two people agree on the hypotheses that have nonzero probability. One person does not think a hypothesis is impossible, with zero probability, while the other thinks that it has positive probability. This clause is essential because of the definition of conditional probability. $\Pr(A/B) = \Pr(A\&B) \div \Pr(B)$, *so long as $\Pr(B) > 0$.* If one person had $\Pr(B) = 0$, while the other had $\Pr(B) > 0$, then the first person's degrees of belief could not be affected, in a Bayesian way, by new evidence.

The Bayesian does not mind this limitation on the convergence theorem.

If Liza starts out thinking that a hypothesis is absolutely impossible (probability 0), while Elaine thinks it is possible, they may never come to agree—not unless Elaine converts Liza. But conversion is something quite different from slow, reasoned change in belief.

WHAT ARE CONDITIONAL BETTING RATES?

There can be all sorts of objections to this Bayesian evasion of the problem of induction. Here we discuss only one.

What is the meaning of conditional probability and conditional betting rates?

The Bayesian says that we can get the idea without even writing out Bayes' Rule in detail. We need only look at the connection between prior probability, posterior probability, and likelihood.

Suppose I am interested in a hypothesis H and some possible evidence E. I have a prior personal betting rate on H, which is represented by a prior probability Pr(H).

In my personal belief structure there is also my conditional betting rate that E will happen, conditional on H being true, represented by the probability of getting E if H is true, Pr(E/H), or the likelihood of E in the light of H.

Then, if I have degrees of belief of this sort for the various possible hypotheses of interest to me, I know by Bayes' Rule that my posterior betting rate when I learn H—that is, my personal posterior probability Pr(H/E)—should be proportional (on pain of being incoherent) to the prior probability times the likelihood: Pr(H/E) is proportional to Pr(H) × Pr(E/H).

OBJECTION

Let us call our objector Hialeah Hume, a great-great- . . . . -granddaughter of one of Hume's nephews.

Hialeah says:

> You are equivocating—using words in two different ways.
>
> You use "Pr(H/E)" to mean two different things, namely,
>
> (i) Your personal rate for betting on H, conditional on E, *before* you know that E is true.
>
> (ii) Your personal rate for betting on H when you know that E is true, that is, *after* you know that E is true.

The three ideas listed at the beginning of this chapter, and presented in Chapters 13–15, showed that betting rates, including conditional betting rates, *all offered at one moment of time*, ought to satisfy the basic rules of probability. That is what might be called a *static* situation.

At one moment of time, or during a period of time in which you don't change your beliefs, the total set of your beliefs should be coherent. All the arguments for coherence, as a kind of inductive consistency, have to do with the static assumption. The arguments are all about (i) above. They do not consider the *dynamic* situation, in which you change your beliefs in the course of time. We would require an argument about (ii) above, in order to do this. Hialeah Hume continues,

> You are fooling us with your notation!
>
> If we are going to talk about **dynamic** learning from experience in the course of time, we should not use the "timeless" abbreviation "Pr(H)" for the probability of H.
>
> We should put in a subscript "*t*" to indicate the subjective probability of a person at time *t*.
>
> $Pr_t(H)$ means your degree of belief in H at time *t*.
>
> $Pr_t(H/E)$ is an indicator of the conditional bets that you would place at time *t*.

All that was proved in Chapters 13–15, is that for any definite t,
$Pr_t(H/E)$ is proportional to $Pr_t(H) \times Pr_t(E/H)$.

Hialeah Hume now gets quite mad.

You can talk about posterior and prior probabilities if you want to, but don't imagine that those words "prior" and "posterior" have their usual temporal sense!

What you Bayesians need for learning across time is a notation such as this:

For a truly posterior (later) probability at time t^*, later than t, where you know evidence E, you want $Pr_{t^*}(H)$.

For a truly prior (earlier) probability at time t when you don't actually know E, you want $Pr_t(H/E)$.

Once you have made that clear, you require the following postulate:

$Pr_{t^*}(H) = Pr_t(H/E)$.

But you haven't given any argument for this postulate!

(Hialeah isn't quite right. Over the past twenty-five years or so, since this objection was first raised, very able responses have been proposed. But none, I think, is convincing.)

UNDOGMATIC RESPONSE

This difficulty shows that the "Bayesian" argument is not so compelling as it might at first have seemed. But the Bayesian can put up a slightly more modest case on the basis of arguments like those found in Chapters 13–15.

◆ At any one time, there is a way of keeping degrees of belief coherent.
◆ If one is going to modify one's beliefs in the light of evidence, the resulting set of beliefs should also satisfy the probability axioms.
◆ No one has suggested a general rule that is more attractive than the straightforward $Pr_{t^*}(H) = Pr_t(H/E)$.

We could propose this as the *rule of conditionalization*, as an additional characterization of the Bayesian approach to probability. There is nothing wrong with regarding it as an additional maxim or axiom of the Bayesian subjective approach—comparable, say, to Jeffrey's rule (pages 182–3). It is not as if we have a better rule in competition with it.

We might even look at the rule of conditionalization as a moral rule. *One should be true to one's former self* (unless one has undergone a radical conversion in one's life and thought).

You should have a certain existential commitment to the person that you have chosen to be. When you are true to your former self, you will in fact learn from experience by following Bayes' Rule.

This is a rather surprising development in the belief perspective. The belief perspective enjoins us to learn from experience by Bayesian thinking. This is now seen as something like a moral injunction. Even more surprising is the fact that the frequency perspective will develop in a similar, moralistic way. That is not what you expect in a logic book. Perhaps that is one last way in which inductive and deductive logic differ.

22 Inductive Behavior as an Evasion of the Problem of Induction

The frequentist agrees that no reasons can be given for inductive inferences, but holds that reasons can be given for inductive behavior, using certain procedures based on the idea of confidence intervals.

The Bayesian is able to attach personal probabilities, or degrees of belief, to individual propositions. The hard-line frequency dogmatist thinks that probabilities can be attached only to a series of events.

Probability, says this dogmatist, just means the relative frequency of some kind of event produced by a chance setup. Or it refers to the propensity of a chance setup to produce events with a certain stable frequency. Or it refers to certain underlying symmetry properties.

At any rate, we cannot talk sensibly about the probability of a single event, for that event either happens or does not happen. It has "probability" 0 or 1, and that is that.

So the frequency dogmatist will never talk about the frequency-type probability that a particular hypothesis is true.

The hypothesis is either true or false, and there is no frequency about it. At most, we can discuss the relative frequency with which hypotheses of a certain kind are true.

Thus far the dogmatic frequentist is happy to agree with Hume.

INDUCTIVE BEHAVIOR

Nevertheless, continues the frequentist, we may sometimes be able to apply a *system* for making inferences or drawing conclusions such that the conclusions are usually right.

We can talk about the relative frequency with which inferences drawn by a certain method are in fact correct.

If we are interested in knowing a certain quantity on the basis of inconclusive data, we may have a method of providing an interval estimate of the quantity. And we may be able to determine the frequency-type probability that, when following that method, we make interval estimates that include the true unknown value of the quantity. These are, of course, just confidence intervals.

There is no (sound) inductive inference, there is only inductive behavior. That is the formulation of Jerzy Neyman in the 1930s, after he and E. S. Pearson had developed their theory of statistical inference. Neyman said:

> It's perfectly true that we cannot generalize on experience in an undisciplined way. But in carefully designed experiments in which we introduce randomized trials, we can use the resultant evidence in a system for drawing conclusions (say, that a desired quantity lies in such and such a confidence interval) so that we will be right most of the time (say, 95% of the time).

Thus Neyman evades Hume's problem by:

- Actively interfering in the course of nature, using a randomized experimental design.
- Using a method of inference which is right most of the time—say, 95% of the time.

Hume is right, says Neyman. I do not have reasons for believing any one conclusion. *But I have a reason for using my method of inference, namely that it is right most of the time.*

THE EVASION

The Bayesian did not claim that premises give sound reasons for an inductive conclusion. Instead, it was claimed that there are sound reasons for modifying one's opinions in the light of new evidence. Moreover, a group of people starting with different opinions will reach consensus if all modify their opinions by the rule of conditionalization over time. This does not solve the problem of induction, but (says the Bayesian) it provides as good a ground for rational opinion as we can sensibly hope for.

Similarly, frequentists like Neyman do not claim to solve the problem of induction. Nor do they even propose that they have a method that can be applied immediately to daily life and the ordinary expectations that Hume said were a matter of custom or habit.

But we are not only creatures of habit. We can regiment our inquiries and design experiments to which we can then apply the confidence idea, using methods that are right most of the time.

That is precisely what we need for an objective, rational science!

That is as good a ground for reasonable behavior as we can sensibly hope for.

THE MODELING OBJECTION

As always in probability and induction, there are difficulties.

One is that the frequentist moves much too fast when talking about doing experiments and imposing the method of confidence intervals. The method can be applied only to models of the experiment and how it works. The models implicitly assume that most features of the world are going to stay constant. They assume that the future will be like the past in all respects needed to keep the model appropriate.

All the assertions of confidence intervals are relative to a vast body of background knowledge which takes for granted that the future will be like the past. So, says this objector, the doctrine of inductive behavior does not evade the problem of induction, it just begs the question.

RESPONSE

The response is oddly similar to that of the Bayesian, when asked about dynamic changes in beliefs.

> Hume was telling us that there is *no* reason or foundation for *any* inductive inferences, wasn't he? He was saying that there is only custom or habit.
>
> Well, we frequentists don't even try to give a foundation for all our knowledge and beliefs. But given certain beliefs that we represent in models used to design experiments, we can prove that some customs or habits are better than others.
>
> Hume's words "custom" and "habit" were supposed to make us throw up our hands. Custom is simply whatever we do, and Hume implied that nothing more could be said about it.
>
> On the contrary! (says Neyman). We can choose to adopt wise habits, ones that lead us to the right conclusions most of the time!
>
> We can't prove absolutely that our customs have this property, but given that we have some beliefs about how the world is, we can prove on the basis of those beliefs that the habits commended by Neyman are more reasonable than other customs.
>
> And that is all that we can sensibly hope for.

THE SINGLE-CASE OBJECTION

There is a quite different and rather philosophical difficulty. It resembles a small problem we saw long ago. Remember the old Coke machine on the South Sea island? (page 146).

For people who lived on the island, it was all right to pay a nickel with a 5/6 chance of getting a bottle of Coke (real cost 6 cents). But why should that satisfy the sailor who was on the island for a day, and wanted only one bottle of Coke?

It is all very well to say that this is a great old Coke machine, if one regularly uses it as one's source of soft drinks.

Likewise, it is all very well to say that confidence intervals give a great method of inductive behavior, thanks to their long-run operating characteristics— if one is using them many times.

But what if I am concerned with something very pressing, a matter of life and death? Is there no better justification than that the method is right most of the time?

Let us take the simplest kind of "inductive behavior." It can be put in the form of a gamble.

Suppose we divide a standard pack of 52 cards into two packs, which we will call red and black. The red pack has one black card, and all the red cards but one. The black pack has the remaining cards, just one of which is red. We shuffle and arrange a chance set up so that the chance of getting a black card from the red pack is 1/26. Now consider this gamble for a prize P:

(i) P if a red card is drawn from the red pack.
(ii) P if a red card is drawn from the black pack.

We would all choose option (i). Why? Neyman would say that this is prudent inductive behavior. Most of the time, if you take option (i) you will get your prize; not so with option (ii).

But suppose you are offered this gamble just once, by a mad kidnapper.

The prize P is your release; if you don't win, he'll murder you in an especially horrible manner.

We would all choose (i) and hope. That is the only reasonable thing to do, in the circumstances. *But not because of the long run*. In the next run, you are dead, or not dead.

This objection was made a century ago by Charles Sanders Peirce, the person who first clearly formulated what we have been calling the confidence idea. He made the idea one of the cornerstones of his theory of logic. But he was also a philosopher, and well aware of pitfalls. Worrying about this, he came to a remarkable conclusion, that in the end, the foundations for logic are *faith, hope, and charity*. He was *not* making a religious point, even though he was quoting from the New Testament. In no ordinary sense was Peirce an adherent of any organized religion. He was instead arguing that the requirements of logic lead us back to some long-standing human ideals that we do not usually associate with logic. Here is what he wrote in the *Popular Science Monthly* in 1878.

THREE LOGICAL SENTIMENTS

But there remains an important point to be cleared up. According to what has been said, the idea of probability essentially belongs to a kind of inference which is repeated indefinitely. An individual inference must be either true or false, and can show no effect in probability; and therefore, in reference to a single case considered in itself, probability can have no meaning. Yet if a man had to choose between drawing a card from a pack containing twenty-five red cards and a black one, or from a pack containing twenty-five black cards and a red one, and if the drawing of a red card were destined to transport him to eternal felicity, and that of a black one to consign him to everlasting woe, it would be folly to deny that he ought to prefer the pack containing the larger proportion of red cards, although, from the nature of the risk, it could not be repeated. It is not easy to reconcile this with our conception of chance. But suppose he should choose the red pack, and should draw the wrong card, what consolation would he have? He might say that he had acted in accordance with reason, but that would only show that his reason was absolutely worthless. And if he should choose the right card, how could he regard it as anything but a happy accident? He could not say that if he had drawn from the other pack he might have drawn the wrong one, because an hypothetical proposition such as, "if A, then B," means nothing with reference to a single case.

Peirce then goes on to consider a number of ways out. If I could just think of my choice of card, in dire circumstances, as one of the many choices I make, then I could still be engaging in rational inductive behavior. Yet every class of actions I perform is finite, my whole life is finite. The difficulty repeats itself. The set of my own entire set of life choices is like a single choice from the pack of cards, and what is to make that rational inductive behavior? Peirce concludes in an astounding way:

It seems to me that we are driven to this, that logicality inexorably requires that our interests shall *not* be limited. They must not stop at our own fate, but must embrace the whole community. This community, again, must not be limited, but must extend to all races of beings with whom we can come into immediate or mediate intellectual relation. It must reach, however vaguely, beyond this geological epoch, beyond all bounds. He who would not sacrifice his own to save the whole world is, as it seems to me, illogical in all his inferences, collectively. Logic is rooted in the social principle.

Peirce ended this discussion by observing that:

It may seem strange that I should put forward three sentiments, namely interest in an indefinite community, recognition of the possibility of this interest being made supreme, and hope in the unlimited continuance of intellectual activity, as indispensable requirements of logic. Yet, when we consider that logic depends on a mere struggle to escape doubt, which, as it terminates in action, must begin in emotion, and that, furthermore, the only cause of our planting ourselves on reason is that other methods of doubt fail on account of the social impulse, why should we wonder to find social sentiment presupposed in reasoning? As for the other two sentiments which I find necessary, they are so only as supports and accessories of that. It interests me to notice that these three sentiments seem to be pretty much the same as that famous trio of Charity, Faith, and Hope, which, in the estimation of St. Paul, are the finest and greatest of spiritual gifts.

CHARLES SANDERS PEIRCE

C. S. Peirce (1839–1914) founded the American philosophy called *pragmatism*, a school developed by William James (1842–1910) and John Dewey (1859–1952) and undergoing a great revival today. He was the first contributor to probability and induction mentioned in this book, right back on page 16. He is a good person to end with. (If you have forgotten how to spell or pronounce his name, look back to page 16 and check.)

Peirce was a philosopher with a profound and original understanding of probability. He acquired some of it from close practical work. For a long time he earned his living with the United States Coast and Geodetic Survey, which meant that he had a great deal of hands-on experience with measurement. He was extremely familiar with the "curve of errors" which came to be called the normal distribution.

Peirce set out the rationale for the theory of confidence intervals very clearly, starting with the normal approximation exactly as we did in Chapter 19. It looks as if Jacques Bernoulli, Laplace, and earlier writers had the basic idea long ago. We also owe technical precision to Jerzy Neyman. But Peirce set out the philosophical foundations before anyone else, and did so with great clarity.

He summed up his idea of deductive and inductive logic in a uniform way:

◆ An argument form is deductively valid if the conclusion of an argument of such a form is always true when the premises are true.
◆ An argument form is inductively good if the conclusion of an argument of such a form is usually true when the premises are true.
◆ An argument form is inductively 95% good if the conclusion of an argument of such a form is true in 95% of the cases where the premises are true.

That leads directly to the "evasion" of the problem of induction discussed in this chapter. And Peirce himself saw that the single-case objection is the most interesting problem about this evasion.

He did not think that all scientific reasoning is either deductive or inductive. His third type of scientific reasoning was, as we saw on page 16, what he called "abduction," trying to find the best explanation of something that is puzzling or problematic.

Peirce made use of probability ideas in many parts of his philosophy. He was impressed by the way in which frequencies tend to stabilize, as when taking measurements, according to Bernoulli's Theorem. He thought this was a good way in which to think about the ways in which we form beliefs. In an experiment, an observed relative frequency may be misleading at first, but at the end settles down to a stable probability. Induction is like that, he thought. It is *self-correcting*.

As a scientific worker, Peirce knew that no one person makes the measurements that become stabilized. Many investigators in many parts of the world contribute. Likewise, it is through *collective inquiry* that beliefs gradually stabilize.

Peirce even suggested that truth itself cannot be distinguished from the beliefs that the community of inquirers is, as he put it, "fated" to arrive at. But you need real faith in our community, and hope that it will endure, to think of this as a way to characterize truth.

There is one fundamental way in which the philosophy of Charles Sanders Peirce differs from that of David Hume. It goes far beyond the problem of induction. Hume thought in a highly individualistic way, of how *my* beliefs are formed by *my* experiences. Peirce thought in a collective and communal way, in terms of how *our* beliefs are formed on the basis of *our* inquiries.

Answers to the Exercises

CHAPTER 1. LOGIC

1. *Propositions.*
   (a) Yes.
   (b) I myself don't know if it is true, unless I trust the newspaper.
   (c) Yes.
   (d) Yes.
   (e) Once again, I don't know if it is true, unless I trust the newspaper. There might be a big debate among snake scientists. Some suggest that the ball python was not named after its tendency to curl up into a ball. Instead, it was named after the famous explorer and snake expert, Emily Ball. The question may never be settled. We may never be really sure why this snake is called a ball python. We may not know whether what the paper wrote is true, or whether it is false. But we know it is true-or-false.
   (f) Yes.
   (g) No. The snakes may be attractive to Joe, but probably some other people think the snakes are repulsive or scary. This statement is not what logicians call a proposition, because it expresses an attitude more than a matter of fact.
   (h) Yes. This is a proposition about what Joe feels or thinks.
   (i) No. It is not even a sentence. Hence it does not express a proposition.
   (j) No. The slang expression "I'm not really too thrilled" is more a way of expressing an attitude than stating a fact, so we will not count this as a proposition.
   (k) No. It is an exclamation, not a proposition.
   (l) No. It is a question, not a proposition.
   (m) This is tricky. It is not always so clear whether something is true-or-false. Joe is not so much making a statement as saying that FedEx ought to reimburse him for their mistake.
   (n) Yes.

2. *False all over.* There are endless silly examples.
   (a) *Valid*: All heads of horses are heads of chickens. All chickens are fish. *So,* All heads of horses are heads of fish.
   (b) *Invalid*: All heads of horses are heads of chickens. All fish are chickens. *So,* All heads of horses are heads of fish.

   Valid arguments like (a) show that there is more to validity than simple syllogisms. The validity of (a) depends on the relation *head of*. This example about animal heads was used to make just this point by Augustus de Morgan (1806–1871), an English logician who made contributions to both deductive and inductive logic.

3. *Unsound.* Any correct answer to (2a) will be unsound because the premises are false. Any correct answer to (2b) will be unsound both because it is invalid, and because it has false premises.

4. *Combinations.* Only (b) is impossible. An argument with all premises true, and a false conclusion is, by definition, invalid.

5. *Soundness.* Only (a) is sound. Sound arguments are valid, and have true premises.

6. *Conditional propositions.* (a) is valid-or-invalid. It is an argument. (b) is true-or-false. It is a conditional, if-then proposition.

7. *Chewing tobacco.* All four arguments are invalid.

8. *Inductive baseball.* None of the four arguments is worthless. (7c) is the strongest, assuming that the number of chewers and the number of nonchewers in 1988 were both quite large, and that the seven teams were chosen haphazardly, by the investigators. We might disagree about which of (7a), (7b), and (7d) is weakest. They can be criticized for different reasons. That is what inductive logic is all about.

CHAPTER 2. WHAT IS INDUCTIVE LOGIC?

1. *Fees.* (a) Population to sample. (b) Sample to population. (c) Population to sample. (d) Sample to sample.

2. *More fees.* (a) and (b) are inferences to a plausible explanation. (c) is an inference based on testimony.

3.1. *Boys and girls.* (a) The argument is risky because all the premises could be true while the conclusion is false.

3.2. *Pia.* (e) is the riskier conclusion. With (a) you are taking just one risk—Pia might not be an active feminist. But with (e) you are taking three risks—she might not be a bank teller, she might not be an active feminist, and she might not take yoga classes.

3.3. *Lotteries.*
   (a) The probability that A wins is exactly the same as the probability that B wins. If two people choose the same combination of numbers, and that combination wins a big prize, they split the prize. People in general don't like regular-looking numbers, so the probability that someone else picks A is less than the probability that someone else picks B. So if I bet on A and win, I'll get a bigger share of the prize than if I bet on B and win. So I choose A.
   (b) This is not obviously a risky decision, since you lose nothing no matter what happens—the lottery tickets are free. But you do risk being regretful—if you chose A, and B wins.

3.4. *Dice.* No, this is not risky. It is a valid argument.

3.5. *Taxicabs.* (a) Yes. (b) You could think of them as risky decisions, because both Amos and Daniel have to decide what to say to the judge or to their fellow jurors.

3.6. *Strep throat.* The risk is that the patient does have strep throat, which will rapidly get worse if treatment is not commenced.

4. *Ludwig van Beethoven.* (a) Inference to a plausible explanation. How plausible? Musicologists are not impressed. (b) Many examples might do, for instance, new letters by Beethoven saying that he composes when he is high on opium. More interesting: a laboratory in Tucson is doing an analysis of a lock of 582 strands of Beethoven's hair, which should reveal trace elements of whatever chemicals the composer ingested.

5. *The slender oarfish.* (a) "If an oarfish, which normally lives in depths of more than 200 meters, is landed in nets, then major tremors are not far behind." It is based on the testimony of Japanese folklore. (b) Conclusion: "Whenever an oarfish is netted, a geological upheaval is in progress or about to occur." (c) From sample to population—from individual oarfish-catches and quakes, to a general statement about oarfish and quakes. (d) Plausible explanation (i): The oarfish, with its elongated shape, may be stunned and then float to the surface. Plausible explanation (ii): Poisonous gases are released from the earth's crust during seismic activity. (e) First, there is an argument from testimony. Second,

there is an inductive argument from sample to population. Third, there are proposals of plausible explanations, either of which, if true, would predict the conclusion. *The conclusion is supported by three different types of risky argument.*

6. *Women engineers.* (a) "That showing is particularly poor." (b) Valid (although the validity may depend on what we mean by "particularly poor").

7. *Plastic surgery.* Inference to the best explanation.

8. *Manitoba marijuana.* This resembles an argument from sample to population. The sample consists of homes that the police have checked for hydroponic marijuana. The population consists of rural homes in Manitoba.

CHAPTER 3. THE GAMBLER'S FALLACY

1. *Roulette wheels.* (a) In North America, the probability of the wheel stopping at red is 18/38. In Europe, the probability is 18/37. So if you are simply betting on red, Europe is better. (b) No.

2. *Shuffling.* (a) Yes. Every card should, in the course of a great many games, be dealt as often as every other. (b) No. (c) No. BUT: Since the players are unlikely to be able to predict the order of the cards after a shuffle, no one has an advantage despite the fact that the deal has a memory. Hence from the player's point of view the game is, in another sense of the word, "fair."

3. *Lotto.* It looks as if this is a good buy: if few people choose this sequence to bet on, then, if it does come up, they will have to share their winnings with fewer people than if they had bought a popular ticket. BUT how do I know this to be a fact? If I got it from a popular book on gambling, you can imagine that the book itself has changed people's habits, so that now, after the book has been around for a while, this is the most popular ticket!

4. *Numerals.*
   (a) *Birth weights.* In grams, we expect the last digit to be unbiased and independent of previous trials. But in pounds, 7 would occur more frequently than any other digit, so the set up would be biased. Trials would, however, still be independent (except for twins, or worse, quintuplets).
   (b) *Telephone poles.* Unbiased and dependent.
   (c) *Books.* 100% biased against 1, 3, 5, 7, and 9.
   (d) *Cruise ships.* Unbiased, independent.

5. Fallacious Gambler *strikes back.*
   (a) No. *Fallacious Gambler* sensibly supposes that "thirteen blacks" counts as a "long run," and concludes that, according to Dr. Marbe's data, a sequence of twelve blacks followed by a red occurs more often than a sequence of twelve blacks followed by a black. Of course when we dig up the records, it may turn out that Marbe was referring to much longer runs, but at any rate *Fallacious Gambler* was not committing the gambler's fallacy.
   (b) Here is *one* possible explanation: the croupiers who spin the roulette wheels think people will imagine the wheel is biased, and so think the house is dishonest. So after a longish run, they do their best to spin the wheel so as to break the long run. *Or* the house itself deliberately puts a mechanical "corrector" behind the wheel, which, when the croupier touches a button, biases the wheel toward black, when red has been appearing many times, and vice versa.

6. *Counting.* Someone who can remember what cards have been dealt for previous hands has an advantage. For example, if you know that most of the low cards have already been dealt, then the probability of getting a high card is greater than it was at the beginning. Using this information, it is possible to improve the odds. You need quite a lot of capital, because you have to make large bets, and will sometimes lose. A mathematician named

Thorpe perfected a gambling system known as "counting." Most casinos have now changed the rules and use a new pack for each deal.

7. *The American draft.*
    (a) Sampling without replacement.
    (b) Statisticians analyzed the data, in fact, and showed that there was bias towards the earlier part of the year.
    (c) The setup was not fair. If you were born early in the year, you would feel that the setup was not "fair to you." But if you thought that birth dates themselves were, in a way, determined randomly, then you might feel the system was fair enough. At least there was no bias for picking poor people over rich ones.
    (d) Here are two fundamentally different types of explanation. *Carelessness*: The balls were not shaken very well. At the beginning the young women did dig and scrabble around in the urn, and so drawing was not seriously biased. But later on they got bored, and just picked the first ball that came to hand, and the low numbers were nearer the top. *Cheating*: The young women had brothers who were born in November and December. They could see enough of a ball to see whether it had one, two, or three digits on it. They took a one or two-digit ball whenever they safely could. Note: There is every reason to choose the first explanation. There was no evidence of deliberate cheating.

8. *X-rays.* For example, *Sara* might insist: "No, no, the effect of X rays is cumulative! That's because when one ray harms a cell, there is only a low probability of cancer developing, but two cells harmed more than doubles the danger, and so on." *Dentist*: "That's silly. The doses of X rays are independent . . ." *Sara* breaks in, "No, that's my point, they are not independent, because your body has a 'memory': if a cell has been harmed, then the effect of a second harmed cell is greater . . ."

9. *A dry August.* This is not an example of the gambler's fallacy, because we are given no reason to assume that monthly trials (whether or not there is a good rainfall in a given month) are independent.

    But the argument is fallacious, even if it does not commit the gambler's fallacy. Here is one way it is fallacious. For all we know, when there has been no rain for six months, there will be no rain the next month either. For example, the conditional probability of rain in month 8, given no rain for months 1–7, could be 0. (This story is taken from a French novel by Marcel Pagnol, which was made into the movie *Jean de Florette*.)

10. *The inverse gambler's fallacy.*
    (a) $1/6 \times 1/6 \times 1/6 \times 1/6 = 1/1296$.
    (b) Yes. Suppose we compare two hypotheses—that he rolled 900 times, and that he rolled just once. The probability of getting four sixes at least once in 900 tosses is almost exactly ½. The probability of getting four sixes in one toss is about 1/1300. So Nelson is right, it is far more likely that Trapper rolled many times, say 900 times, than that he rolled just once. (Where did we get that figure of ½ from? Well, the probability of *not* getting four sixes in two tosses is $[1295/1296 \times 1295/1296]$. The probability of *not* getting four sixes in 900 tosses is $[1295/1296]^{900} \approx 0.499$, so the probability of getting at least one roll of four sixes is about 0.501.)
    (c) No. For example, suppose Lucie guesses Albert has made 899 tosses and this is the 900th. No matter what happened on the 899 tosses, the probability of Albert rolling four sixes on toss 900 is about 1/1300—exactly the same as on the first roll of the evening. We can call Lucie's error **the inverse gambler's fallacy.**

11. *Lucky aunt.* (a) Yes. (b) Strictly, no, for the same reasons as in question 10. But you might use more information, a little human psychology. Aunt might have simply decided, "now I'm seventy, time for a little fling." But typically people who buy a lottery ticket do so regularly. And there is a "selection effect." Aunt does not call up when she does not win. So it might be reasonable to guess that your aunt has been playing for many weeks—but not *simply* on the evidence that she won this time.

12. *The argument from design.* No. It commits the inverse gambler's fallacy. You may think that this is all out of date, since we now believe in the Big Bang origin of our universe.

But John Wheeler, a distinguished cosmologist, urged that we should think of serial universes, with universes being created and dying, followed by a new Big Bang ... He argued that we can understand our present "fine-tuned" universe on the hypothesis that there have been many universes, so that by mere chance we'd finally get a fine-tuned one like ours.

CHAPTER 4. ELEMENTARY PROBABILITY IDEAS

1. *Galileo.* Since both 9 and 10 can be made up in six ways, you might think that they are equally probable:

    [9]: {1,2,6} {1,3,5} {2,3,4} {1,4,4} {2,2,5} {3,3,3}
    [10]: {1,3,6} {1,4,5} {2,3,5} {2,2,6} {2,4,4} {3,3,4}.

    Indeed, the first three italicized outcomes, with three different numerals, are equally probable. The next two outcomes, with only two different numerals, are equally probable. But {3,3,3} has only one arrangement, and a probability of 1/216. {3,3,4} = {(3,3,4) or (3,4,3) or (4,3,3)} with probability (3/216 = 1/72). So 10 is more probable than 9.

2. *One card.* (a) 4/13. (b) 11/26.

3. *Two cards.* (a) 1/16. (b) (1/4) × (12/51) = 3/51.
   (c) 9/16. (d) (3/4) × (38/51) = 19/34.

4. *Archery.* (a) 0.02. (b) 0.04. There is a .02 chance that she hits the bull's-eye and then the third circle, and there is .02 chance that she hits the third circle and then the bull's-eye, for a total of .04. (c) 0.1.

5. *Polio from diapers.* The only *literal* meaning I attach to this is that catching polio from a diaper is very, very unusual. Maybe Dr. Wale meant that in the last three million polio shots, there has been only one case like this. He might have meant that if you looked after your niece and went to an insurance company and asked for a $3 million insurance policy against your catching polio from her diapers, they should charge you a premium of only $1. He might mean that the relative frequency of catching polio from diapers is only one per three million shots. But tiny improbabilities like this, based on a single very rare item, mean almost nothing, except "very rare." You should usually treat remarks like this as rhetoric, not science.

6. *Languages.* The question is not very sharp. Question 2 asked, "What is the probability that so and so (is true)": *proposition* talk. Question 3 asked about the probability of so and so (happening): *event* talk. But clearly questions 2 and 3 are just two different ways of asking similar questions. Similarly, you could say that question 4 used the proposition language, and question 5 used the event language.

CHAPTER 5. CONDITIONAL PROBABILITY

1. *Phony precision about tennis.* So many places of decimals don't make much sense. Perhaps Ivan meant 37.5% = 3/8 or odds of 5-to-3 against Stefan. Moral: don't get bamboozled by numbers. Sometimes they only sound good. Ivan is a well-known show-off. By the way, Stefan won.

2. *Heat lamps.* When a lamp is taken from the store, let T = made by *Tropicana*, F = made by *Florida*, B = below standards.

    Pr(T) = 0.4 Pr(F) = 0.6 Pr(B/T) = 0.03 Pr(B/F) = 0.06

   (a) Pr(T&B) = 0.012.
   (b) Pr(B) = Pr[(T&B)v(F&B)] = Pr(T&B) + Pr(F&B) = 0.012 + 0.036 = 0.048.
   (c) Pr(T/B) = 1/4.

3. *The Triangle.* Let T = a city child lives in the Triangle. Let ~T = a city child does not live in the Triangle. Let P = a child tests positive.

    Pr(T) = 0.02 Pr(P/T) = 0.14 Pr(P/~T) = 0.01

(a) Pr(T&P) = 0.0028.
(b) Pr(P) = 0.0028 + 0.0098 = 0.0126.
(c) Pr(T/P) = 2/9 (≈ 0.22). Notice how the fractions cancelled. 28/126 = 14/63 = 2/9. You can do most of these exercises more quickly in your head than with a calculator.

4.   *Taxicabs.*

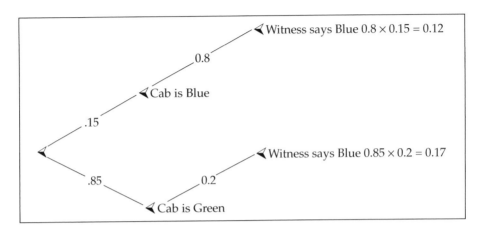

Probability (Cab is blue/Witness says blue) = .12/(.12 + .29) ≈ .41.

In Chapter 6, 0.15 is called the **base rate** for blue taxicabs. The diagram shows that if there were 100 cabs in town, 15 blue and 85 green, then an "80% reliable" witness would on average pick 12 randomly presented blue cabs as blue, and 29 randomly presented green cabs as blue. The base rate overwhelms the reliability of the witness.

5.   *Laplace's trick question.* We already know from pages 44–5 that:

Pr(First ball drawn is red) = 1/2.
Pr(First ball drawn is red & Second ball drawn is red) = 5/16.

Hence, Pr(Second ball drawn is red/First ball drawn is red) = 10/16 = 5/8.

6.   *Understanding the question.* The conditional probability of drawing a second red, given that we drew a first red, is greater than ½. So even though the probability of drawing a first Red is ½, the probability of drawing two Reds is NOT ½ × ½. In fact, it is ½(5/8) = 5/16.

CHAPTER 6. THE BASIC RULES OF PROBABILITY

1.   *Venn Diagrams.* (a) Pr(LvS)

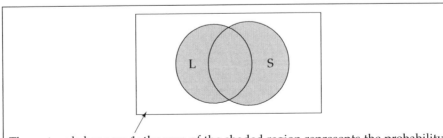

The rectangle has area 1; the area of the shaded region represents the probability that a person smokes or contracts lung disease or both.

(b) Pr(L/S)

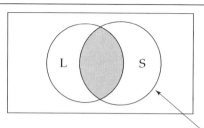

The proportion of the area of overlap, shaded, to the area of S, represents the conditional probability.

(c) Pr(S/L)

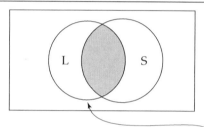

The proportion of the area of overlap, shaded, to the area of L, represents the conditional probability.

2. *Total probability.*

    Pr(A) + Pr(~A) = Pr(Av~A) by additivity.
    Av~A is logically equivalent to Ω.
    Pr(Ω) = 1 by normality.
    Hence by the assumption of logical equivalence (page 58),
    Pr(A) + Pr(~A) = 1.

3. *Multiplying.* When 0 < Pr(A), and 0 < Pr(B), then

    Pr(A/B) = Pr(A&B)/Pr(B) by definition.
    So Pr(A&B) = Pr(A/B)Pr(B).
    If A and B are statistically independent, Pr(A/B) = Pr(A).
    Hence Pr(A&B) = Pr(A)Pr(B).

4. *Conventions.* There are several possibilities. Here are two:

    (i) *Infinite probabilities.* Probability of a certain proposition or event is +∞. Probability of an impossible proposition or event is −∞.

        You might think this was better than our convention that Pr(Ω) = 1. You'd say, no proposition about the real world is *really completely* certain. So the probability of any real-world proposition can be a large finite number, as big as you want, but never infinite.

        In this convention, for any event or proposition A,

    (i) If A and ~A are equally probable, then Pr(A) = Pr(~A) = 0.
    (ii) If A is more probable than ~A, then 0 ≤ Pr(A).
    (iii) If ~A is more probable than A, then Pr(A) ≤ 0.

That, however, does not take us very far. The beauty of the usual convention is that addition and multiplication are so tidy for mutually exclusive or independent events.

(ii) *Upper and lower probabilities*. The probability of an event is represented by an interval, (p_*, p^*). This seems especially sensible for belief-type probabilities. Most of our beliefs don't seem to be very exact. Really certain events would still have probability $p_* = p^* = 1$, and we would have:

$$0 \leq p_* \leq p^* \leq 1.$$

There is a viable theory of upper and lower probabilities, but it has not conquered mainstream probability theory.

5. *Terrorists*. You can't explain a joke without killing it! The joke is a play on conditional probability and statistical independence.

   Observation 1. Say the probability of a terrorist placing a bomb on a plane is minute. The probability of two terrorists independently placing bombs on the same plane is some meaninglessly small number, call it one in a trillion. So Black is right: "The risk that there would be two independent bombs on your plane is virtually zero."

   Observation 2. But the student who considers taking a bomb on the plane, to reduce the risk to practically zero, needs to know the probability that a terrorist places a bomb in her plane, given that she takes a bomb on the plane. If these two events are statistically independent, the conditional probability of a terrorist bomb, given her bomb, is just the probability of a terrorist bomb. The risk has not changed.

CHAPTER 7. BAYES' RULE

1. [2(c)]: *Heat lamps*.

$$Pr(T/B) = \frac{Pr(T)Pr(B/T)}{Pr(T)Pr(B/T) + Pr(F)Pr(B/F)}$$

$$= \frac{0.4 \times 0.03}{(0.4 \times 0.03) + (0.6 \times 0.06)} = 1/4$$

   [3(c)]: *Triangle*.

$$Pr(T/P) = \frac{Pr(T)Pr(P/T)}{Pr(T)Pr(P/T) + Pr(\sim T)Pr(P/\sim T)}$$

$$= \frac{0.02 \times 0.14}{(0.02 \times 0.14) + (0.98 \times 0.01)} = 2/9$$

2. *Double dipping*.
   (a) With replacement:

$$Pr(A/RR) = \frac{Pr(A)Pr(RR/A)}{Pr(A)Pr(RR/A) + Pr(B)Pr(RR/B)}$$

$$= \frac{0.5 \times (0.6 \times 0.6)}{0.5 \times (0.6 \times 0.6) + 0.5 \times (0.1 \times 0.1)} = 36/37 \approx 0.973$$

   (b) Without replacement:

$$Pr(A/RR) = \frac{0.5 \times (0.6 \times 59/99)}{0.5 \times (0.6 \times 59/99) + 0.5 \times (0.1 \times 9/99)} = 354/363 \approx 0.975$$

   Notice how little difference there is in sampling with and without replacement, even with a small population of 100.

3. *Tests*. Let S = A student is serious. ~S = A student is not serious. C = A question is answered correctly. CC = Two questions are answered correctly. Since the teacher looks at two questions haphazardly, we can assume independence.

$$Pr(S) = 3/4 \qquad Pr(\sim S) = 1/4$$
$$Pr(C/S) = 3/4 \qquad Pr(C/\sim S) = 1/2$$

$$Pr(S/CC) = \frac{Pr(S)Pr(CC/S)}{Pr(S)Pr(CC/S) + Pr(\sim S)Pr(CC/\sim S)}$$

$$= \frac{(3/4) \times (3/4) \times (3/4)}{[3/4 \times 3/4 \times 3/4] + [1/4 \times 1/2 \times 1/2]} = 27/31$$

4. *Weightlifters.*
   (a) The coach sent the Cleaner team, but the committee randomly selected a user, and decided that the Steroid team had been sent.
   (b) Pr(Cleaner team/one user detected): $Pr(C/U) = 0.2$.
   (c) Using the results of page 54, $Pr(C/U_1 \& U_2) = 1/29 < 0.04$.

5. *Three hypotheses.*

   (a) $Pr(F/E) = \dfrac{Pr(F)Pr(E/F)}{Pr(F)Pr(E/F) + Pr(G)Pr(E/G) + Pr(H)Pr(E/H)}$

   (b) By definition, $Pr(F/E) = Pr(F\&E)/Pr(E)$.
   By logical equivalence, $Pr(F\&E) = Pr(E\&F)$, which equals $Pr(F)Pr(E/F)$.
   That is the required numerator. As for the denominator,

   E is logically equivalent to $(E\&F)v(E\&G)v(E\&H)$.

   Since the disjuncts are mutually exclusive, by additivity,

   $Pr(E) = Pr(F)Pr(E/F) + Pr(G)Pr(E/G) + Pr(H)Pr(E/H)$.

6. *Computer crashes.* Let: C = Sophia's computer crashes.

   F = Sophia's computer is running Fog. G = running Golem. H = running Hotshot.
   $Pr(C/F) = 0.1$ $Pr(C/G) = 0.2$ $Pr(C/H) = 0.3$
   $Pr(F) = 0.6$ $Pr(G) = 0.3$ $Pr(H) = 0.1$
   $Pr(H/C) = (0.1 \times 0.3) \div [(0.1 \times 0.3) + (0.3 \times 0.2) + (0.6 \times 0.)1] = 1/5 = 0.2$

7. *Deterring burglars.* Let A = Ali was chosen at random, J = Jenny was chosen at random, and L = Larry was chosen at random. Let B = the person chosen at random was burgled last year.

   $Pr(B/A) = 0.4$ $Pr(B/J) = 0.1$ $Pr(B/L) = 0.6$ $Pr(A) = Pr(J) = Pr(L) = 1/3$
   We require $Pr(A/B) = \dfrac{Pr(A)Pr(B/A)}{Pr(A)Pr(B/A) + Pr(J)Pr(B/J) + Pr(L)Pr(B/L)} = 4/11$.

   This probability is based on the amazing information provided by the sociologist. Since I did not believe what was stated in his letter, I wrote him and discovered that he had more complicated statistics in mind. Thus the argument to the probability is *unsound* because one of the premises, about burglary rates, is totally false.

CHAPTER 8. EXPECTED VALUE

1. *Winter travel.* It may well have been both, but the utility disagreement is most important.
   Probability disagreement: I'm a pessimist, I think snow is likely, and I think traffic will be terribly snarled if there is a bad storm. Oliver does not think a bad storm is so likely, and he does not think traffic chaos will be as great as I do.
   Utility disagreement. I think the inconvenience and hassle—negative utility—of getting stuck in the snow is very great. Oliver does not mind much. But he thinks the negative utility of a very long subway ride is quite great. I prefer taking the subway to driving.

2. *Gimmicks.* −20¢. Even free coupons are worth less than the paper they are printed on.

3. *Street vendor: fines not enforced.* $Exp(W) = \$200 − [(0.4)(0.2)(\$100)] = \$192$.

4. *Street vendor with a bad boss.* $Exp(W) = \$150 − (0.4)(0.25)(0.2)(\$100) = \$148$.

5. *The best of possible worlds.* The best arrangement is (3), the worst is (4).

6. *Insurance.*
   (a) Probability of losing both watch and car: $(1/900)(1/30) = 1/27{,}000$.

   Probability of losing watch only: $(1/30)(899/900) = 899/27{,}000$.

   Probability of losing car only: $(1/900)(29/30) = 29/27{,}000$.

   Probability of no theft at all: $(899/900)(29/30) = 26{,}071/27{,}000$.

   (b) The four possible consequences of D are: nothing stolen, watch only is stolen, car only is stolen, both are stolen.

   $$\text{Exp}(D) = 0 - \$(1/27000)(899)(600) + 29(5400) + 6000) = -\$(234)/9$$
   $$\approx -\$26.00$$

   (c) Consequences of I. William has to pay out \$60 in any event; his losses are only 10% of the previous loss in the event of theft: $\text{Exp}(I) = -\$60 - \$2.60 = -\$62.60$.

   (d) The expected value of the act, "insure," is really much worse, more than twice as bad, as the expected value of not insuring. But William may insure, because he is risk-averse. Or because the utility value of losing his cherished possessions is much more than the cash value. Or because he really can afford the \$60, but if he loses his car, he simply cannot buy another one.

   (e) No, by definition they are not statistically independent.

   (f) Exp(D) becomes significantly more negative. The insurance means the effect is much less on Exp(I), which becomes a little more negative. Nevertheless, Exp(I) <Exp(D).

7. *Doubling up.* This is a variation on a martingale. Sooner or later *Slick Jim* will lose all his capital.

8. *The Moscow Game.*
   (a) $(1/2)^{40} \approx 9 \times 10^{-13}$, or about one in 10 million million.
   (b) Yes.
   (c) \$40.
   (d) You have to win more than \$40. So you will lose if heads comes up on the first, second, third, fourth, or fifth toss. (At the sixth toss, when you get tails, you win \$24.) You also lose if tails comes up 40 times in a row. Hence the probability of winning some money is:

   $$[1 - (\text{probability of not getting H in tosses 1, 2, 3, 4, 5, or 40})] = 1/32 - 2^{-40}$$

   (e) 29 tails followed by a heads. But if the bank is speculating in spot oil futures, you might not have to wait for 30 tails in a row before it goes bankrupt.

CHAPTER 9. MAXIMIZING EXPECTED VALUE

1. *Locking.* Act K: Buy a Kryptonite lock. Act L: Buy a cheap chain and lock. Consequence S: your bike is stolen. Consequence N: your bike is not stolen.
   $U(S) = -\$80$. You have already spent your money, so the further utility of not losing your bike is $U(N) = 0$.

   $\text{Exp}(K) = [\text{Pr}(S/K)][U(S) - \$20] + [\text{Pr}(N/K)][U(N) - \$20]$
   $\qquad = 0 + (-\$20) = -\$20$.
   $\text{Exp}(L) = [\text{Pr}(S/L)][U(S) - \$8] + [\text{Pr}(N/L)][U(N) - \$8]$
   $\qquad = 0.1(-\$88) + 0.9(-\$8) = -\$16$.

   So if you want to maximize expected value, you should buy the cheap lock.

2. *Inconvenience.* More than \$40.

3. *Repeated losses.* No. The expected values are exactly the same as before. The only way it would be rational to buy the Kryptonite lock would be if:
   • The fact that your bike was stolen made you realize that the chance of theft with a cheap lock was greater than 10%. (But how could one experience of a rare event lead you to that conclusion?) Or,
   • You realized that losing your bike when you are visiting a friend four miles from home

is a real hassle. You do not want to have that happen again. You value the inconvenience as worse than −$40.

4. *Planning ahead.* No, but the calculation gets complicated. Then the consequences of buying the cheap lock are:

    N: not stolen.
    SN: bike stolen, buy new bike, chain, and lock for $88, but the second bike is not stolen.
    SS: bike stolen, buy new bike, chain, and lock for $88, but the second bike is also stolen.

    Exp(L) = −$8−(0.1)[$88 + (0.1)($80)] = −$17.60.

    So you still maximize expected value by buying the cheap lock.

5. *Be wise the first time?* The cheap lock *still* maximizes expected value, with Exp(L) = −$8−(0.1)[$108] = −$18.80.

6. *No insurance.* My friend did carry catastrophic health insurance—that is, he was generously covered if he were to endure catastrophic illness or accident. When he was a bachelor, at most he risked losing all his assets, and he was so gifted he could easily start over again. Hence for him the disutility of an accident was quite small. My friend thought he was perfectly rational, because the expected value of buying insurance was, as it often is, less than the expected value of not buying insurance. When he married, he risked losing his home, harming his family, for it would take some time for him to start up again. So now his utility structure changed, even though his assessment of probabilities did not.

7. *Uty and Duty.* *Uty* might agree with my friend. *Duty* would disapprove. My friend was very selfish, for he did not cover the risks to anyone he hurt while driving, beyond his actual assets. *Duty* would say we have an obligation to be able to help those whom we may harm by our actions.

8. *Atoms and coal.* Your discussion will resemble the one about the space probe.

9. *The longest bridge.* Among other things, the critic will claim that you cannot properly quantify the possibility of complete disaster, either to the climate or to the pillars of the bridge. The consultant will argue that every remote "possibility" has been properly quantified as a small probability.

    Although disagreements about probabilities influence the discussion, one needs a lot more information to know the details. For example,

    > The fact that the bridge is built at the narrowest point between the island and New Brunswick complicates the predictions. Critics point to one report that estimated the effective channel width will be reduced by nearly 20%, and the final ice-out date will be much delayed.

    Note that behind the critics' ire is a profound unhappiness—that an idyllic island, site of the fantasy *Anne of Green Gables*, once reached only by ferry, will be paved over by tourist malls, mini-golf courses, and gigantic Anne of Green Gables theme parks. For some, that is a positive utility—money in the bank. For others, that is a massive negative utility, a destruction of irreplaceable values.

    By the way, the bridge is now in service. No problems. Yet.

10. *Allais.* No. The dollar utilities in the paradox were $5 million and $1 million. But in fact the paradox is quite general. Instead of $5 million and $1 million, let the utilities, in utiles, be x and y.

    Show that so long as $x > (1 + [Pr(N)/Pr(H)])y$, there is no consistent way to maximize expected utility by preferring A to B, while preferring G to F. Why? We see that

    Exp(A) = Pr(L)0 + Pr(N)0 + Pr(H)x.
    Exp(B) = Pr(L)0 + Pr(N)0 + Pr(H)y.

    Since x must exceed y by [Pr(N)/Pr(H)])y,

    Pr(N)0 + Pr(H)x > Pr(N)0 + Pr(H)y.

and hence $\text{Exp}(A) > \text{Exp}(B)$. **But now add** $\text{Pr}(L)y$ to the above inequality:

$$\text{Pr}(L)y + \text{Pr}(N)0 + \text{Pr}(H)x > \text{Pr}(L)y + \text{Pr}(N)0 + \text{Pr}(H)y.$$

On the left-hand side we have $\text{Exp}(F)$, and on the right-hand side we have $\text{Exp}(G)$, so $\text{Exp}(F) > \text{Exp}(G)$.

CHAPTER 10. DECISION UNDER UNCERTAINTY

Some questions asked you to use *your own* utilities and probabilities. What follows are *my* judgments. They are not right or wrong. Your numbers will be different, but the resulting arguments should be similar.

1. *Mercenary Sarah.* Suppose Sarah's estimates of annual salary five years after graduation are as in this table:

	B	G
C	$80K	$120K
P	$8K	$50K

    The $8,000 is what she thinks she will get on welfare. Neither act C nor act P has any causal influence on the economy, so the dominance rule can be applied. Sarah decides to take a degree in computer science, using the dominance rule.

2. *Dreamer Peony.* Peony has two different sources of utility: income and job contentment. She might represent her utilities this way:

	B	G
C	4	6
P	1	10

    There is no dominating act. Hence she requires probabilities of good and bad times. She is an optimist. She judges that

    $\text{Pr}(B) = 0.3. \ \text{Pr}(G) = 0.7.$
    $\text{Exp}(C) = 5.4$ utiles.
    $\text{Exp}(P) = 0.3(1) + 0.7(10) = 7.3$ utiles.

    She applies the expected value rule, and decides to take a degree in philosophy.

3. *Idealist Maria.* Maria might represent her utilities in this way.

	B	G
C	50	50
P	100	1,000

    Clearly act P dominates. Since neither act affects the economy, she applies the dominance rule and decides to take a philosophy degree.

4. *Criticizing Pascal.*
    (a) The partition is wrong. There are obviously many more live possibilities, at least for us. There are many more religions. Buddhism has nothing like the reward values of Pascal's Catholicism. Someone might even think this is possible: God is malicious, and actually punishes those who believe in Him. Or He punishes those who sincerely believe in him if they have come to believe as a consequence of decision theory.
    (b) This criticism is not applicable, for we do not think our personal acts of belief affect the existence or nonexistence of Pascal's God.
    (c) The gambler challenges Pascal's claim that the utilities of not-belief are zero, and thus forces expected value considerations.

5. *Study or not.* No, because the decision affects the outcome. If he thought that

    $\text{Pr}(A/R) = 0.2, \ \text{Pr}(B/R) = 0.6, \ \text{Pr}(C/R) = 0.2.$
    $\text{Pr}(A/S) = 0.7, \ \text{Pr}(B/S) = 0.3, \ \text{Pr}(C/S) = 0.$

Then, weighting the pluses and minuses in the table as 1, 2, 3, etc., his expected values are:

$$\text{Exp}(R) = 0.2(4) + 0.6(2) = 2.0.$$
$$\text{Exp}(S) = 0.7(3) + 0.3(1) = 2.4.$$

So he should decide to study.

6. *Twenty-first-century gloom.* Let S = stop work on robotics, genetic engineering, nanotechnology, etc., now.
Let C = Carry on with that work.
Let T = Terrible results ensue from carrying on.
Let ~T = There are no terrible results from carrying on.
There are many possible assignments of utilities which would yield an argument from dominance. Here is one:

	T	~T
C	$-\infty$	0
S	0	0

A high U(C,T) is just as good as $-\infty$, and any utility assignment that leaves U(C,~T) no lower than U(S,~T) is fine.

The most obvious criticism is that if there are no terrible consequences, then the utility of carrying on will be greater than the utility of doing nothing. U(C,~T) is greater than U(S,~T), and so there is no sound argument from dominance. But there are other criticisms, for example, that there are more alternatives—you would have to spell out what alternatives you have in mind.

CHAPTER 11. WHAT DO YOU MEAN?

1. *Shock absorbers again.*
   (a) Perhaps Acme has union workers, who are well paid with excellent benefits, while Bolt uses nonunion labor and pays less well with no benefits. Maybe it is the opposite. Bolt is unionized and the workers have lost incentive, while at Acme, you get fired for the least slip-up. Maybe Acme has newer (or older!) machines that are more trustworthy. Perhaps Acme has a hotshot quality control engineer.
   (b) Whatever the cause, we think there is a definite tendency for Acme to produce more reliable shock absorbers than Bolt. We are concerned not with what anyone believes, but with some in-the-world fact about the two manufacturers.

2. *Influenza.*
   (a) Frequency-type. This is a statement about "the world," about the natural course of influenza under current conditions.
   (b) "Likely" here seems to mean that for most young people who catch the disease, it runs its course in a week or less. A frequency-type probability ($> 75\%$?) seems to be implied.
   (c) Frequency-type.
   (d) This statement seems to be a claim about what can be expected to happen regularly under current conditions. So it seems to be frequency-type, perhaps with a propensity interpretation.
   (e) All three statements are plainly frequency-type.

3. (a) *January 31, 1996.* Belief-type. The probability stated is *relative to* the evidence available in 1996. We now have a lot more evidence.

   (b) *February 1, 2006.* Belief-type, relative to evidence available in 2006.

4. *The Fed.*
   (a) Clearly a single case. Belief-type. Intended to be impersonal, and perhaps relative to available evidence.

   (b) Belief-type.
   (c) Betting here suggests a purely personal belief-type probability.

5.   *Clones.* Frequency-type.

CHAPTER 12. THEORIES ABOUT PROBABILITY

1.   *Indifference.* There is no "right" answer, for this is a matter of Mario's personal probabilities. If he goes for Eatemup at terminal 3, his personal probabilities for Sonia coming on that airline are greater than the sum of his personal probability for Alpha, plus his personal probability for Beta. But if his personal probability for Eatemup is not that high, he should go to terminal 1 (or 2, depending on his beliefs about Gamma and Delta) rather than 3.

For variety, the answers to Exercises 2–4 give slightly different verbal expressions of the interpretations made by our theorists.

2.   *Happy Harry.*
      Venn: The relative frequency of success, among students who use the kit, is 90%.
      Popper: There is a 90% tendency or propensity to produce success, using the kit.
      De Finetti: Happy Harry (or his advertisers) are saying that their personal probability for success is 0.9—they'd bet 9 to 1 that any arbitrarily chosen student who uses the kit will succeed.
      Keynes: Given the evidence that a student has used the kit, the logical probability that he or she will succeed is 0.9.

3.   *The Informed Source.*
      Venn: I don't think you should speak of probability here at all. If you insist, you mean that the relative frequency of lasting settlements in the Middle East, in two-year periods like the upcoming one, is very low.
      Popper: There is no tendency, in this situation, for a lasting settlement in the next two years.
      De Finetti: My personal probability for a lasting settlement over the next two-year period is zilch.
      Keynes: Relative to the available evidence, it is not reasonable to have a high degree of belief that there will be a lasting peace settlement arising in the next two years.

4.   *Conditional Happy Harry.*
      Venn: The relative frequency of success is 75%, in a reference class of students among whom the relative frequency of success is only 0.5, and who then use the kit.
      Popper: If a student has a propensity for success of only 50%, then, if she uses the kit, her propensity for success climbs to 75%.
      De Finetti: The advertiser is saying something like this: If my personal betting rate on a student's succeeding is even, 1:1, then when she uses the kit, my personal betting rate changes to 3:1 on her success.
      Keynes: I start with some information about the student that makes the logical probability of her success ½. Relative to the further information that she uses the kit, the logical probability of her success is ¾.
      You should be able to continue with Exercises 5–8 in much the same vein.

CHAPTER 13. PERSONAL PROBABILITIES

1.   *Nuclear power.*
      (a) No. The bet cannot be settled for more than half a century.
      (b) Yes, if you don't mind waiting for a couple of years.

2.   *Chocoholic.* No, because the value of the prize—to Alice—is affected by the outcome of the gamble.

3. *Intelligent aliens.*
    (a) Yes, if you think of one year as soon enough. The conditions for settling the bet are entirely definite, and the bet will be settled in one year precisely.
    (b) Skuli is faced with two options. He can give $49 to Ladbroke's. He thinks he is virtually certain to collect $1 in a year. Or he can put $49 in a one-year deposit account at the bank, which at present pays a measly 4% (say). At the end of a year he collects almost $2 in interest. So he would rather put his money in the bank than make a bet that he is guaranteed to win.

4. *Bets.* $3.   ¼.

5. *Raising the ante.* −$25.

6. *Fair bet.* ¾.

7. *Make-up tests.* Once again, it is your choice of numbers. The only requirement is that:

    $$Pr(B) > Pr(B/M).$$

    You might have:

    $$Pr(B) = 0.5 \text{ and } Pr(B/M) = 0.3.$$

    Then a payoff matrix for the conditional bet would be:

	Payoff for bet on B, given M	Payoff for bet against B, given M
B&M	$7	−$7
(~B)&M	−$3	$3
~M	0	0

8. *"Not" reverses preferences.* $10 if (2) does not occur. This seems to be a matter of logic: a preference for "$10 if (1) occurs" is the same as a preference for "$10 if (2) does not occur."

CHAPTER 14. COHERENCE

1. *Diogenes.* You bet $1 against B. He bets $9 on B. You also bet $8 on B. He bets $2 against B.
    If the Leafs come in last, his net payoff is $1 − $2 = −$1.
    If the Leafs do not come in last, his net payoff is $8 − $9 = −$1.

2. *Epicurus.* You bet $7 on T. He bets $3 against T (using his first betting rate of .7).
    You bet $2 against T. He bets $8 on T (using his second betting rate).
    If T occurs, his net payoff is $2 − $3 = −$1.
    If T does not occur, his net payoff is $7 − $8 = −$1.

3. *Optimistic Cinderella.* For coherence, we require that the conditional betting rate equals the betting rate on P&S, divided by the rate on S. The conditional betting rate is ½. But $(0.2)/(1/3) = 0.6$, so the conditional rate is *too small*. (It should be 0.6, not 0.5.)
    This is the situation in the payoff matrix on the other side. So Cinderella is asked to bet:

    > Bet $2 on P&S (to win $8).
    > Bet $4 against S (to win $2).
    > Bet $5 against P given S (to win $5).

    If P&S occurs, she wins $8, but loses her other two bets for a net loss of $1.
    If (~P)&S occurs, she loses $2 on P&S, loses $4 against S, and wins $5 on the conditional bet, for a net loss of $1.
    If S does not occur, she loses and wins $2, for a net loss of 0.
    How did we get these numbers? In terms of p, q, r on the other side,

    > $p = ½, q = 0.2$, and $r = 1/3$.
    > The net loss should be $q − pr = 1/5 − 1/6 = −1/30$.
    > So we should multiply by 30 to get a net loss of $1.

We bet $qr(\$30)$ on P&S, or $(1/5)(1/3)(\$30) = \$2$.
We bet $(1 - r)q(\$30)$ against S, or $(2/3)(1/5)(\$30) = \$4$
We bet $(1-p)r(\$30)$ against P conditional on S, or $(\frac{1}{2})(1/3)(\$30) = \$5$.

4. *Pessimistic Cinderella.*
   Here, the conditional rate is *too large*. (It should be 0.3, not 0.5.) She is asked to bet the opposite way from the way she would bet if the conditional rate were too small. So she is asked to:

   Bet $4.50 against P&S (to win $0.50).
   Bet $0.50 on S (to win $1).
   Bet $2.50 on P given S (to win $2.50).

   If P&S occurs, she loses $4.50, but wins her other two bets to win $3.50, for a net loss of $1.
   If (~P)&S occurs, she wins $0.50 on P&S, $1 on S, and loses $2.50 on the conditional bet, for a net loss of $1.
   If S does not occur, she loses and wins $0.50, for a net loss of 0.

5. *A mysterious gift.* A sure-loss contract, where you lose $100 for sure:
   Let q = betting rate on C&H = 0.3.
   Let r = betting rate on C = 0.8.
   Let p = betting rate on H given C = 0.5.
   The loss is to be $(\$x)(q-pr) = (\$x)(0.3 - 0.4) = -\$100$, so $x = \$1000$.

   Bet $(1-q)r(\$1,000) = \$560$ against C&H to win $qr(\$1,000) = \$240$.
   Bet $(qr)\$1,000 = \$240$ on C to win $(1-r)q(\$1,000) = \$60$.
   Bet $pr(\$1,000) = \$400$ on H, conditional on C, to win $400.

   If H&C occurs, you lose $56, win $60, and win $400, to lose $100.
   If ~H&C occurs, you win $240, win $60, and lose $400, to lose $100.
   If C does not occur, you win $240, and lose $240.
   Therefore if C occurs, you are sure to lose $100.

CHAPTER 15: LEARNING FROM EXPERIENCE

1. *Likelihoods.*
   (a) Priors: $Pr(G) = 0.6$. $Pr(H) = 0.4$. Posteriors: $Pr(G/T) = 3/4$. $Pr(H/T) = 1/4$.
       Likelihoods: $Pr(T/G) = 0.6$. $Pr(T/H) = 0.3$. The sum of the likelihoods is 0.9, and not 1.
   (b) Priors: $Pr(G) = 0.85$. $Pr(B) = 0.15$. Posteriors: $Pr(G/W_b) = 0.59$. $Pr(B/W_b) = 0.41$.
       Likelihoods: $Pr(W_b/G) = 0.2$. $Pr(W_b/B) = 0.8$.
       The sum of the likelihoods is, as it happens, just 1. But that fact is of no significance. Likelihoods in general do not add to 1.

2. *Lost notes.* Here are my own personal assignments. Yours will be different.
   (a) $Pr(L) = 0.2$. $Pr(C) = 0.8$. I assign these numbers because I seldom take my notes to the library, and I often leave stuff in the classroom.
   (b) Likelihood of L $= Pr(E/L) = 0.3$. Likelihood of C $= Pr(E/C) = 0.1$. I put both of these quite low, because L does not make it especially likely that my friend is going to see some notes in the library. And C really does not make it especially likely at all—just the probability of seeing some notes in the library.

   (c) $$Pr(L/E) = \frac{Pr(L)Pr(E/L)}{Pr(L)Pr(E/L) + Pr(C)Pr(E/C)]} = 3/7 \approx 0.43.$$

   So: $Pr(C/E) = 4/7 \approx 0.57$.
   (d) Likelihood of L given F $= Pr(F/L\&E) = 0.5$.
       Likelihood of C given F $= Pr(F/C\&E) = 0.1$.

       These are all personal probabilities. The first likelihood is not large, for me, but middling: given that some notes were seen in the library, and the hypothesis that I left my notes in the library, it would not be surprising if my friend saw those very notes. Leaving my notes in the classroom, however, does not give much probability to F.

(e) $\quad$ Pr(L/E&F) $= \dfrac{\text{Pr(L/E)Pr(F/L\&E)}}{[\text{Pr(L/E)Pr(F/L\&E)} + \text{Pr(C/E)Pr(F/C\&E)}]} = 15/19 \approx 0.79.$

Pr(C/E&F) $= 4/19 \approx 0.21.$

3. *Mushrooms.* Presumably Jack's eating the tasty *Caesar* makes no difference to your assessment of the probability of appendicitis: Pr(A/Y) = Pr(A).

   On the other hand, if he ate the *Death Cap*, he has surely not got appendicitis, but has been poisoned: Pr(A/~Y) = 0.

   Pr*(A) = Pr(A/~Y)Pr(~Y)+ Pr(A/Y)Pr(Y) = 0.56.

   That is a terrible result! You have no idea what to do.

   This example of learning from experience does not lead us closer to certainty, but leaves us in a desperate quandary.

4. *Rumors, rumors.* (a) By Jeffrey's rule:

   Pr*(G/I) = Pr(G/I)Pr*(I) + Pr(G/~I)Pr*(~I).
   Pr(~G/I) = 0.9. So Pr(G/I) = 0.1.
   Pr(G/~I) = 0.3.
   Pr*(I) = 0.8. So Pr*(~I) = 0.2.
   Pr*(G/I) = (0.1 × 0.8) + (0.3 × 0.2) = 0.08 + 0.06 = 0.14.

   (b) Expectation before the rumor is

   Pr(G)U(S/G) + Pr(~G)(U/~G)
   = (0.3 × 20) + (0.7 × −5) = 6 − 3.5 = 2.5.
   Pr*(G)U(S/G) + Pr*(~G)(U/~G)
   = (0.14 × 20) + (0.86 × −5) = 2.8 − 4.3 = −1.5.

   No, she does not review.

5. *Buses.*
   (a) Everyone will have his or her own personal probabilities. Here are mine. Pr([200]) = 0.9. Pr([20]) = 0.1.
   (b) Pr(n) = Pr(n&[200]) + Pr(n&[20]).
       For $1 \leq n \leq 20$, Pr(n) = 19/2000 = 0.0095.
       For $21 \leq n \leq 200$, Pr(n) = 9/2000 = 0.0045.
   (c) Pr($0 \leq n \leq 20$) = 0.19. Pr($21 \leq n \leq 200$) = 0.81.
   (d) The likelihood of [200] is Pr(19/[200]) = 1/200.
       The likelihood of [20] is Pr(19/[20]) = 1/20.
       The relative likelihood of [20] to that of [200] is ten to one.
   (e) Starting with *my* personal probabilities, Pr([200]/19) = 9/19. Pr([20]/19) = 10/19. Thus the posterior probabilities are almost equal.
   (f) Virtually zero—if I personally take for granted that I have been just about everywhere in the city, at all times when all routes are operating.
   (g) It seems to. I start with the plausible opinion that the larger city, Gotterdam, has 200 bus routes. After I see bus number 19, I conclude that the chances are only about fifty-fifty that Gotterdam has 200 routes. After I have seen many buses numbered 20 or less, and none numbered more, I become virtually certain that Gotterdam has only 20 bus routes.

6. *Doom.*
   (a) About 67%.
   (b) Better than 50%.
   (c) If 1/10 is a plausible proportion of:

$$\frac{\text{People who are alive in the 1990s}}{\text{People in the history of the human race, up to 2150.}}$$

Then the plausible proportion of:

$$\frac{\text{People who are alive in the 1990s}}{\text{People in the history of the human race, up to now}}$$

should be much higher than 1/10. (If the population explosion continues, most of the people who are born by 2150 will actually have been born after 2000!) With a higher proportion, Bayes' Rule, as used by Leslie, will make it even more probable that the human race will become extinct soon.

(d) No. Recall from Chapter 1 that you can have a true conclusion but an invalid argument. Even if Leslie convinced us that the human race will come to an end by 2150, that would not provide a single shred of evidence that his argument using Bayes' Rule is sound.

(e) Virtual certainty! Is that plausible?

7. *Fallacy.* There are many problems with Leslie's argument. Here we will do a painstaking job on **one** fallacy. *We will show that Leslie uses an incorrect likelihood in his computation.* (You may have found **other** fallacies.)

Recall the succinct summary of Bayes' Rule:

Posterior Probability $\propto$ *Prior Probability* $\times$ *Likelihood.*

The likelihood of hypothesis H, in the light of evidence E, is $\Pr(E/H)$. From the perspective of personal probabilities, likelihoods are personal too. First recall the correct use of likelihoods, in the bus problem. Here is a sensible statement of personal probabilities:

(I) My personal conditional probability that the first bus I see is a No. 19, conditional on the hypothesis that Gotterdam has 20 bus routes, is 1/20.

Since a likelihood is $\Pr(E/H)$, 1/20 is thus a plausible personal *likelihood* of the hypothesis that Gotterdam has 20 bus routes, in the light of the evidence that the first bus I see is a No. 19.

Likewise, 1/200 is a plausible likelihood, for me, of the hypothesis that Gotterdam has 200 bus routes, in the light of the evidence that the first bus I see is a No. 19. These are the likelihoods that we use for Bayes' Rule, in the bus problem.

Betting version of (I). Although betting is artificial, it often helps to clarify our ideas. Corresponding to the personal conditional probability (I):

It would be fair to contract a conditional bet at rate 1/20—betting $1 to win $19—that the first bus I see is a No. 19, conditional on Gotterdam having 20 bus routes. (Bets off if Gotterdam has 200 bus routes! I don't want this bet at all, if there are 200 routes in Gotterdam.)

It would be fair to contract a conditional bet at rate 19/20—betting $19 to win $1—that the first bus I see is not a No. 19, conditional on Gotterdam having 20 bus routes. (Bets off, unfortunately, if Gotterdam has 200 bus routes).

Now contrast Leslie's use of Bayes' Rule. Corresponding to (I) we have (II). Read (II) aloud as about *your* personal probability and as about *you*, as Leslie intends.

(II) My personal conditional probability that I was alive in (at least part of) the 1990s, conditional on the hypothesis that the human race comes to an end in 2150, is 1/10.

This is not a plausible conditional personal probability. Your conditional probability that you were alive in the 1990s is 1! Hence 1/10 is *not* your personal likelihood of the hypothesis that the human race will end by 2150, in the light of the evidence that I am alive in (at least part of) the 1990s.

Betting version of (II). Some students will see the problem with (II) more clearly in terms of bets. We cannot sensibly bet, because 2150 is too far away for payoff time. Disregard that for a moment. Parallel to the buses, (II) would suggest these contracts. As before, we are dealing with personal probabilities, and the "I" in question is you:

(iii) It would be fair to contract a conditional bet at rate 1/10—betting $1 to win $9—that I am alive in (at least part of) the 1990s, conditional on the human race becoming extinct by 2150.

(iv) It would be fair to contract a conditional bet at rate 9/10—betting $9 to win $1—that I am not alive in (at least part of) the 1990s, conditional on the human race becoming extinct by 2150.

The second contract is plainly not fair! Ask Professor Leslie to take contract (iv) and also to make a bet conditional on the alternative he proposes, that the race goes on long after 2150:

(v) It would be fair to contract a conditional bet at rate 999/1000—betting $999 to win $1—that I am not alive in (at least part of) the 1990s, conditional on the human race continuing long after 2150.

You say to Professor Leslie: Please bet $9.99 using contract (v), and $9 using contract (iv).

"Since I was alive in the 1990s, I win one or the other conditional bet, no matter which alternative turns out to be true. So please pay me my minimum winnings now, namely $9."

To return to (II), Leslie wrote, as we quoted him, "Let us say that the chance that a human being will be alive in the 1990s is 1/10 in the case of the short-lasting race."
Fine. I, and perhaps you, go along with that. To be more formal:

(III) "My personal conditional probability that an arbitrarily chosen human being, about whom we know nothing, was alive in the 1990s, conditional on the hypothesis that the human race comes to an end in 2150, is 1/10."

(III) is a good enough personal probability for me, and perhaps for you. However, the evidence is not about an arbitrarily chosen human being. It is about me. We know more about ourselves than about arbitrarily chosen people, and so my personal probabilities about me differ from my personal probabilities about arbitrarily chosen people.

We could say that in this presentation of his argument, Leslie commits *the fallacy of equivocation*. He equivocates between:

(III), which is a sensible personal probability, and (II), which is not a sensible personal probability.

It is thus a mistake to use the probability (II) as the likelihood to plug into Bayes' Rule in Leslie's calculation.

8. *Total evidence.* We discussed Leslie's Doomsday Argument from the perspective of personal probabilities. As you know, there are many other Bayesian approaches. From the perspective of the logical probability approach of Carnap and Keynes, things are much simpler. Carnap insisted on a *requirement of total evidence* to be used for any practical decision. The conditional probabilities that you use must always be conditional on the total available evidence. The fact that you are alive in at least part of the 1990s is certainly part of your total available evidence, so any usable conditional probability will always equal 1. That is:

Pr(I am alive in at least part of the 1990s/total evidence available to me) = 1.

CHAPTER 16. STABILITY

1. *Hungry Clara.* (a) 5 oz. (b) $\sqrt{20/7}$.

2. *Sick Sam.* (a) 3 oz. (b) 6/7. (c) The mean is smaller because, on average, Sam eats less than Clara, but the standard deviation is larger because the average difference from the mean is larger, thanks to that one big feed of 8 ounces.

3. *Median income.* (a) $61,000. (b) $56,000.

4. *Incomes.* The median is lower than the average *in all countries* because there is a relatively small number of high incomes. This is because the median does not weight higher incomes; it just counts them. The greater the difference between the average and the median, then, usually, the greater the disparity in income between ordinary income earners and the rich. But a different social system could change that. For example, if 20% of households had a fixed income of $60,000, 60% had a fixed income of $50,000, while 20% (the elderly, say) had a fixed income of $20,000, then the average income would be $46,000, and the median would be $50,000.

5. *Poverty lines.* The Canadian family poverty line computed by the median is about $25,000. Computed by the mean, it is about $28,600. In either event, it is lower than the low-income cut off in use for the time period when the same statistics were the basis of calculation.

6. *Quick fixes.* (a) One simple method is to slightly raise the income of the 30% best-off poor people, that is, the top income earners in the group whose income falls below 50% of the present average income. This would not raise the average income significantly. But it would not make anyone much better off, and would leave the poorest just as poor as ever. (b) No, this method would not work for a poverty line based on the median; just as many would be below the line as before.

7. *Most probable numbers.*
   (a) 32 ranging from no green (the outcome 0 green, or RRRRR) to all green (the outcome 5 green, or GGGGG).
   (b) $\Pr(0) = \Pr(5) = 1/32$. (c) $\Pr(1) = \Pr(4) = 5/32$. (d) $\Pr(2) = \Pr(3) = 10/32$. (e) 2 and 3.
   (f) $np - (1 - p) \le k_o \le np + p$.
   $\quad (5)(\frac{1}{2}) - (1 - \frac{1}{2}) \le k_o \le (5)(\frac{1}{2}) + \frac{1}{2}$.
   $\quad 2 \le k_o \le 3$.

8. *Most probable number.* k_o is that integer or pair of integers such that,
   $$np - (1-p) \le k_o \le np + p.$$
   $$(13)(0.3) - (1 - 0.3) \le k_o \le (13)(0.3) + 0.3.$$
   $$3.2 \le k_o \le 4.2.$$
   So 4 is the most probable number of greens in 13 Bernoulli trials with $\Pr(G) = 0.3$.

9. *Success.*
   (a) When $n = 11$ and $p = 0.3$, $np - (1 - p) = 2.6$, $np + p = 3.6$, so the most probable number of successes is 3.
   (b) The expected number of successes is 3.3.

10. *Coastal rain.* When $n = 50$ and $p = 4/17$, $np - (1 - p) = 11$, and $np + p = 12$. Hence the most probable numbers of rainy July the firsts in Victoria, over the next 50 years, are 11 and 12.

11. *Particle accelerators.* In conditions A, $n = 60$, $p = 0.7$. So $np - (1 - p) = 41.7$, and $np + p = 42.7$. Hence $k_o = 42$.
    In conditions B, $n = 50$, $p = 0.8$. So $np - (1 - p) = 39.8$, and $np + p = 40.8$. Hence $k_o = 40$.
    (b) No. It is unusual for most probable and expected numbers to coincide. It happens only when the expected number is an integer.
    (c) You expect slightly more fast particles per second with B, despite having more particles per second with A.

CHAPTER 17. NORMAL APPROXIMATIONS

1. *Bimodal:*
   • Distribution of rainfall by month in a place where there are two rainy seasons and two dry seasons.

- Distribution of ages in a large evening class at a university, a class that includes many typical undergraduates and a small number of older people taking continuing education courses.
- Distribution of number of games won in a season, in a league with some good teams and some bad teams. (This could be applied for any group of contests, chess, bridge, etc.)

2. *Normal.* (a) Roughly normal. (b) Roughly bimodal (a peak for males, and a peak for females). (c) In many temperate regions, including Toronto, it is neither. In places with one clearly marked rainy season, the curve is very roughly bell-shaped, but some parts of the world have two rainy seasons, and are bimodal. (d) Normal.

3. *Inferior products.* (a) 3600.
   (b) $d = \sqrt{[p(1 - p)n]} = \sqrt{[3/4 \times 1/4 \times 4800]} = 30$. Hence the probability is 0.95 that the number of long-life bulbs in a production batch is within 60 of 3600.

4. *Showers after sports.* $d = \sqrt{[p(1 - p)n]} = \sqrt{[½ \times ½ \times 3136]} = 28$. $3d = 84$. Hence $x = 84$. The probability is only 1% that in our sample more than 1652 or fewer than 1484 boys do not shower after sports.

5. *Other regions.* (a) 77. (b) 77. (c) 51. (d) 51.

6. *Worst-case scenario.* In general, if p differs from ½, then $p = ½ + z$, where z is positive or negative.
   $$p(1 - p) = (½ + z)(½ - z) = ¼ - z^2.$$
   This is a maximum when $z = 0$, so d is a maximum when $p = ½$.

CHAPTER 18. SIGNIFICANCE AND POWER

1. *Birthdays.* In principle, the calculation is the same as for the signs of the zodiac. The probability that in a group of k people, all k birthdays are different, is:
   $$(1 - 1/365)(1 - 2/365) \ldots (1 - [k - 1]/365).$$
   You were not asked to work this out. Most people are astonished to learn that there is a better than 50:50 chance that in a group of *twenty-three* people, two individuals have the same birthday. This idea can be generalized to a wide-ranging analysis of coincidences. When should you be surprised by a seeming coincidence? When should you look for an explanation? Well, you should *not* look for an explanation if it is the sort of thing that happens half the time by sheer chance.

2. *Statistics in law.* The null hypothesis must be: *A certain coefficient is zero.*
   "The chances are less than one in 20 . . ." must mean: *the probability is less than 5% that the true coefficient is zero.* **That is a mistake.** Correct statement: *If the true coefficient is zero, an event of probability less than 5% occurred.*

3. *Vitamin E and heart failure.*
   (a) Hypothesis 1: Taking vitamin E in assigned doses has no effect on the incidence of nonfatal heart attacks. Hypothesis 2: Taking vitamin E in assigned doses has no effect on the incidence of death by heart disease.
   (b) Apparently the data are significant for hypothesis 1. Taking vitamin E may, then, cut down on nonfatal heart attacks. But it is not significant for hypothesis 2.
   (c) Because it does not make clear that it is only *nonfatal* heart attacks that seem to be affected. Someone with heart disease who read the first sentence only would think, Great! Vitamin E will prolong my life! Instead, that person learns only that life will be better, while they are alive—fewer nonfatal heart attacks. But no difference (it seems) in life expectancy.

4. *Vitamins: two tests.*
   (a) 1%.
   (b) If the two hypotheses are not related to each other, and there are two sets of results, then it seems that the significance level should be about 2%. That is, about 2% of the time you would get an unusual result.

In this example, however, the relation between the two hypotheses is more complicated. The same results are taken as evidence bearing on two distinct hypotheses. And the two hypotheses, though distinct, are connected, not only because they are about, respectively, fatal and nonfatal heart attacks, but because a nonfatal attack might predispose a patient to a fatal one (or, conversely, might create tissue that protected against a future attack).

5. *Fat and beans.* The point of the p-values for the fats was to see which aspect of fat consuming might be most relevant for lung cancer. The important feature is not that some significance was found, but that saturated fat was so much more significant, in this survey, than any other type of fat. As for the peas and beans, the investigators did not select these vegetables out of a hat. They had already conjectured that the legumes might be relevant, and derived significant results. If they had, by contrast, been applying a statistical software package across dozens of foodstuffs, to find associations with lung cancer, they would be bound to turn up something with a low p-value sooner or later. That would in itself show very little, but would suggest another survey, with a better design, to test a specific hypothesis about a particular foodstuff.

6. *Psychology: one hundred tests.* The point is, of course, that an experimenter who does 200 experiments testing 200 well-specified statistical hypotheses can expect to get a couple of sets of results that happen only one time in a hundred. Does this show that Jerry's results are worthless? If all his fellow graduate students do the same sort of work, is the work of their entire department worthless? There is a real disagreement about this question, with some statisticians being very skeptical of repeated uses of significances level tests.

7. *The department at work.* It certainly sounds as if the department—and by implication, a good deal of experimental psychology—is bound to get a lot of seemingly significant results, no matter where the truth lies. There is a great deal of disagreement about this issue.

8. *Power.* This continues the controversy. It is not obvious that the Neyman–Pearson framework is a sure cure for the problem raised by questions 5 and 6. What is true is that the larger framework does force more careful thought about rival hypotheses. The temptation to publish meaningless p-values would diminish if investigators were obliged to design statistically powerful tests.

9. *Vitamins again.* The power of a test is the probability that it will reject the hypothesis under test when it is false. The size, or significance level, is the probability that the test will be rejected if true.

   The question does not state precise families of hypotheses H_E, K_E, H_A, or K_A. For actual tests we would have to be more precise. *We cannot normally achieve high significance (low significance level) and high power.*

   H_E is good news. We do not want to reject H_E if it is true. Hence we will reject H_E only if the significance is great, say, a significance level of .01. If H_E is false, then, so far as the rival hypotheses K_E go, it does not matter much. So we do not especially care about high power.

   According to K_A, it is bad news if H_A is false. So we do want to reject H_A if it is false. So we want a high power, and do not care so much about significance level.

10. *More statistics in law.* The point is the same as that in question 2. This is a common error, not just from beginners, but from experts. On this example, Freedman comments:

    > No. If the true coefficient is zero, there is only one chance in a hundred that [the statistic] $t > 2.5$. The author of the textbook is a well-known econometrician who often testifies as an expert witness.

11. *Bayesian lawyers?* To paraphrase David Freedman (reference on page 297), we should say instead that:

    > From the frequency perspective, a statement like $Pr(\text{coefficient}=0/\text{data})$ makes no sense; parameters like the coefficient do not exhibit chance variation.

From the belief perspective, Pr(coefficient=0/data) makes good sense, but its computation via a significance test is grossly wrong, because the prior probability that the coefficient equals 0 has not been taken into account; the calculation exemplifies the *base rate fallacy*. Power matters too. (Recall the meaning of *base rates* from the taxicab problem, page 73.)

12. *Overconfident physics.* It is simply not true that when we present a result as $x \pm \sigma$, "the true value [of what we are measuring] has (about) 68% probability of lying between the limits $x - \sigma$ and $x+\sigma$." The true value is some definite number, which is either in the stated interval, or not, and there is no frequency-type probability about it. The correct statement is that if we repeatedly measured the quantity of interest using the same techniques, and obtained an interval estimate with a margin of error of $\pm\sigma$, then about 68% of these intervals would cover the true, unknown value.

CHAPTER 19. CONFIDENCE AND INDUCTIVE BEHAVIOR

1. *Missed tests.* (a) 0.04. (b) .06. The 95% confidence interval estimate of the proportion who had missed a test because of illness would be the interval 0.04 on either side of the observed proportion, $^{125}/_{625} = ^{1}/_{5} = 0.20$, namely (0.16, .24). (b) The 99% estimate is the interval (0.14, 0.26).

2. *Smaller sample.* (a) About 0.111. (b) About 0.167. The observed proportion is almost 0.197, much the same as the proportion of 0.2 in question 1. But now the 95% estimate is the interval (0.086, 0.308), in other words, even less "precise" than saying, "the true unknown proportion of students who missed one test because of illness is between 10% and 30%."

  The 99% estimate is extremely "imprecise": (0.03, 0.364). That is not much better than saying that the true proportion might be anywhere from almost nothing to as much as 35%.

3. *Parapsychology.*

  The 95% confidence interval for the proportion of San Franciscans who believe in parapsychological phenomena is (0.60, 0.66).

  The 95% confidence interval for the proportion of San Franciscans who believe in telepathy is (0.55, 0.61).

  The 95% confidence interval for the proportion of San Franciscans who believe that mediums can make contact with the dead is (0.28, 0.34).

  The 95% confidence interval for the proportion of San Franciscans who believe in ghosts is (0.40, 0.46).

  The 95% confidence interval for the proportion of San Franciscans who believe in poltergeists is (0.23, 0.29).

  The 95% confidence interval for the proportion of San Franciscans who believe in psychokinesis is (0.34, 0.40).

  In each case, the estimate is made by a method that gives correct intervals at least 95% of the time.

Further Reading

Aside from a few textbooks and a few articles on special topics, many of the works described here are classics that will stay in the repertory for decades to come.

CHAPTERS 1 AND 2

There are a great many textbooks of deductive reasoning, and more appear every year. One useful textbook that touches on induction is:

> Robert J. Fogelin and Walter Sinnott-Armstrong. *Understanding Arguments: An Introduction to Informal Reasoning.* Fort Worth: Harcourt Brace, 5th edn., 1997.

There are very few textbooks of inductive logic. One excellent one is:

> Brian Skyrms. *Choice and Chance: An Introduction to Inductive Logic.* Belmont, Calif.: Dickenson, 2nd edn., 1975.

A textbook that overlaps with, but also supplements, ours is:

> Davis Baird. *Inductive Logic: Probability and Statistics.* Englewood Cliffs, N. J.: Prentice Hall, 1992.

Baird emphasizes the frequency approach. The best textbook with a belief-type, personal probability orientation is:

> Colin Howson and Peter Urbach. *Scientific Reasoning: The Bayesian Approach.* Chicago: Open Court, 2nd edn., 1993.

CHAPTERS 3–5

These chapters start us on the way to thinking about probabilities. There are at least as many introductions to probability and statistics as there are introductions to deductive logic, and more come out every year. One excellent older example is:

> David Freedman, Robert Pisani, and Roger Purves. *Statistics.* New York: Norton, 1978.

The true classic, which starts with simple intuitions and fascinating examples, but leads on to some of the most profound results in probability theory, is:

> William Feller. *An Introduction to Probability Theory and Its Applications.* New York: Wiley, 1950.

If you have a taste for more difficult problems with unexpected solutions, try:

> Frederick Mosteller. *Fifty Challenging Problems in Probability*. Reading, Mass.: Addison-Wesley, 1965.

The Inverse Gambler's Fallacy was developed in Chapter 3, exercises 8–10. It is further explained in:

> Ian Hacking. The inverse gambler's fallacy: The argument from design. The Anthropic Principle applied to Wheeler universes. *Mind* 97 (1987): 331–340. (See subsequent issues of *Mind* for criticisms.)

CHAPTER 6

Odd Question 2 has elicited quite a lot of discussion. Many people give the "wrong" answer. Some authors believe this shows that human beings are innately bad probability reasoners. Others think that we are tricked by the way the question is asked. Here is a sampling of the literature. Tversky and Kahneman started the ball rolling:

> Daniel Kahneman and Amos Tversky. On the psychology of prediction. *Psychological Review* 80 (1973): 237–251.

> Amos Tversky and Daniel Kahneman. Extensional versus intuitive reasoning: The conjunction fallacy in probability judgment. *Psychological Review* 90 (1983): 293–315.

Some say the problem lies in the language used to state the question:

> K. Fiedler. The dependence of the conjunction fallacy on subtle linguistic factors. *Psychological Research* 50 (1988): 123–129.

Some say the problem has to do with background knowledge of the frequencies with which people have various careers and hobbies.

> Gerd Gigerenzer. How to make cognitive illusions disappear: Beyond 'Heuristics and Biases.' *European Review of Social Psychology* 2 (1991): 83–115.

Many of the Tversky–Kahneman cognitive illusions are further presented in:

> Amos Tversky, Paul Slovic, and Daniel Kahneman, eds. *Judgment under Uncertainty*. Cambridge: Cambridge University Press, 1982.

CHAPTER 7

The "taxicab problem" and the base-rate fallacy have also generated a large literature. It began with:

> Amos Tversky and Daniel Kahneman. Judgement under uncertainty: Heuristics and biases. *Science* 185 (1974): 1124–1131.

For a defense of common sense against the psychologists, see this article, together with the comments by numerous authors that follow it.

> L. J. Cohen. Can human irrationality be experimentally demonstrated? *The Behavioral and Brain Sciences* 4 (1981): 317–331.

This article contains discussion and criticism by many experts in the field. See also the Gigerenzer paper cited for Chapter 6.

For a survey of all sorts of cognitive illusions, and more extensive bibliography, see:

Massimo Piattelli-Palmarini. *Inevitable Illusions: How Mistakes of Reason Rule Our Minds*. New York: Wiley, 1994.

Howard Margolis. *Patterns, Thinking, and Cognition: A Theory of Judgment*. Chicago: University of Chicago Press, 1982.

CHAPTER 8

Further exercises on expectation can be found in any elementary textbook. The quotations at the end of the chapter are from:

Antoine Arnauld and Pierre Nicole. *Logic or the Art of Thinking. Containing, besides Common Rules, Several New Observations Appropriate for Forming Judgment*. Translated and edited by Jill Buroker. Cambridge: Cambridge University Press, 1994, pages 273–274.

CHAPTER 9

The Allais paradox, examined at the end of the chapter, mentions comments found on pages 102–103 of:

L. J. Savage. *The Foundations of Statistics*. New York: Wiley, 1954.

This is one of the classic expositions of probability theory, and contains the full statement of Savage's theory of personal probability.

CHAPTER 10

There are many editions and translations of Pascal's *Pensées*. (That means *Thoughts* in French, but many English translations use the French title.) Unfortunately, different editions sometimes number the fragments differently. Here is one widely available translation:

Blaise Pascal. *Pensées*. Translated with an introduction by A. J. Krailsheimer. New York: Penguin, 1966. The "wager" is #418 in this edition, pp. 149–153.

There are many philosophical and historical discussions of the wager. The one closest to the discussion in Chapter 10 is:

Ian Hacking. *The Emergence of Probability*. Cambridge: Cambridge University Press, 1975, Chapter 9.

CHAPTERS 11 AND 12

Here are classic philosophical expositions of the theories of probability described in Chapter 12.

(1) *Frequency Theory*. We will mention just one classic:

Richard von Mises. *Probability, Statistics and Truth*. London: Allen and Unwin, 1957.

(2) *Propensity Theory*.

Karl Popper. The propensity interpretation of probability. *British Journal for the Philosophy of Science* 10 (1959): 25–42.

(3) *Personal Theory*. As is sometimes the case, the very first presentations of these ideas remain fresh seventy-five years later.

> F. P. Ramsey. Truth and probability. In *The Foundations of Mathematics and Other Logical Essays*. London: Routledge and Kegan Paul, 1931. Also in H. E. Kyburg and Howard E. Smokler, eds. *Studies in Subjective Probability*. New York: Wiley, 1964, pages 61–92.
>
> Bruno de Finetti. Foresight: Its logical laws, its subjective sources. In ibid. 97–158.

L. J. Savage's book cited for Chapter 9 is the classic full exposition of the personal theory.

(4) *Logical Theory*. Keynes is still a wonderful read not only for his theory, but for his historical background and philosophical insight.

> John Maynard Keynes. *A Treatise on Probability*. London: Macmillan, 1921.

CHAPTERS 13 AND 14

The ideas of these two chapters originate with Ramsey and de Finetti. Their papers in the Kyburg and Smokler collection, just cited for Chapters 11–12, remain excellent sources. Ramsey is the more readable, and de Finetti has more rigorous detail.

CHAPTER 15

Howson and Urbach, cited earlier for Chapters 1–2, is the best elementary exposition of Bayesian ideas. Another introduction, containing Jeffrey's rule, is:

> Richard Jeffrey. *The Logic of Decision*. Chicago: University of Chicago Press, 2nd edn., 1983.

A more advanced philosophical book investigating Bayesian methods is:

> John Earman. *Bayes or Bust: A Critical Examination of Bayesian Confirmation Theory*. Cambridge, Mass.: MIT Press, 1992.

Instant doom

Exercises 4–7 developed John Leslie's paradoxical arguments, and suggested that they were a mistake. To get the original version from his point of view, see his papers and books:

> The doomsday argument. *The Mathematical Intelligencer* 14 (1992): 48–51.
> Is the end of the world nigh? *The Philosophical Quarterly* 40 (1996): 65–72.
> *The End of the World*. London: Routledge, 1996.

Miracles

Philosophy and Bayes' Theorem intersect in another curious way. David Hume argued that we can never have good reasons for believing in a miracle.

> David Hume. *An Enquiry Concerning Human Understanding*. 1748, available in many editions. See section X.

Some philosophers use Bayesian reasoning to argue that Hume was right, while others argue that he was wrong. One version of the debate starts in these two papers; you can use a search engine to find many further contributions to this discussion.

J. H. Sobell. On the evidence of testimony for miracles: A Bayesian reconstruction of Hume's analysis. *The Philosophical Quarterly* 37 (1987): 166–186.

David Owen. Hume *versus* Price on miracles and prior probabilities: Testimony and the Bayesian calculation. Ibid., 187–202.

CHAPTER 16

The successive connections between probability and relative frequency, stated in this chapter, are steps in an elementary proof of Bernoulli's Theorem due to the Russian mathematician P. L. Chebyshev (1821–1894). This proof is given in a Russian textbook written by two important contributors to the theory of probability. It has been translated into English in what is still one of the most direct practical introductions to probability ideas. The proof given here requires no advanced mathematics whatsoever.

B. V. Gnedenko and A. Ya. Khinchin. *An Elementary Introduction to the Theory of Probability.* New York: Dover, 1962, pages 38–59.

Their exposition, although primarily written for engineering students in the former Soviet Union, and strictly taking a frequency perspective, follows exactly the same chain of probability notions that we have been using throughout this book, and in the same order. Their book has no explicit philosophy, but it goes further with probabilities than we do, and is only 122 pages long—a real plus!

For a more thorough investigation of laws of large numbers, see the Feller textbook cited for Chapters 3–5.

CHAPTER 17

Any textbook of probability or statistics will tell you more about the normal distribution.

CHAPTER 18

Significance levels and Neyman–Pearson tests are often run together. For one account of how this has happened, see:

Gerd Gigerenzer and David J. Murray. *Cognition as Intuitive Statistics.* Hillsdale, N. J.: Lawrence Erlbaum, 1987.

Many of the examples of abuses of significance levels are taken from an article by a statistician writing in part for philosophers:

David Freedman. Some issues in the foundations of statistics. *Foundations of Science* 1 (1995): 19–39, with comments by other contributors, 41–67, and a rejoinder by Freedman, 69–83.

A recent philosophical book explaining the frequency-type approach to inference and decision by Deborah Mayo is cited for Chapter 22.

Questions 6 and 7 raise an important worry about significance tests, first posed in:

Paul Meehl. Theory testing in psychology and physics: A methodological paradox. *Philosophy of Science* 34 (1967): 103–115.

Meehl has developed his criticisms for many years; a more recent discussion is:

Paul Meehl. Why summaries of research on psychological theories are often un-interpretable. *Psychological Reports* 66 (1990): 195–244.

A spirited philosophical defense of traditional statistical methods is to be found in:

J. D. Trout. *Measuring the Intentional World: Realism, Naturalism and Quantitative Methods in the Behavioral Sciences.* New York: Oxford University Press, 1998.

CHAPTER 19

For a *very* elementary introduction to the theory of confidence intervals, in the framework of scientific reasoning, see:

Ronald Giere. *Understanding Scientific Reasoning.* New York: Holt, Rinehart and Winston, 1979, Chapters 11 and 12.

CHAPTER 20

The classic statement of the problem of induction is by David Hume. Perhaps the best introduction is in:

David Hume. *An Enquiry Concerning Human Understanding.* 1748, many editions, sections IV, V.

A more complex argument is found in:

David Hume. *A Treatise of Human Nature.* 1739, many editions, Part III.

The quotations on pages 249–251 are from Hume's own anonymous advertise-ment for the *Treatise.* He called his advertisement "An abstract of a treatise of human nature." You can find it in a number of places, including Charles W. Hendel's student edition of the *Enquiry*—but note that in this edition, the spelling has been modern-ized: *An Inquiry Concerning Human Understanding,* New York: Liberal Arts Press, 1955.

A delightful version of the problem of induction is in Chapter 6 of:

Bertrand Russell. *The Problems of Philosophy.* Many editions since 1912.

One collection of papers (including Russell's chapter) about the problem of induction is:

Richard Swinburn. *The Justification of Induction.* Oxford: Oxford University Press, 1974.

For Popper's evasion, see a paper of his that begins with the words, "Of course I may be mistaken, but I think I have solved a major philosophical problem, the problem of induction."

Karl Popper. Conjectural knowledge: My solution of the problem of induction. *Objective Knowledge: An Evolutionary Approach.* Oxford: Clarendon Press, 1972, Chapter 1.

CHAPTER 21

Howson and Urbach, cited earlier for Chapters 1–2, is the best elementary discussion of the Bayesian approach to the problem of induction.

The objection raised by Hialeah Hume was first put forward in:

Ian Hacking. Slightly more realistic personal probability. *Philosophy of Science* 34 (1967): 311–325.

There have been many technical attempts to meet the objection, but Howson and Urbach, Chapter 6, find that none of them work.

CHAPTER 22

Charles Sanders Peirce had an enormous number of fertile ideas, but he was not good at getting them in order. There are several anthologies of his philosophy of science; this one includes more of his work on probability than others:

Justus Buchler. *The Philosophical Writings of Peirce.* New York: Dover, 1955. See especially papers 11–14. The quotations on pages 264–266 are from pages 160–164 of Buchler. See also *Writings of Charles S. Peirce*, edited by C. J. W. Kloesel. Bloomington: Indiana University Press, 1982, vol. 3, pages 276–281.

For an explanation of how Peirce's philosophy of probability anticipated the theory of confidence intervals, see:

Ian Hacking. Neyman, Peirce and Braithwaite. In *Science, Belief and Behavior*, ed. D. H. Mellor. Cambridge: Cambridge University Press, 1980, pages 141–160.

For an account of Peirce's views about probability and their relation to his overall philosophy, see:

Ian Hacking. *The Taming of Chance.* Cambridge: Cambridge University Press, 1990, Chapter 17.

A recent book that explains how frequency probability applies to the problem of induction is:

Deborah Mayo. *Error and the Growth of Experimental Knowledge.* Chicago: University of Chicago Press, 1996.

ON THE HISTORY OF PROBABILITY

The best history from the mathematical point of view is:

Stephen M. Stigler. *The History of Statistics: The Measurement of Uncertainty before 1900.* Cambridge, Mass.: Harvard University Press, 1986.

Although this is a history of mathematics, it is remarkably accessible to the general reader. Some more philosophical or cultural histories of probability cover nonmathematical topics. Among them are Hacking's *The Emergence of Probability* and *The Taming of Chance*, cited for Chapters 10 and 22, respectively. A fascinating book about the life and times of probability in the seventeenth century is:

Lorraine Daston. *Classical Probability in the Enlightenment.* Princeton: Princeton University Press, 1988.

An equally fascinating book for the nineteenth century is:

Theodore Porter. *The Rise of Statistical Thinking, 1820–1900.* Princeton: Princeton University Press, 1986.

Index

1788690R00170

Made in the USA
San Bernardino, CA
31 January 2013